Cambridge School Shakespeare

Romeo and Juliet

Edited by Rex Gibson

Series Editor: Rex Gibson
Director, Shakespeare and Schools Project

CAMBRIDGE
UNIVERSITY PRESS

CAMBRIDGE UNIVERSITY PRESS

Cambridge, New York, Melbourne, Madrid, Cape Town, Singapore, São Paulo

Cambridge University Press
The Edinburgh Building, Cambridge CB2 2RU, UK

www.cambridge.org
Information on this title: www.cambridge.org/9780521618700

First published 1992
Second edition 1998
Third edition 2005
Reprinted 2006

Printed in the United Kingdom at the University Press, Cambridge

A catalogue record for this publication is available from the British Library

ISBN-13   978-0-521-61870-0 paperback
ISBN-10   0-521-61870-3 paperback

ACKNOWLEDGEMENTS
Thanks are due to the following for permission to reproduce illustrations:
Cover, v, vi*t*, vii, viii, ix, x, xi*b*, xii*t*, 24, 38, 47, 58, 64, 82, 89, 139, 174, 190, 201, 205, 206, 220, 221, 223, 224, Donald Cooper/Photostage; vi*b*, xi*t*, 140, 225, 20th Century Fox/The Kobal Collection/Merrick Morton; xii*b*, 204, Paramount/The Kobal Collection; 6, MGM/The Kobal Collection; 16, V & A Images; 22, 50, Mansell/Time Life Pictures/Getty Images; 60, Mary Evans Picture Library; 70 Giacomo Di Grassi his true Arte of Defence, Englished by I.G. gentleman, Printed at London 1594 (SSS.24.31(2)), reproduced by permission of the Syndics of Cambridge University Library; 90*l*, Romeo and Juliet © Paramount Pictures all rights reserved; 90*r*, Joe Cocks Studio Collection © Shakespeare Birthplace Trust; 100, 124*r*, 148, John Haynes; 108, Ivan Kyncl; 110, Topham Picturepoint; 124*l*, 169, 222, The Harvard Theater Collection, Houghton Library.

Cover design by Smith

Contents

Cambridge School
Shakespeare

This edition of *Romeo and Juliet* is part of the **Cambridge School Shakespeare** series. Like every other play in the series, it has been specially prepared to help all students in schools and colleges.

This *Romeo and Juliet* aims to be different from other editions of the play. It invites you to bring the play to life in your classroom, hall or drama studio through enjoyable activities that will increase your understanding. Actors have created their different interpretations of the play over the centuries. Similarly, you are encouraged to make up your own mind about *Romeo and Juliet*, rather than having someone else's interpretation handed down to you.

Cambridge School Shakespeare does not offer you a cut-down or simplified version of the play. This is Shakespeare's language, filled with imaginative possibilities. You will find on every left-hand page: a summary of the action, an explanation of unfamiliar words, a choice of activities on Shakespeare's language, characters and stories.

Between each act and in the pages at the end of the play, you will find notes, illustrations and activities. These will help to increase your understanding of the whole play.

There are a large number of activities to give you the widest choice to suit your own particular needs. Please don't think you have to do every one. Choose the activities that will help you most.

This edition will be of value to you whether you are studying for an examination, reading for pleasure, or thinking of putting on the play to entertain others. You can work on the activities on your own or in groups. Many of the activities suggest a particular group size, but don't be afraid to make up larger or smaller groups to suit your own purposes.

Although you are invited to treat *Romeo and Juliet* as a play, you don't need special dramatic or theatrical skills to do the activities. By choosing your activities, and by exploring and experimenting, you can make your own interpretations of Shakespeare's language, characters and stories. Whatever you do, remember that Shakespeare wrote his plays to be acted, watched and enjoyed.

Rex Gibson

This edition of *Romeo and Juliet* uses the text of the play established by G. Blakemore Evans in the **New Cambridge Shakespeare** edition.

'Star-crossed lovers'. *Romeo and Juliet* dramatises the story of two young people who fall deeply in love. But their families are locked in an age-old bitter feud. As Romeo and Juliet seek happiness, the hatred of the Montagues and Capulets, together with chance and accident, makes everything go wrong. They kill themselves rather than be parted.

'Foot it, girls'. Capulet orders dancing at his lavish party. Lady Capulet, the Nurse and Juliet take him at his word.

'If I profane with my unworthiest hand'. Romeo has gatecrashed Capulet's party. He falls in love at first sight with Juliet. He takes her hand and begs a kiss.

'What light through yonder window breaks?' After the party, Romeo catches sight of Juliet as she thinks of him. Shakespeare never mentions a balcony, but all productions strive to find an inventive way of staging Act 2 Scene 2, and it has become known as the 'balcony' scene.

'Parting is such sweet sorrow'. Juliet has agreed to marry Romeo tomorrow, and bids him a reluctant farewell. Some stagings of the 'balcony' scene use a non-realistic set, as in this Royal Shakespeare Company production in 2000.

'Tybalt, you rat–catcher, will you walk?' Mercutio (right), disgusted by Romeo's refusal to fight Tybalt, challenges Tybalt to a duel.

'Hold, Tybalt! Good Mercutio!' Romeo tries to stop the duel, but as he restrains Mercutio, Tybalt (right) thrusts in his sword, and fatally wounds Mercutio. Romeo, furious at Mercutio's death, will shortly kill Tybalt and be banished from Verona.

'Good father, I beseech you on my knees'. Juliet, already married to Romeo, refuses to marry Paris, her father's choice. She pleads for her father to listen to her, but he is deaf to her entreaty.

'God's bread, it makes me mad!' Capulet is enraged by Juliet's refusal to marry Paris, and subjects her to a tirade of abuse. His fury will lead to Juliet agreeing to Friar Lawrence's hazardous plan in which she will drink a potion that makes her appear as dead.

'What if this mixture do not work at all?' Juliet fears that the Friar's 'poison' may not act, and she will be married to Paris. But in spite of her misgivings, and her dread of the horrors that may await her in the Capulets' tomb, she finally drinks the potion. She hopes that, seeming dead, she will be placed in the tomb and Romeo will rescue her when she wakes.

'Her beauty makes / This vault a feasting presence full of light'. In his 1996 film *William Shakespeare's Romeo + Juliet*, Baz Luhrmann makes Romeo's image very visual. The 'dead' Juliet lies in a cathedral, radiantly lit by hundreds of encircling candles.

'O happy dagger, / This is thy sheath'. Juliet prepares to stab herself, unwilling to live without Romeo. In Shakespeare's play, Romeo is already dead, having poisoned himself. But in Gounod's opera *Romeo et Juliette*, he lives long enough to bid farewell to Juliet. The lovers die together praying for God's forgiveness.

'Poor sacrifices of our enmity!' Capulet takes Montague's hand as they look on
the bodies of their children, tragic victims of their families' feud. The
traumatised Lady Capulet gazes on the dead Paris.

'For never was a story of more woe / Than this of Juliet and her Romeo'.
Franco Zeffirelli's 1968 film set the play in Renaissance Italy and used outdoor
locations in Tuscany and Umbria (but not in Verona). The film ended with the
funeral procession of Romeo and Juliet.

List of characters

The house of Capulet

JULIET
CAPULET her father
LADY CAPULET her mother
TYBALT her cousin
NURSE to Juliet
PETER the Nurse's servant
COUSIN CAPULET Juliet's kinsman
SAMPSON servant to Capulet
GREGORY servant to Capulet
CLOWN servant to Capulet
PETRUCHIO Tybalt's friend

The house of Montague

ROMEO
MONTAGUE his father
LADY MONTAGUE his mother
BENVOLIO his friend
BALTHASAR his servant
ABRAM Montague's servant

The Court

ESCALES Prince of Verona
MERCUTIO his kinsman, Romeo's friend
PARIS his kinsman, suitor to Juliet
PAGE to Paris

The Church

FRIAR LAWRENCE Franciscan priest
FRIAR JOHN Franciscan priest

The City

Musicians, Gentlemen and Gentlewomen, Maskers, Torch-bearers, Citizens and Officers of the Watch, Captain of the Watch

Mantua

An apothecary

The Play is set in Verona and Mantua

Chorus (a narrator) gives a preview of the play: the bitter quarrels of the Montagues and Capulets are ended only by the death of their children, Romeo and Juliet.

---

1 What began the feud? (in small groups)

But *why* were the Montagues and Capulets such bitter enemies? Shakespeare never tells us and no one really knows. Talk together about why you think these two families should have been at each other's throats for so long. Prepare a short scene to show what long-ago incident sparked off the age-old hatred ('ancient grudge') between two of Verona's leading families. Present your scene to the class.

2 Oppositions – antithesis

Romeo and Juliet is full of oppositions: Montagues versus Capulets, parents versus children, for example. The language reflects those oppositions by the use of antithesis (opposing words or phrases, see also p. 216), as in line 3 where 'ancient' is set against 'new'. Identify the opposition in line 14, and look out for other oppositions as you read through the play.

3 Perform the whole play! (in groups of six or more)

The Prologue gives an outline of the play. Work out your own short drama to show all the action described. One person reads the Prologue aloud, a line or section at a time. The others mime what is described. Each group shows its Prologue in turn.

4 Write your own sonnet

The Prologue is in the form of a **sonnet** (fourteen lines). There are several sonnets in *Romeo and Juliet*. Turn to page 217 to learn more about sonnets, and try your hand at writing one.

---

alike in dignity   equal in high
  status
From forth . . . foes   conceived by
  deadly enemies
star-crossed   ill-fated
take their life   are born

misadventured piteous overthrows
  unlucky tragic accidents
fearful passage   tragic unfolding
traffic   business, performance
miss/mend   fail/improve

The tragedy of Romeo and Juliet

The prologue

Enter CHORUS.

Two households, both alike in dignity,
In fair Verona (where we lay our scene),
From ancient grudge break to new mutiny,
Where civil blood makes civil hands unclean.
From forth the fatal loins of these two foes   5
A pair of star-crossed lovers take their life;
Whose misadventured piteous overthrows
Doth with their death bury their parents' strife.
The fearful passage of their death-marked love,
And the continuance of their parents' rage,   10
Which but their children's end nought could remove,
Is now the two hours' traffic of our stage;
The which if you with patient ears attend,
What here shall miss, our toil shall strive to mend.   [*Exit*]

Capulet's servants, Sampson and Gregory, joke together and boast that they are superior to the Montagues. Suddenly two of Montague's servants appear. Sampson urges Gregory to pick a quarrel with them.

1 Brave or cowardly? (in pairs – as Gregory and Sampson)

Read lines 1–36 aloud together several times, changing roles. Try to emphasise all their wordplay of puns and double meanings. For example, in lines 3–4 Sampson's 'we be in choler, we'll draw' means 'being angry, we'll draw our swords'. But Gregory's reply, 'draw your neck out of collar', turns the meaning into 'pull your head out of the hangman's noose' ('choler' = anger, 'collar' = noose).

After you have spoken the lines, talk together about these two characters. Are they really as brave as they brag they are?

2 What do you think?

Here's what one student wrote about Sampson and Gregory:

> Times never change! Like typical men these boneheads boast about their sexual prowess and turn everything into a sex-joke ('stand', 'thrust', 'maidenheads', 'tool', 'weapon'). Why on earth did Shakespeare put such crude characters and language into a play that's about love, not sex?

Write your reply to her question.

3 Set the scene

At the beginning of each scene, a location is given (here it is 'Verona A public place'). But in Shakespeare's theatre the action took place on a bare stage, with little or no scenery. Suggest a simple way in which you could convey to the audience that this scene takes place in the open air in Verona.

---

bucklers small round shields
carry coals suffer insults, do dirty work
take the wall not be near the gutter
thrust to the wall cowardly, dominated

poor-John dried hake, cheap food that Elizabethans linked with lack of sex-drive
two other **Servingmen** Abram and, probably, Balthasar
naked weapon sword

4

Act 1 Scene 1
Verona A public place

Enter SAMPSON and GREGORY, with swords and bucklers.

SAMPSON Gregory, on my word, we'll not carry coals.
GREGORY No, for then we should be colliers.
SAMPSON I mean, and we be in choler, we'll draw.
GREGORY Ay, while you live, draw your neck out of collar.
SAMPSON I strike quickly, being moved.   5
GREGORY But thou art not quickly moved to strike.
SAMPSON A dog of the house of Montague moves me.
GREGORY To move is to stir, and to be valiant is to stand: therefore
    if thou art moved thou runn'st away.
SAMPSON A dog of that house shall move me to stand: I will take the   10
    wall of any man or maid of Montague's.
GREGORY That shows thee a weak slave, for the weakest goes to the
    wall.
SAMPSON 'Tis true, and therefore women being the weaker vessels are
    ever thrust to the wall: therefore I will push Montague's men from   15
    the wall, and thrust his maids to the wall.
GREGORY The quarrel is between our masters, and us their men.
SAMPSON 'Tis all one, I will show myself a tyrant: when I have fought
    with the men, I will be civil with the maids; I will cut off their
    heads.   20
GREGORY The heads of the maids?
SAMPSON Ay, the heads of the maids, or their maidenheads, take it in
    what sense thou wilt.
GREGORY They must take it in sense that feel it.
SAMPSON Me they shall feel while I am able to stand, and 'tis known   25
    I am a pretty piece of flesh.
GREGORY 'Tis well thou art not fish; if thou hadst, thou hadst been
    poor-John. Draw thy tool, here comes of the house of Montagues.

Enter two other SERVINGMEN, [*one being* ABRAM].

SAMPSON My naked weapon is out. Quarrel, I will back thee.
GREGORY How, turn thy back and run?   30

Sampson and Gregory begin a quarrel with the Montagues. Benvolio (a Montague) tries to make peace, but Tybalt (a Capulet) adds flames to the fire, seizing the opportunity to fight.

1 Where would you set the play? (in pairs)

The American musical film *West Side Story* was based on *Romeo and Juliet*. It was set in modern New York, with the lovers belonging to opposing gangs, the Jets and the Sharks (see picture below). Baz Luhrmann's film *William Shakespeare's Romeo + Juliet* sets the action in Verona Beach, a mythical modern Hispanic-American city (see pictures on pp. vi, xi and 225).

Talk together about other possible settings where the quarrels (that Shakespeare set in Verona) could take place. Look through the illustrations in this edition and decide which location and period you prefer. Set out the reasons for your preference in writing.

2 Tybalt – what's he like? (in small groups)

Tybalt speaks only five lines (lines 57–8 and lines 61–3), but they tell a great deal about him. Choose one word from each line and work out a short mime using those five words to show Tybalt's character.

as they list   as they wish
bite my thumb   a rude gesture in Elizabethan times. What are similar provocative gestures today?
sir   (repeatedly spoken contemptuously)

washing   slashing
hinds   young female deer. Tybalt is punning on 'heart' (hart = a male deer), mocking Benvolio for fighting with servants (see 'Puns', p. 219)

SAMPSON Fear me not.

GREGORY No, marry, I fear thee!

SAMPSON Let us take the law of our sides, let them begin.

GREGORY I will frown as I pass by, and let them take it as they list.

SAMPSON Nay, as they dare. I will bite my thumb at them, which is   35
disgrace to them if they bear it.

ABRAM Do you bite your thumb at us, sir?

SAMPSON I do bite my thumb, sir.

ABRAM Do you bite your thumb at us, sir?

SAMPSON [*Aside to Gregory*] Is the law of our side if I say ay?   40

GREGORY [*Aside to Sampson*] No.

SAMPSON No, sir, I do not bite my thumb at you, sir, but I bite my
thumb, sir.

GREGORY Do you quarrel, sir?

ABRAM Quarrel, sir? No, sir.   45

SAMPSON But if you do, sir, I am for you. I serve as good a man as
you.

ABRAM No better.

SAMPSON Well, sir.

Enter BENVOLIO.

GREGORY [*Aside to Sampson*] Say 'better', here comes one of my   50
master's kinsmen.

SAMPSON Yes, better, sir.

ABRAM You lie.

SAMPSON Draw, if you be men. Gregory, remember thy washing blow.
They fight.

BENVOLIO Part, fools!   55
Put up your swords, you know not what you do.
[*Beats down their swords.*]

Enter TYBALT.

TYBALT What, art thou drawn among these heartless hinds?
Turn thee, Benvolio, look upon thy death.

BENVOLIO I do but keep the peace. Put up thy sword,
Or manage it to part these men with me.   60

TYBALT What, drawn and talk of peace? I hate the word,
As I hate hell, all Montagues, and thee.
Have at thee, coward.
[*They fight.*]

A furious riot develops. Capulet and Montague join in. Prince Escales, angry and exasperated, stops the fight. He rebukes Montague and Capulet, and threatens death if they fight in public again.

1 A snapshot at the height of the riot (in large groups)

Each group member takes a part. There are at least eleven speaking characters so far. You can add as many other servants and officers as you wish. Use the hall or drama studio if you can, but it will work well in the classroom if you clear some space.

Each group prepares and presents a snapshot photograph (a 'tableau' or 'frozen moment') showing the height of the riot at line 72, 'Rebellious subjects, enemies to peace'.

Your group 'snapshot' shows precisely what each character is doing at *that* moment. This means thinking carefully about what *your* character has said so far, then 'freezing' as that person at this moment in the riot. Remember, each character is doing something in relation to other characters, so try to show those relationships. For example, both Lady Capulet and Lady Montague seem to rebuke and mock their husbands. It takes time to think out, experiment and then present the most dramatic picture.

Hold your 'freeze' for at least sixty seconds – with no movement whatever. The other groups watch for that time. They identify exactly who is who.

2 The all-powerful Prince (in groups of four)

The Prince holds the power of life or death over his subjects. He uses elaborate language (e.g. bloodstained swords are 'neighbour-stainèd steel'). Read the speech aloud, each person reading just one line at a time. Read it again around the group, with a different person beginning the speech. After your readings, write notes advising an actor playing the Prince how to speak the different sections of the speech.

Clubs, bills, and partisans weapons: bills are long-handled pikes, partisans are long, broad-headed spears

train attendants to the Prince

Profaners abusers (because they stain their swords with neighbours' blood)

mistempered disorderly or badly made

movèd angry

Cast by throw aside

Enter [several of both houses, who join the fray, and] three or four
Citizens [as OFFICERS *of the Watch,] with clubs or partisans.*

OFFICERS Clubs, bills, and partisans! Strike! Beat them down!
    Down with the Capulets! Down with the Montagues!   65

Enter old CAPULET *in his gown, and his wife [*LADY CAPULET*].*

CAPULET What noise is this? Give me my long sword, ho!
LADY CAPULET A crutch, a crutch! why call you for a sword?
CAPULET My sword, I say! old Montague is come,
    And flourishes his blade in spite of me.

Enter old MONTAGUE *and his wife [*LADY MONTAGUE*].*

MONTAGUE Thou villain Capulet! – Hold me not, let me go.   70
LADY MONTAGUE Thou shalt not stir one foot to seek a foe.

Enter PRINCE ESCALES *with his train.*

PRINCE Rebellious subjects, enemies to peace,
    Profaners of this neighbour-stainèd steel –
    Will they not hear? – What ho, you men, you beasts!
    That quench the fire of your pernicious rage   75
    With purple fountains issuing from your veins:
    On pain of torture, from those bloody hands
    Throw your mistempered weapons to the ground,
    And hear the sentence of your movèd prince.
    Three civil brawls, bred of an airy word,   80
    By thee, old Capulet, and Montague,
    Have thrice disturbed the quiet of our streets,
    And made Verona's ancient citizens
    Cast by their grave beseeming ornaments
    To wield old partisans, in hands as old,   85
    Cankered with peace, to part your cankered hate;
    If ever you disturb our streets again,
    Your lives shall pay the forfeit of the peace.
    For this time all the rest depart away:
    You, Capulet, shall go along with me,   90
    And, Montague, come you this afternoon,
    To know our farther pleasure in this case,
    To old Free-town, our common judgement-place.
    Once more, on pain of death, all men depart.
        Exeunt [all but Montague, Lady Montague, and Benvolio]

Benvolio recounts the story of the riot. He tells Lady Montague how Romeo has avoided meeting him. Montague confirms that Romeo has been keeping to himself, preferring night to day.

1 Show Benvolio's story of the riot (in small groups)

Take each moment in the developing fight as Benvolio tells it ('Here . . . adversary'; 'And . . . approach'; 'I . . . them'; 'in . . . prepared', and so on). Notice how Benvolio mocks Tybalt's style of fighting in lines 100–3.

Present a slow-motion version and a fast-motion version of the story, showing each action described in lines 97–106. It helps to appoint a narrator who speaks the words as the other group members present the mime.

As you watch other groups presenting their mimes, see if they perform every incident that Benvolio mentions. You'll have to watch the fast-motion versions very carefully!

2 Give Lady Montague a voice

Lady Montague speaks only two lines, then is silent. She never speaks again in the play. Her silence suggests the powerlessness of women in Verona. Step into role as Lady Montague and write an entry in her diary. In it she expresses her concern for Romeo and also says what she thinks about the feud and the fight she has just witnessed.

3 What's the matter with Romeo? (in pairs)

Take parts as Benvolio and Montague and speak lines 109–33 several times, changing characters. Talk together about Romeo's behaviour as described in the speeches. Why is he behaving like this? Suggest a number of possible reasons.

abroach open and flowing like a wine-barrel
sycamore tree associated with melancholy lovers
ware wary, aware
covert concealment
shunned avoided

augmenting adding to
Aurora Roman goddess of dawn
heavy sad, melancholy
pens shuts
portentous ominous
humour mood

MONTAGUE Who set this ancient quarrel new abroach?   95
     Speak, nephew, were you by when it began?
BENVOLIO Here were the servants of your adversary,
     And yours, close fighting ere I did approach:
     I drew to part them; in the instant came
     The fiery Tybalt, with his sword prepared,   100
     Which, as he breathed defiance to my ears,
     He swung about his head and cut the winds,
     Who, nothing hurt withal, hissed him in scorn;
     While we were interchanging thrusts and blows,
     Came more and more, and fought on part and part,   105
     Till the Prince came, who parted either part.
LADY MONTAGUE O where is Romeo? saw you him today?
     Right glad I am he was not at this fray.
BENVOLIO Madam, an hour before the worshipped sun
     Peered forth the golden window of the east,   110
     A troubled mind drive me to walk abroad,
     Where underneath the grove of sycamore,
     That westward rooteth from this city side,
     So early walking did I see your son;
     Towards him I made, but he was ware of me,   115
     And stole into the covert of the wood;
     I, measuring his affections by my own,
     Which then most sought where most might not be found,
     Being one too many by my weary self,
     Pursued my humour, not pursuing his,   120
     And gladly shunned who gladly fled from me.
MONTAGUE Many a morning hath he there been seen,
     With tears augmenting the fresh morning's dew,
     Adding to clouds more clouds with his deep sighs,
     But all so soon as the all-cheering sun   125
     Should in the farthest east begin to draw
     The shady curtains from Aurora's bed,
     Away from light steals home my heavy son,
     And private in his chamber pens himself,
     Shuts up his windows, locks fair daylight out,   130
     And makes himself an artificial night:
     Black and portentous must this humour prove,
     Unless good counsel may the cause remove.

Benvolio promises to find out the cause of Romeo's sadness. Romeo says it is because his love for Rosaline (whom he doesn't name) is not returned. He suddenly notices the signs of the riot.

1 Parents question children (in small groups)

Montague says that he and his friends have questioned Romeo about why he keeps so much to himself, but without success. Romeo just won't tell.

Improvise this questioning of Romeo by his father and other adults who wish to find out the cause of his sadness. After the improvisation, each group member reads Montague's speech (lines 137–46) to the group to see if it comes over as exasperation or puzzlement, or as some other mood.

2 Imagery: 'bit with an envious worm'

In lines 142–4, Montague compares Romeo to a bud which is destroyed by a malicious ('envious') worm before it can fully flower. And in lines 162–3 Romeo says that although Love is blind ('muffled') it can still impose its will on lovers. Both are vivid images typical of many to be found throughout the play.

As you read on you will find it helpful to compile your own list of images which particularly appeal to you (see 'Imagery', pp. 214–15).

3 What's the play all about?

Here's what one student said of line 166:

> This line ('Here's much to do with hate, but more with love') is really what the play is all about. It's the most important line of all.

From what you know of the play so far, write a response agreeing or disagreeing with her view.

---

importuned questioned
sounding investigating (fathoming, an image from measuring the depth of the sea)

shrift confession (by Romeo)
so gentle . . . proof so seemingly kind, is so harsh in experience
muffled still always blindfolded

BENVOLIO My noble uncle, do you know the cause?
MONTAGUE I neither know it, nor can learn of him.   135
BENVOLIO Have you importuned him by any means?
MONTAGUE Both by myself and many other friends,
        But he, his own affections' counsellor,
        Is to himself (I will not say how true)
        But to himself so secret and so close,   140
        So far from sounding and discovery,
        As is the bud bit with an envious worm
        Ere he can spread his sweet leaves to the air,
        Or dedicate his beauty to the sun.
        Could we but learn from whence his sorrows grow,   145
        We would as willingly give cure as know.

Enter ROMEO.

BENVOLIO See where he comes. So please you step aside,
        I'll know his grievance or be much denied.
MONTAGUE I would thou wert so happy by thy stay
        To hear true shrift. Come, madam, let's away.   150
             Exeunt [*Montague and Lady Montague*]
BENVOLIO Good morrow, cousin.
ROMEO   Is the day so young?
BENVOLIO But new struck nine.
ROMEO   Ay me, sad hours seem long.
        Was that my father that went hence so fast?
BENVOLIO It was. What sadness lengthens Romeo's hours?
ROMEO Not having that, which, having, makes them short.   155
BENVOLIO In love?
ROMEO Out –
BENVOLIO Of love?
ROMEO Out of her favour where I am in love.
BENVOLIO Alas that Love, so gentle in his view,   160
        Should be so tyrannous and rough in proof!
ROMEO Alas that Love, whose view is muffled still,
        Should, without eyes, see pathways to his will!
        Where shall we dine? O me! what fray was here?
        Yet tell me not, for I have heard it all: 165
        Here's much to do with hate, but more with love:
        Why then, O brawling love, O loving hate,
        O any thing of nothing first create!

Romeo, melancholy because he loves a girl (Rosaline) who does not love him, plays with words to express how love confuses and mixes up all kinds of things, turning order into chaos.

1 The contradictions of love (in pairs)

Take a closer look at Romeo's language. Here is a different way of setting out parts of lines 167–72:

'loving' v. 'hate'
'heavy' v. 'lightness'
'serious' v. 'vanity'
'Misshapen chaos' v. 'well-seeming forms'
'Feather' v. 'lead'
'bright' v. 'smoke'
'cold' v. 'fire'
'sick' v. 'health'
'Still-waking' v. 'sleep'

The love poetry of Shakespeare's time put together such contradictory words to express the turmoil that love causes. These strange oppositions (e.g. 'loving hate') are called **oxymorons** (see p. 216). You can think of them as very compressed antitheses.

With your partner, choose one pair of words from the list above and prepare three tableaux. These three frozen pictures in turn show the two separate words (e.g. 'loving' and 'hate'), then show the oxymoron ('loving hate'). The class guesses which oxymoron each pair has chosen.

Afterwards, write down five or six oxymorons of your own. Here are two adjectives to get you started: fill in the blanks with suitable 'opposing' nouns.

slow _____
cowardly _____

---

coz cousin
propagate increase
fume breath
gall bitter poison
sadness seriousness (notice Romeo's wordplay in lines 193–5)

mark-man marksman: an archer who hits the target (mark)
Dian Diana, goddess of hunting and chastity. She avoided Cupid's arrows
proof armour

```
                  O heavy lightness, serious vanity,
                  Misshapen chaos of well-seeming forms,              170
                  Feather of lead, bright smoke, cold fire, sick health,
                  Still-waking sleep, that is not what it is!
                  This love feel I, that feel no love in this.
                  Dost thou not laugh?
BENVOLIO                            No, coz, I rather weep.
ROMEO  Good heart, at what?
BENVOLIO                            At thy good heart's oppression.   175
ROMEO  Why, such is love's transgression:
                  Griefs of mine own lie heavy in my breast,
                  Which thou wilt propagate to have it pressed
                  With more of thine; this love that thou hast shown
                  Doth add more grief to too much of mine own.        180
                  Love is a smoke made with the fume of sighs,
                  Being purged, a fire sparkling in lovers' eyes,
                  Being vexed, a sea nourished with loving tears.
                  What is it else? a madness most discreet,
                  A choking gall, and a preserving sweet.             185
                  Farewell, my coz.
BENVOLIO                   Soft, I will go along;
                  And if you leave me so, you do me wrong.
ROMEO  Tut, I have lost myself, I am not here,
                  This is not Romeo, he's some other where.
BENVOLIO  Tell me in sadness, who is that you love?                   190
ROMEO  What, shall I groan and tell thee?
BENVOLIO                                 Groan? why, no;
                  But sadly tell me, who?
ROMEO  Bid a sick man in sadness make his will –
                  A word ill urged to one that is so ill:
                  In sadness, cousin, I do love a woman.              195
BENVOLIO  I aimed so near, when I supposed you loved.
ROMEO  A right good mark-man! and she's fair I love.
BENVOLIO  A right fair mark, fair coz, is soonest hit.
ROMEO  Well, in that hit you miss: she'll not be hit
                  With Cupid's arrow, she hath Dian's wit;            200
                  And in strong proof of chastity well armed,
                  From Love's weak childish bow she lives uncharmed.
```

Romeo complains that because she refuses to marry, the woman he loves will leave no children. Her beauty dies with her. Benvolio advises him to look at other girls – that will cure him! Romeo isn't convinced.

1 Is Romeo really in love? (in small groups)

Romeo uses the language of classical poetry, and many people today think that because he uses this elaborate way of speaking, his emotions are 'artificial', not coming from the heart. But what do you think? Does this manner of speaking (for example, using fanciful imagery, wordplay, antitheses and rhyming couplets) show that he is really in love, as he claims to be, or just infatuated? Speak Romeo's language opposite, and talk about whether it strikes you as really sincere and heartfelt.

Nicholas Hilliard's painting of an Elizabethan courtier echoes the melancholy mood of Romeo. He leans languorously on a tree, hand on heart, and caught by rosebush thorns, the symbol of unrequited passion.

---

stay the siege submit to the assault (notice Romeo's military metaphor)
bide th'encounter endure the battle
ope her lap to sell her chastity for

posterity descendants, children
forsworn to love taken an oath not to fall in love
passing exceedingly
pay that doctrine teach that lesson

She will not stay the siege of loving terms,
Nor bide th'encounter of assailing eyes,
Nor ope her lap to saint-seducing gold.   205
O, she is rich in beauty, only poor
That when she dies, with beauty dies her store.
BENVOLIO Then she hath sworn that she will still live chaste?
ROMEO She hath, and in that sparing makes huge waste;
For beauty starved with her severity   210
Cuts beauty off from all posterity.
She is too fair, too wise, wisely too fair,
To merit bliss by making me despair.
She hath forsworn to love, and in that vow
Do I live dead, that live to tell it now.   215
BENVOLIO Be ruled by me, forget to think of her.
ROMEO O teach me how I should forget to think.
BENVOLIO By giving liberty unto thine eyes,
Examine other beauties.
ROMEO   'Tis the way
To call hers (exquisite) in question more: 220
These happy masks that kiss fair ladies' brows,
Being black, puts us in mind they hide the fair;
He that is strucken blind cannot forget
The precious treasure of his eyesight lost;
Show me a mistress that is passing fair,   225
What doth her beauty serve but as a note
Where I may read who passed that passing fair?
Farewell, thou canst not teach me to forget.
BENVOLIO I'll pay that doctrine, or else die in debt.

                                              Exeunt

Paris wishes to marry Juliet. Capulet says his daughter is still only thirteen, but he will agree if Juliet consents. He invites Paris to a party that night, where there will be many beautiful women.

1 What were Capulet and Paris talking about? (in pairs)

Capulet and Paris enter in the middle of a conversation. Improvise some of the things they have been saying together before they entered. Remember, Capulet has already been involved in the action of Scene 1; Paris has not been involved. Try to make your improvised conversation lead up naturally to the opening line: 'But Montague is bound as well as I' (the Prince has ordered both me and Montague to keep the peace).

2 More vivid imagery

Juliet is Capulet's only child. Line 14 suggests that all his other children have died. Make a drawing to illustrate the line:

Earth hath swallowed all my hopes but she

3 Help the audience – lines 32–3

Most people find these two lines very difficult, so don't worry if you have problems with them. They echo Benvolio's advice to Romeo in Scene 1 ('Examine other beauties' – look at other girls). The general sense seems to be: 'When you see the other girls at my party, my daughter might or might not be the one you'll like most'. If you were the actor playing Capulet and wished to make the meaning as clear as possible to Paris and the audience, what would you do?

Clown (servant) in most modern productions this is usually Peter, the Nurse's servant
bound ordered
In penalty alike both subject to the same punishment
at odds as enemies

suit request to marry
marred spoilt
Earth-treading stars lovely ladies
well-apparelled well-dressed
fennel buds fennel (a herb) was thought to provoke passion. Here it implies 'young women'

Act 1 Scene 2
Capulet's mansion

Enter CAPULET, COUNTY PARIS, and the CLOWN [SERVANT to
CAPULET].

CAPULET But Montague is bound as well as I,
   In penalty alike, and 'tis not hard, I think,
   For men so old as we to keep the peace.
PARIS Of honourable reckoning are you both,
   And pity 'tis, you lived at odds so long.   5
   But now, my lord, what say you to my suit?
CAPULET But saying o'er what I have said before:
   My child is yet a stranger in the world,
   She hath not seen the change of fourteen years;
   Let two more summers wither in their pride, 10
   Ere we may think her ripe to be a bride.
PARIS Younger than she are happy mothers made.
CAPULET And too soon marred are those so early made.
   Earth hath swallowed all my hopes but she;
   She's the hopeful lady of my earth.   15
   But woo her, gentle Paris, get her heart,
   My will to her consent is but a part;
   And she agreed, within her scope of choice
   Lies my consent and fair according voice.
   This night I hold an old accustomed feast, 20
   Whereto I have invited many a guest,
   Such as I love, and you among the store,
   One more, most welcome, makes my number more.
   At my poor house look to behold this night
   Earth-treading stars that make dark heaven light. 25
   Such comfort as do lusty young men feel
   When well-apparelled April on the heel
   Of limping winter treads, even such delight
   Among fresh fennel buds shall you this night
   Inherit at my house; hear all, all see;   30
   And like her most whose merit most shall be;
   Which on more view of many, mine, being one,
   May stand in number, though in reck'ning none.

Capulet orders his servant to deliver party invitations. But the servant can't read! Benvolio again urges Romeo to look at other women to cure his love-sickness. The servant asks Romeo to read the letter.

1 Prose and verse

Notice that the servant speaks in prose. In plays written in Shakespeare's time it was conventional for lower-status characters to use prose (as Sampson and Gregory did in Scene 1). High-status characters spoke verse. See page 218 for more on the use of verse and prose.

2 Is the servant clever or stupid? (in pairs)

The servant, who cannot read, is given a list of names. As he talks (lines 39–40), he muddles up workers and their tools (a shoemaker uses a last, a tailor a yard, and so on). Imagine you are directing the play. The actor playing the servant asks whether he should play him as dull-witted or clever. Is the servant in fact cleverer than he seems? What do you say, and why?

To help you, read lines 38–43 with your partner: first, as if the servant were stupid, then as if he were quick-witted.

3 Make Benvolio's advice active (in groups of four)

Benvolio's advice to Romeo (lines 44–9) is that the cure for love is to look at other girls because new love drives out old. Here, he says the same thing in five different ways. Work out how you can show, without words, each part of the advice. A hint: it's probably easiest to begin with 'pain' (line 45 – new pain makes you forget earlier suffering), then 'giddy', then 'grief', then 'infection'. Finally, see if you can make up a mime for 'fire'.

Show your five actions to the class.

---

yard a tailor's measuring rod
last a shoemaker's device to hold a shoe
holp helped
rank foul-smelling

plantain leaf a leaf used to heal cuts and grazes
God-den good evening
gi' give you
rest you merry farewell

Come go with me. [*To Servant*] Go, sirrah, trudge about
Through fair Verona, find those persons out   35
Whose names are written there [*Gives a paper.*], and to
    them say,
My house and welcome on their pleasure stay.

                                        Exit [*with Paris*]

SERVANT Find them out whose names are written here! It is written
that the shoemaker should meddle with his yard and the tailor with
his last, the fisher with his pencil and the painter with his nets;   40
but I am sent to find those persons whose names are here writ, and
can never find what names the writing person hath here writ. I must
to the learnèd. In good time!

                Enter BENVOLIO *and* ROMEO.

BENVOLIO Tut, man, one fire burns out another's burning,
    One pain is lessened by another's anguish;   45
    Turn giddy, and be holp by backward turning;
    One desperate grief cures with another's languish:
    Take thou some new infection to thy eye,
    And the rank poison of the old will die.
ROMEO Your plantain leaf is excellent for that.   50
BENVOLIO For what, I pray thee?
ROMEO   For your broken shin.
BENVOLIO Why, Romeo, art thou mad?
ROMEO Not mad, but bound more than a madman is:
    Shut up in prison, kept without my food,
    Whipt and tormented, and – God-den, good fellow.   55
SERVANT God gi' god-den. I pray, sir, can you read?
ROMEO Ay, mine own fortune in my misery.
SERVANT Perhaps you have learned it without book; but I pray, can
    you read any thing you see?
ROMEO Ay, if I know the letters and the language.   60
SERVANT Ye say honestly, rest you merry.
ROMEO Stay, fellow, I can read.
               He reads the letter.
    'Signior Martino and his wife and daughters,
    County Anselme and his beauteous sisters,
    The lady widow of Vitruvio,   65
    Signior Placentio and his lovely nieces,
    Mercutio and his brother Valentine,

Romeo discovers that Rosaline has been invited to Capulet's party. Benvolio urges Romeo to go. There he will see women more beautiful than Rosaline. Romeo refuses to believe Benvolio's claim.

---

1 Make a grand entry! (in large groups)

The names on the list of guests (lines 63–71) roll off the tongue. One person acts as Master (or Mistress) of Ceremonies. He or she will announce the guests, line by line. Everyone else chooses a part and decides how their character will make their grand entrance to Capulet's party. At least twenty-three persons are listed, so double up parts and make two entrances!

2 How does Romeo react to 'Rosaline'? (in pairs)

Romeo, reading the list, suddenly discovers (line 69) that Rosaline, the woman he thinks he loves, is coming to the party. How does he react at that moment? Read the list to your partner and react to the name 'Rosaline' as you think Romeo would.

3 'Transparent heretics, be burnt for liars'

Romeo continues to protest that his love for Rosaline will never change. He even says (lines 88–91) that if he did see someone more beautiful than Rosaline, his eyes would burn out because they would be liars, unfaithful to the 'devout religion' they serve: his adoring belief in Rosaline's beauty. Romeo's lines seem to be inspired by the practice of burning heretics at the stake.

---

unattainted unbiased
devout religion adoring belief
Transparent heretics obvious
 disbelievers

poised balanced, weighed
crystal scales (Romeo's eyes)
scant scarcely
mine own (Rosaline's beauty)

Mine uncle Capulet, his wife and daughters,
My fair niece Rosaline, and Livia,
Signior Valentio and his cousin Tybalt,   70
Lucio and the lively Helena.'
A fair assembly: whither should they come?
SERVANT Up.
ROMEO Whither? to supper?
SERVANT To our house.   75
ROMEO Whose house?
SERVANT My master's.
ROMEO Indeed I should have asked thee that before.
SERVANT Now I'll tell you without asking. My master is the great rich
  Capulet, and if you be not of the house of Montagues, I pray come   80
  and crush a cup of wine. Rest you merry.   [*Exit*]
BENVOLIO At this same ancient feast of Capulet's
Sups the fair Rosaline whom thou so loves,
With all the admirèd beauties of Verona:
Go thither, and with unattainted eye   85
Compare her face with some that I shall show,
And I will make thee think thy swan a crow.
ROMEO When the devout religion of mine eye
Maintains such falsehood, then turn tears to fires;
And these who, often drowned, could never die,   90
Transparent heretics, be burnt for liars.
One fairer than my love! the all-seeing sun
Ne'er saw her match since first the world begun.
BENVOLIO Tut, you saw her fair, none else being by,
Herself poised with herself in either eye;   95
But in that crystal scales let there be weighed
Your lady's love against some other maid
That I will show you shining at this feast,
And she shall scant show well that now seems best.
ROMEO I'll go along no such sight to be shown,   100
But to rejoice in splendour of mine own.
                                              [*Exeunt*]

Lady Capulet and the Nurse discuss Juliet's age. She is not yet fourteen. The Nurse remembers her own daughter, Susan, now dead. She recalls that Juliet was weaned eleven years ago.

1 The Nurse – first impressions (in small groups)

Speak aloud all the Nurse says from line 2 to line 63. Each person reads only a little of the Nurse's language (not more than two or three lines, sometimes only one or two words), then hands the speech on to the next group member. Just read a short piece that makes sense on its own, then hand on. Speak your own short extracts as you think the Nurse would say them.

Afterwards, write down a list of words or phrases your group thinks would best describe the Nurse. Compare your list with those of other groups. Add to your list as you learn more about her in other scenes.

The Nurse, Lady Capulet and Juliet. What line might be being spoken here?

---

maidenhead virginity
thou s' hear you shall hear
teen sorrow
Lammas-tide 1 August (Lady Mass). Juliet will be fourteen on Lammas-eve (31 July)

marry by the Virgin Mary (a mild oath)
laid wormwood to my dug rubbed bitter-tasting plant on her nipple (to wean Juliet)
bear a brain have a good memory

Act 1 Scene 3
A room in Capulet's mansion

Enter CAPULET'S WIFE and NURSE.

LADY CAPULET Nurse, where's my daughter? call her forth to me.
NURSE Now by my maidenhead at twelve year old,
    I bade her come. What, lamb! What, ladybird!
    God forbid, where's this girl? What, Juliet!

Enter JULIET.

JULIET How now, who calls?   5
NURSE Your mother.
JULIET Madam, I am here, what is your will?
LADY CAPULET This is the matter. Nurse, give leave a while,
    We must talk in secret. Nurse, come back again,
    I have remembered me, thou s' hear our counsel.   10
    Thou knowest my daughter's of a pretty age.
NURSE Faith, I can tell her age unto an hour.
LADY CAPULET She's not fourteen.
NURSE   I'll lay fourteen of my teeth –
    And yet to my teen be it spoken, I have but four –
    She's not fourteen. How long is it now   15
    To Lammas-tide?
LADY CAPULET   A fortnight and odd days.
NURSE Even or odd, of all days in the year,
    Come Lammas-eve at night shall she be fourteen.
    Susan and she – God rest all Christian souls! –
    Were of an age. Well, Susan is with God,   20
    She was too good for me. But as I said,
    On Lammas-eve at night shall she be fourteen,
    That shall she, marry, I remember it well.
    'Tis since the earthquake now aleven years,
    And she was weaned – I never shall forget it –   25
    Of all the days of the year, upon that day;
    For I had then laid wormwood to my dug,
    Sitting in the sun under the dove-house wall.
    My lord and you were then at Mantua –
    Nay, I do bear a brain – but as I said,   30

The Nurse reminisces about Juliet's childhood and tells how her husband joked about Juliet's sexuality. Lady Capulet begins to talk to Juliet about marriage.

---

1 Juliet's age (in small groups)

The opening of Scene 3 creates the impression of just how young Juliet is. She is still only thirteen, even though Lady Capulet has plans that she shall soon marry. One production made Juliet seem almost childlike. She entered eating chocolates, then sat cross-legged on the floor ignoring all that the Nurse and her mother said. She continued to eat, and her face became more and more smeared with chocolate.

Talk together about how you think Juliet should enter, and what first impression of her (and her age) you would wish the audience to have.

2 Lady Capulet's view of the Nurse

Imagine you are Lady Capulet. Write the letter she sends later that day to a close friend telling her about the Nurse's story. Make clear her attitude towards the Nurse's talkativeness. Remember, she has very high status in Verona, so that will influence her style of writing.

3 Write the stage directions (in pairs)

Write detailed stage directions for this scene so far. For example, how does the Nurse behave at lines 8–10 when Lady Capulet dismisses her, then calls her back to share in the conversation? And how should Juliet and Lady Capulet behave during the Nurse's long story (lines 17–63)? Identify which lines or words you think they would most obviously respond to and write directions for the actors.

---

tetchy   irritable
Shake!   Look lively! (Shake a leg!)
I trow   I'm sure
high-lone   unaided
th'rood   Christ's cross
'A   he

holidam   'holiness', or Virgin Mary (holy dame)
stinted   stopped (crying)
cock'rel's stone   cockerel's testicle
perilous knock   terrible lump
dispositions   inclinations

When it did taste the wormwood on the nipple
Of my dug, and felt it bitter, pretty fool,
To see it tetchy and fall out wi'th'dug!
'Shake!' quoth the dove-house; 'twas no need, I trow,
To bid me trudge.   35
And since that time it is aleven years,
For then she could stand high-lone; nay, by th'rood,
She could have run and waddled all about;
For even the day before, she broke her brow,
And then my husband – God be with his soul,   40
'A was a merry man – took up the child.
'Yea', quoth he, 'dost thou fall upon thy face?
Thou wilt fall backward when thou hast more wit,
Wilt thou not, Jule?' And by my holidam,
The pretty wretch left crying, and said 'Ay'.   45
To see now how a jest shall come about!
I warrant, and I should live a thousand years,
I never should forget it: 'Wilt thou not, Jule?' quoth he,
And, pretty fool, it stinted, and said 'Ay'.

LADY CAPULET Enough of this, I pray thee hold thy peace.   50
NURSE Yes, madam, yet I cannot choose but laugh,
    To think it should leave crying, and say 'Ay':
    And yet I warrant it had upon it brow
    A bump as big as a young cock'rel's stone,
    A perilous knock, and it cried bitterly.   55
    'Yea', quoth my husband, 'fall'st upon thy face?
    Thou wilt fall backward when thou comest to age,
    Wilt thou not, Jule?' It stinted, and said 'Ay'.
JULIET And stint thou too, I pray thee, Nurse, say I.
NURSE Peace, I have done. God mark thee to his grace,   60
    Thou wast the prettiest babe that e'er I nursed.
    And I might live to see thee married once,
    I have my wish.
LADY CAPULET Marry, that 'marry' is the very theme
    I came to talk of. Tell me, daughter Juliet,   65
    How stands your dispositions to be married?
JULIET It is an honour that I dream not of.
NURSE An honour! were not I thine only nurse,
    I would say thou hadst sucked wisdom from thy teat.

Lady Capulet gives her reasons why Juliet should think of marriage. She tells her daughter of Paris's love, praising him in elaborate style. A servant tells them the party guests have arrived.

___

1 Juliet's diary entry

Juliet speaks only five times in this scene and has a total of only seven lines. But what is she thinking? Remind yourself of her seven lines and what she has heard her mother and Nurse say. Write her diary entry about how she feels about what happened in Scene 3.

2 Something like a sonnet (in pairs)

Lady Capulet's lines 82–95 praising Paris are rather like a sonnet: there are fourteen lines, but the pattern of the rhymes is different from the usual sonnet form (see p. 217). Lady Capulet elaborately compares Paris to an attractive book. To explore her imagery more closely, try the following activity.

Sit facing each other and read the lines aloud, each person reading just one line at a time. As you read your line, try to perform an action with the book you have in your hand. Some lines you'll find quite easy to accompany with an action. Others are more difficult, especially lines 90–1, 'The fish lives in the sea . . . / . . . the fair within to hide'. This seems to mean that just as fish are at home in the sea, so good books deserve good covers, and handsome men deserve beautiful wives.

3 Ages: Lady Capulet, the Nurse . . . and Romeo

Shakespeare tells us Juliet's age. But how old are other characters? Use lines 73–4 to work out the approximate age of Juliet's mother. Then suggest how old you think the Nurse might be . . . and Romeo.

___

man of wax perfect man (like a sculptor's wax model)
married lineament harmonious feature
margent margin
fair without handsome appearance

bigger women . . . men pregnancy makes women larger
endart pierce like a dart (or Cupid's arrow)
extremity crisis
the County stays Count Paris is waiting

LADY CAPULET Well, think of marriage now; younger than you,   70
        Here in Verona, ladies of esteem,
        Are made already mothers. By my count,
        I was your mother much upon these years
        That you are now a maid. Thus then in brief:
        The valiant Paris seeks you for his love.   75
NURSE A man, young lady! lady, such a man
        As all the world – Why, he's a man of wax.
LADY CAPULET Verona's summer hath not such a flower.
NURSE Nay, he's a flower, in faith, a very flower.
LADY CAPULET What say you, can you love the gentleman?   80
        This night you shall behold him at our feast;
        Read o'er the volume of young Paris' face,
        And find delight writ there with beauty's pen;
        Examine every married lineament,
        And see how one another lends content;   85
        And what obscured in this fair volume lies
        Find written in the margent of his eyes.
        This precious book of love, this unbound lover,
        To beautify him, only lacks a cover.
        The fish lives in the sea, and 'tis much pride   90
        For fair without the fair within to hide;
        That book in many's eyes doth share the glory
        That in gold clasps locks in the golden story:
        So shall you share all that he doth possess,
        By having him, making yourself no less.   95
NURSE No less! nay, bigger women grow by men.
LADY CAPULET Speak briefly, can you like of Paris' love?
JULIET I'll look to like, if looking liking move;
        But no more deep will I endart mine eye
        Than your consent gives strength to make it fly.   100

                        Enter SERVINGMAN.

SERVINGMAN Madam, the guests are come, supper served up, you
        called, my young lady asked for, the Nurse cursed in the pantry,
        and every thing in extremity. I must hence to wait, I beseech you
        follow straight.   [*Exit*]
LADY CAPULET We follow thee. Juliet, the County stays.   105
NURSE Go, girl, seek happy nights to happy days.

                                Exeunt

Romeo and his friends, carrying masks and torches, prepare for their visit to Capulet's party. Romeo declares his unhappiness and says he will not dance. Mercutio tries to laugh Romeo out of his sadness.

1 Focus on Benvolio, the peacekeeper

Romeo and his friends are about to gatecrash Capulet's party. It was the custom of such uninvited guests to have a speech prepared and to perform a dance for the guests. Benvolio argues that such speeches are old-fashioned and long-winded ('The date is out of such prolixity'). His lines 7–8 may be Shakespeare's private joke about actors who speak the Prologue being unable to remember their lines. Benvolio says they should just perform their dance and leave ('We'll measure them a measure and be gone').

Benvolio's name means 'well-wishing' (the opposite of Malvolio in *Twelfth Night*, whose name means 'ill-wishing'). He seems to be a peacekeeper: in Scene 1, he tried to stop the brawling. Here, he seems to want to avoid trouble. As you read on, look out for ways in which Benvolio tries to prevent conflict.

2 Introducing Mercutio, the joker

In contrast to Benvolio, Mercutio is never bothered about getting into trouble. He seeks excitement and revels in living on the edge. His language is rich in imaginative imagery, and like Shakespeare's contemporaries he loves wordplay and puns (words which sound the same but have different meanings, see p. 219). All three young men use puns in the dialogue opposite: for example, 'soles'/'soul', 'soar'/'sore', 'pricks'/'prick', 'visor'/'visor'; and in Shakespeare's time 'heavy' (line 22) also meant 'sad'. As you read on, look out for how Mercutio's dazzling imagination produces sparkling language.

Tartar's painted bow of lath an oriental bow (shaped like an upper lip). Here, made of thin wood and held by Cupid
crow-keeper scarecrow
measure (line 9) judge
measure (line 10) (1) perform (2) dance
bound (line 18) limit
bound (line 20) tied up
bound (line 21) leap
case mask
A visor for a visor! a mask for an ugly face
cote notice

Act 1 Scene 4

A street outside Capulet's mansion

Enter ROMEO, MERCUTIO, BENVOLIO, with five or six other MASKERS, TORCH-BEARERS.

ROMEO What, shall this speech be spoke for our excuse?
　　　Or shall we on without apology?
BENVOLIO The date is out of such prolixity:
　　　We'll have no Cupid hoodwinked with a scarf,
　　　Bearing a Tartar's painted bow of lath,　　　　　　　5
　　　Scaring the ladies like a crow-keeper,
　　　Nor no without-book prologue, faintly spoke
　　　After the prompter, for our entrance;
　　　But let them measure us by what they will,
　　　We'll measure them a measure and be gone.　　　　　10
ROMEO Give me a torch, I am not for this ambling;
　　　Being but heavy, I will bear the light.
MERCUTIO Nay, gentle Romeo, we must have you dance.
ROMEO Not I, believe me. You have dancing shoes
　　　With nimble soles, I have a soul of lead　　　　　　15
　　　So stakes me to the ground I cannot move.
MERCUTIO You are a lover, borrow Cupid's wings,
~　　　And soar with them above a common bound.
ROMEO I am too sore enpiercèd with his shaft
　　　To soar with his light feathers, and so bound　　　　20
　　　I cannot bound a pitch above dull woe:
　　　Under love's heavy burden do I sink.
MERCUTIO And to sink in it should you burden love,
　　　Too great oppression for a tender thing.
ROMEO Is love a tender thing? it is too rough,　　　　　　25
　　　Too rude, too boist'rous, and it pricks like thorn.
MERCUTIO If love be rough with you, be rough with love:
　　　Prick love for pricking, and you beat love down.
　　　Give me a case to put my visage in, [*Puts on a mask.*]
　　　A visor for a visor! what care I　　　　　　　　　　30
　　　What curious eye doth cote deformities?
　　　Here are the beetle brows shall blush for me.

Romeo refuses to be cheered up, in spite of Mercutio's joking. He has no wish to join in the dance. Mercutio begins to tell of Queen Mab, queen of the fairies. He describes the intricate detail of her coach.

An artist's vision of Queen Mab. Compare it closely with Mercutio's description in lines 54–68, identifying details.

senseless rushes green rushes used to cover floors – try to work out why Romeo calls them 'senseless'
grandsire phrase old saying
dun mouse-coloured

Dun horse or 'stick in the mud'. An Elizabethan Christmas game was 'Dun-in-the-mire': partygoers pulled a log out of an imaginary marsh
burn daylight waste time

BENVOLIO Come knock and enter, and no sooner in,
　　　　But every man betake him to his legs.
ROMEO A torch for me: let wantons light of heart　　　　35
　　　　Tickle the senseless rushes with their heels;
　　　　For I am proverbed with a grandsire phrase,
　　　　I'll be a candle-holder and look on:
　　　　The game was ne'er so fair, and I am done.
MERCUTIO Tut, dun's the mouse, the constable's own word.　　40
　　　　If thou art Dun, we'll draw thee from the mire,
　　　　Or (save your reverence) love, wherein thou stickest
　　　　Up to the ears. Come, we burn daylight, ho!
ROMEO Nay, that's not so.
MERCUTIO　　　　　　I mean, sir, in delay
　　　　We waste our lights in vain, like lights by day.　　45
　　　　Take our good meaning, for our judgement sits
　　　　Five times in that ere once in our five wits.
ROMEO And we mean well in going to this mask,
　　　　But 'tis no wit to go.
MERCUTIO　　　　　　　Why, may one ask?
ROMEO I dreamt a dream tonight.
MERCUTIO　　　　　　　And so did I.　　50
ROMEO Well, what was yours?
MERCUTIO　　　　　　　That dreamers often lie.
ROMEO In bed asleep, while they do dream things true.
MERCUTIO O then I see Queen Mab hath been with you:
　　　　She is the fairies' midwife, and she comes
　　　　In shape no bigger than an agate-stone　　55
　　　　On the forefinger of an alderman,
　　　　Drawn with a team of little atomi
　　　　Over men's noses as they lie asleep.
　　　　Her chariot is an empty hazel-nut,
　　　　Made by the joiner squirrel or old grub,　　60
　　　　Time out a'mind the fairies' coachmakers:
　　　　Her waggon-spokes made of long spinners' legs,
　　　　The cover of the wings of grasshoppers,
　　　　Her traces of the smallest spider web,
　　　　Her collars of the moonshine's wat'ry beams,　　65
　　　　Her whip of cricket's bone, the lash of film,
　　　　Her waggoner a small grey-coated gnat,
　　　　Not half so big as a round little worm

Mercutio continues his description of Queen Mab, telling of the dreams she creates in the minds of all kinds of sleepers. He dismisses dreams as nothing but idle fantasies.

1 Act out Queen Mab's trickery (in pairs)

In lines 70–94, Mercutio describes what Queen Mab does to different people: lovers, courtiers, lawyers, churchmen, soldiers and others. One person reads the speech a line at a time, the other mimes the actions described. Then change over reader and mimer.

Talk together about which actions you think best fit each line. Show your final version to the class.

2 Write a modern version of Queen Mab (in pairs)

Take lines 59–94 and write your own version of Queen Mab in today's language. Notice that the speech is very structured. It has two main sections:

• the description of her carriage (lines 59–69)
• what she does to people (lines 70–94).

Passages within those sections begin with 'Her', 'O'er', 'Sometime', and 'This is'.

Use Shakespeare's language as the basis of your own version. You might wish to substitute one word at a time, or rewrite whole lines. Alternatively, you may prefer to write the entire speech in your own style.

Put actions to your version and show it to the other pairs.

3 Notes for Mercutio – then speak the speech!

Imagine you have been chosen to act the role of Mercutio. Write notes on how to deliver each section of the Queen Mab speech (lines 53–94). Afterwards, use your notes to rehearse and speak the lines.

---

cur'sies curtsies, bowing and scraping
smelling out a suit gaining money by helping someone at court
tithe-pig pigs were sometimes given to clergymen as tithes (a tenth part of one's income)

benefice source of income, a paid position in a church
Spanish blades high-quality swords or fashionable young men
healths drinks (or toasts, as in 'cheers')
elf-locks tangled, knotted hair

Pricked from the lazy finger of a maid.
And in this state she gallops night by night   70
Through lovers' brains, and then they dream of love,
O'er courtiers' knees, that dream on cur'sies straight,
O'er lawyers' fingers, who straight dream on fees,
O'er ladies' lips, who straight on kisses dream,
Which oft the angry Mab with blisters plagues,   75
Because their breaths with sweetmeats tainted are.
Sometime she gallops o'er a courtier's nose,
And then dreams he of smelling out a suit;
And sometime comes she with a tithe-pig's tail
Tickling a parson's nose as 'a lies asleep,   80
Then he dreams of another benefice.
Sometime she driveth o'er a soldier's neck,
And then dreams he of cutting foreign throats,
Of breaches, ambuscadoes, Spanish blades,
Of healths five fathom deep; and then anon   85
Drums in his ear, at which he starts and wakes,
And being thus frighted, swears a prayer or two,
And sleeps again. This is that very Mab
That plats the manes of horses in the night,
And bakes the elf-locks in foul sluttish hairs,   90
Which, once untangled, much misfortune bodes.
This is the hag, when maids lie on their backs,
That presses them and learns them first to bear,
Making them women of good carriage.
This is she –

ROMEO   Peace, peace, Mercutio, peace!   95
Thou talk'st of nothing.

MERCUTIO   True, I talk of dreams,
Which are the children of an idle brain,
Begot of nothing but vain fantasy,
Which is as thin of substance as the air,
And more inconstant than the wind, who woos   100
Even now the frozen bosom of the north,
And being angered puffs away from thence,
Turning his side to the dew-dropping south.

BENVOLIO This wind you talk of blows us from ourselves:
Supper is done, and we shall come too late.   105

In spite of his fearful misgivings, Romeo decides to go along with the others to Capulet's party. The following scene begins with Capulet's servants joking together as they prepare for the dancing.

1 Romeo's fearful dream – what was it? (in pairs)

Romeo looks uneasily into the future and has a premonition of death. His tone is ominous, filled with foreboding. He uses legal language prophesying that his premature ('untimely') death will result from what he begins tonight ('date') by going to Capulet's feast. His life will be the penalty ('forfeit') he must pay when the time is up ('expire the term').

Earlier (line 50), Romeo spoke of his dream. Talk together about lines 106–11 and then write an account of what you think Romeo's dream might have been. You may find it helpful to pick out all the words in these six lines that describe fear or loss. No one knows what Romeo dreamed, so don't be afraid to use your imagination.

2 Act out the servants' lines 1–14 (in groups of four)

You'll find you can perform this tiny bustling scene-opening (only fourteen lines) in all kinds of ways. In groups of four, act out the lines, inventing as much 'business' as you like to suit the words.

3 Change the scene swiftly

The stage direction that ends Scene 4 suggests that Romeo and his friends do not leave the stage. But how is the scene change made from outside Capulet's house to inside? Step into role as director and write how you would make the scene change so that there is no long pause, but Scene 4 flows swiftly into Scene 5.

He that hath the steerage of my course God, who guides my life
trencher wooden dish
join-stools wooden stools
look to the plate clear away the silverware
marchpane marzipan
Susan Grindstone and Nell girlfriends (or prostitutes) invited to the servants' party after the feast

ROMEO I fear too early, for my mind misgives
       Some consequence yet hanging in the stars
       Shall bitterly begin his fearful date
       With this night's revels, and expire the term
       Of a despisèd life closed in my breast,   110
       By some vile forfeit of untimely death.
       But He that hath the steerage of my course
       Direct my sail! On, lusty gentlemen.
BENVOLIO Strike, drum.
       They march about the stage [and stand to one side].

Act 1 Scene 5
The Great Hall in Capulet's mansion

       SERVINGMEN come forth with napkins.

FIRST SERVINGMAN Where's Potpan, that he helps not to take away?
   He shift a trencher? he scrape a trencher?
SECOND SERVINGMAN When good manners shall lie all in one or two
   men's hands, and they unwashed too, 'tis a foul thing.
FIRST SERVINGMAN Away with the join-stools, remove the court-   5
   cupboard, look to the plate. Good thou, save me a piece of
   marchpane, and as thou loves me, let the porter let in Susan
   Grindstone and Nell.
                       [Exit Second Servingman]
   Anthony and Potpan!

       [Enter two more SERVINGMEN.*]*

THIRD SERVINGMAN Ay, boy, ready.   10
FIRST SERVINGMAN You are looked for and called for, asked for and
   sought for, in the great chamber.
FOURTH SERVINGMAN We cannot be here and there too. Cheerly,
   boys, be brisk a while, and the longer liver take all.
                       [They retire behind]

Capulet welcomes the dancers. He reminisces with his cousin about past times. Their conversation suggests that Capulet is well into middle age. Romeo catches sight of Juliet for the first time.

In this production, Lady Capulet (centre) flirts openly with Tybalt (right).

1 Relationships: 'business' during the dance (in pairs)

Some productions use the dance to suggest a sexual relationship between Lady Capulet and Tybalt. Other productions show that during the dance Juliet becomes aware of Romeo's fascinated attention. Talk together about what you think are the dramatic advantages and disadvantages of these two options. Then suggest what stage 'business' you would introduce into the dance to convey something about character relationships. (See the picture of the dance on p. vi in the colour section.)

Maskers masked dancers	**nuptial** wedding
walk a bout dance	**Pentecost** Whit Sunday, fifty days after Easter
visor mask	
Berlady by our Lady (the Virgin Mary)	**ward** under twenty-one (and so having a guardian)

Enter [CAPULET, LADY CAPULET, JULIET, TYBALT *and his* PAGE, NURSE, *and*] *all the* GUESTS *and* GENTLEWOMEN *to the Maskers.*

CAPULET Welcome, gentlemen! Ladies that have their toes   15
    Unplagued with corns will walk a bout with you.
    Ah, my mistresses, which of you all
    Will now deny to dance? She that makes dainty,
    She I'll swear hath corns. Am I come near ye now?
    Welcome, gentlemen! I have seen the day   20
    That I have worn a visor and could tell
    A whispering tale in a fair lady's ear,
    Such as would please; 'tis gone, 'tis gone, 'tis gone.
    You are welcome, gentlemen. Come, musicians, play.
                Music plays.
    A hall, a hall, give room! and foot it, girls.   25
                And they dance.
    More light, you knaves, and turn the tables up;
    And quench the fire, the room is grown too hot.
    Ah, sirrah, this unlooked-for sport comes well.
    Nay, sit, nay, sit, good Cousin Capulet,
    For you and I are past our dancing days.   30
    How long is't now since last yourself and I
    Were in a mask?
COUSIN CAPULET   Berlady, thirty years.
CAPULET What, man, 'tis not so much, 'tis not so much:
    'Tis since the nuptial of Lucentio,
    Come Pentecost as quickly as it will,   35
    Some five and twenty years, and then we masked.
COUSIN CAPULET 'Tis more, 'tis more, his son is elder, sir;
    His son is thirty.
CAPULET   Will you tell me that?
    His son was but a ward two years ago.
ROMEO [*To a Servingman*] What lady's that which doth enrich the hand   40
    Of yonder knight?
SERVINGMAN I know not, sir.

Romeo is entranced by Juliet's beauty. Tybalt, recognising Romeo's voice, is outraged that a Montague should dare gatecrash Capulet's party. Capulet scolds Tybalt for wanting to pick a fight.

1 'O she doth teach the torches to burn bright!'

Line 43 is an example of hyperbole: extravagant and exaggerated language ('hype'). Romeo makes other flamboyant comparisons ('cheek'/'jewel', 'snowy dove' / 'crows'), all of which are contrasts of light versus dark. Make up several of your own comparisons in similar style.

2 Love at first sight (in pairs)

Do you believe in love at first sight? Romeo loves Juliet from the first moment he sees her. Talk together about what happens in that electrifying moment when two people fall head over heels in love. Then take the title 'Love at first sight' and write a short story about it. See if you can end your story with Romeo's line 'For I ne'er saw true beauty till this night'.

3 Revealing character: Tybalt and Capulet (in pairs)

Lines 53–91 dramatise an episode in which Capulet is increasingly angered by Tybalt's intention to pick a fight with Romeo. The incident reveals much about the characters of the two men.

Take parts and speak the lines. Then repeat, but this time speak only one word from each line. Simply say whatever word strikes you as being the most important in the line – for any reason.

Try the exercise another time, changing roles. Afterwards talk together about whether you think there are 'typical' Tybalt words, and 'typical' Capulet words, and what they suggest about the character of each man.

Ethiop Elizabethans used this word for any black African
measure dance
antic face fantastic mask
fleer sneer
solemnity celebration

portly dignified
disparagement discourtesy
semblance appearance, behaviour
goodman yeoman, not a gentleman (so 'goodman boy' would be a double insult to Tybalt)

ROMEO O she doth teach the torches to burn bright!
    It seems she hangs upon the cheek of night
    As a rich jewel in an Ethiop's ear –   45
    Beauty too rich for use, for earth too dear:
    So shows a snowy dove trooping with crows,
    As yonder lady o'er her fellows shows.
    The measure done, I'll watch her place of stand,
    And touching hers, make blessèd my rude hand.   50
    Did my heart love till now? forswear it, sight!
    For I ne'er saw true beauty till this night.
TYBALT This, by his voice, should be a Montague.
    Fetch me my rapier, boy.

                                                              [*Exit Page*]
                     What dares the slave
    Come hither, covered with an antic face,   55
    To fleer and scorn at our solemnity?
    Now by the stock and honour of my kin,
    To strike him dead I hold it not a sin.
CAPULET Why, how now, kinsman, wherefore storm you so?
TYBALT Uncle, this is a Montague, our foe: 60
    A villain that is hither come in spite,
    To scorn at our solemnity this night.
CAPULET Young Romeo is it?
TYBALT   'Tis he, that villain Romeo.
CAPULET Content thee, gentle coz, let him alone,
    'A bears him like a portly gentleman;   65
    And to say truth, Verona brags of him
    To be a virtuous and well-governed youth.
    I would not for the wealth of all this town
    Here in my house do him disparagement;
    Therefore be patient, take no note of him;   70
    It is my will, the which if thou respect,
    Show a fair presence, and put off these frowns,
    An ill-beseeming semblance for a feast.
TYBALT It fits when such a villain is a guest:
    I'll not endure him.
CAPULET   He shall be endured.   75
    What, goodman boy, I say he shall, go to!
    Am I the master here, or you? go to!
    You'll not endure him? God shall mend my soul,

Tybalt, rebuked by Capulet, leaves the party. He threatens vengeance. Romeo and Juliet talk together for the first time. Romeo learns from the Nurse that Juliet is a Capulet.

---

1 First meeting of Romeo and Juliet (in pairs)

The first fourteen lines (92–105) of the lovers' meeting are written in sonnet form (the first twelve lines rhyme alternately; the last two lines are a rhyming couplet). It is helpful to know that:

- Sonnet writing was a popular and highly esteemed activity at Queen Elizabeth's court (see p. 217).
- Pilgrims, to show their faith, made long journeys to the shrines of the Holy Land. They brought back palm leaves as proof of their visits, and so were known as 'palmers'.
- Romeo compares Juliet to a shrine or saint. Religious imagery runs through their conversation ('profane', 'holy shrine', 'sin', 'pilgrims', 'wrong', 'devotion', 'palmers', 'faith', 'despair', 'purged', 'trespass').

Take parts and sit facing each other. Speak your lines slowly, pointing at yourself or your partner (or to your own or your partner's hands or lips) on each appropriate mention. Use your imagination to perform actions you feel are appropriate to the words.

Afterwards, talk together about this first meeting of Romeo and Juliet. For example, discuss:

- why you think Romeo uses this religious imagery
- how Romeo's language is different from that of earlier scenes
- whether you feel he's now genuinely in love
- how you think Juliet feels on this first meeting.

Finally, write how you would stage this first meeting (see p. vi in the colour section and p. 47).

---

set cock-a-hoop   create a riot
scathe   injure
contrary   oppose
princox   cocky youngster
choler   anger
gall   poison

profane   desecrate, dishonour
palmers   pilgrims (see above)
trespass   sin
by th'book   expertly (or without passion)
Marry   by St Mary (a mild oath)

You'll make a mutiny among my guests!
You will set cock-a-hoop! you'll be the man!   80

TYBALT Why, uncle, 'tis a shame.

CAPULET   Go to, go to,
You are a saucy boy. Is't so indeed?
This trick may chance to scathe you, I know what.
You must contrary me! Marry, 'tis time. –
Well said, my hearts! – You are a princox, go,   85
Be quiet, or – More light, more light! – For shame,
I'll make you quiet, what! – Cheerly, my hearts!

TYBALT Patience perforce with wilful choler meeting
Makes my flesh tremble in their different greeting:
I will withdraw, but this intrusion shall,   90
Now seeming sweet, convert to bitt'rest gall.   *Exit*

ROMEO [*To Juliet*] If I profane with my unworthiest hand
This holy shrine, the gentle sin is this,
My lips, two blushing pilgrims, ready stand
To smooth that rough touch with a tender kiss.   95

JULIET Good pilgrim, you do wrong your hand too much,
Which mannerly devotion shows in this,
For saints have hands that pilgrims' hands do touch,
And palm to palm is holy palmers' kiss.

ROMEO Have not saints lips, and holy palmers too?   100

JULIET Ay, pilgrim, lips that they must use in prayer.

ROMEO O then, dear saint, let lips do what hands do:
They pray, grant thou, lest faith turn to despair.

JULIET Saints do not move, though grant for prayers' sake.

ROMEO Then move not while my prayer's effect I take.   105
Thus from my lips, by thine, my sin is purged.
[*Kissing her.*]

JULIET Then have my lips the sin that they have took.

ROMEO Sin from my lips? O trespass sweetly urged!
Give me my sin again.
[*Kissing her again.*]

JULIET   You kiss by th'book.

NURSE Madam, your mother craves a word with you.   110

ROMEO What is her mother?

NURSE   Marry, bachelor,
Her mother is the lady of the house,
And a good lady, and a wise and virtuous.

Romeo realises with dismay that Juliet is a Capulet. The party ends and Juliet feels similar foreboding on learning Romeo's name. She has fallen in love with one of her family's hated enemies.

1 Making excuses

The stage direction '*They whisper in his ear*' means that Romeo and his masked friends make an excuse for leaving the party before the banquet is served. Write four lines in Shakespearian style that they might have spoken.

2 Should the audience smile? (in pairs)

Juliet wants to find out Romeo's name, but does it indirectly. Take parts and speak lines 127–36. Afterwards, write notes for Juliet advising her how to make her questions amusing for the audience.

3 Imagery: 'My grave is like to be my wedding bed'

Line 134 is the first time Juliet speaks in such a sombre mood, imagining Death as her bridegroom. You'll find that this personification of Death marrying Juliet keeps appearing in the play (see Act 4 Scene 5, lines 35–40 and p. 215). Make a sketch to illustrate the line.

4 'My only love sprung from my only hate!' (in pairs)

Line 137 echoes line 166 in Act 1 Scene 1 ('Here's much to do with hate, but more with love'). Juliet's lines 137–40 contain examples of the many oppositions (antitheses) that run through the play: 'love'/'hate', 'early'/'late', 'unknown'/'known', 'love'/'loathèd' (see pp. 209–11 and 216).

Does the Nurse hear what Juliet says? Decide whether you think that Juliet speaks her four lines to herself, to the Nurse or to the audience. Give reasons for why you think your chosen style of delivery is dramatically effective.

---

withal with
lay hold of grasp (marry)
the chinks money (Rattle a handful of coins to hear why the Nurse says this)

dear account terrible reckoning
fay faith
waxes grows
Prodigious ominous, monstrous
Anon at once

        I nursed her daughter that you talked withal;
        I tell you, he that can lay hold of her   115
        Shall have the chinks.

ROMEO   Is she a Capulet?
        O dear account! my life is my foe's debt.

BENVOLIO Away, be gone, the sport is at the best.

ROMEO Ay, so I fear, the more is my unrest.

CAPULET Nay, gentlemen, prepare not to be gone,   120
        We have a trifling foolish banquet towards.
        [They whisper in his ear.]
        Is it e'en so? Why then I thank you all.
        I thank you, honest gentlemen, good night.
        More torches here, come on! then let's to bed.
        Ah, sirrah, by my fay, it waxes late,   125
        I'll to my rest.
        [Exeunt all but Juliet and Nurse]

JULIET Come hither, Nurse. What is yond gentleman?

NURSE The son and heir of old Tiberio.

JULIET What's he that now is going out of door?

NURSE Marry, that I think be young Petruchio.   130

JULIET What's he that follows here, that would not dance?

NURSE I know not.

JULIET Go ask his name. – If he be marrièd,
        My grave is like to be my wedding bed.

NURSE His name is Romeo, and a Montague,   135
        The only son of your great enemy.

JULIET My only love sprung from my only hate!
        Too early seen unknown, and known too late!
        Prodigious birth of love it is to me,
        That I must love a loathèd enemy.   140

NURSE What's tis? what's tis?

JULIET   A rhyme I learnt even now
        Of one I danced withal.
        One calls within, 'Juliet!'

NURSE   Anon, anon!
        Come let's away, the strangers all are gone.

        Exeunt

Looking back at Act 1
Activities for groups or individuals

1 Design the stage set

Design a stage set to show your idea of Verona. Will it have towers, battlements, turrets, balconies? How can you create the narrow, threatening alleys of the old town, the large public spaces, the grand mansions of the Capulets and Montagues?

Make sure your design allows scene changes to be made swiftly.

2 Write an agony aunt's advice to Romeo

Benvolio tells Romeo that the cure for his infatuation with Rosaline is to look at other girls ('Examine other beauties'). Imagine you are an 'agony aunt' for a magazine. Romeo writes to you with his problem (using the language of the play in Act 1 Scene 1, lines 154–227). Write his letter and your advice in reply.

3 Rosaline's diary

Until he sees Juliet, Romeo believes he is in love with Rosaline. She never appears in the play, so give her a voice. Write a few entries in Rosaline's diary. How does she feel about Romeo's infatuation? What did she say as she kept him at a distance (see Act 1 Scene 1, lines 199–215), refusing his advances? And how does she feel when she hears he has fallen for Juliet? Remember, she is Juliet's cousin, so she's a Capulet too.

4 The television reporter at the Capulet party

Shakespeare's Verona certainly didn't have television. But don't be afraid to explore the play using your experience of television.

You have been sent by a television station to report on Capulet's party (Scene 5). Your news editor says 'Don't forget to interview the servants – they're the ones who will really know! And "the lively Helena" is a real chatterbox! You'll be given a five-minute slot in tomorrow's *News*.' Work in a group to prepare and deliver your report.

5 Tybalt's point of view

Tybalt meets his friends as he leaves Capulet's party. Tell his story of the party and his past experience of the Montagues.

If I profane with my unworthiest hand (*Scene 5, line 92*)

Romeo's mood changes to joyful anticipation when he first catches sight of Juliet at Capulet's party. Determined to speak to her, he begins a dialogue which will become a sonnet shared between them.

The first meeting of the lovers has been staged in all kinds of ways. For example, in Baz Luhrmann's film, Leonardo DiCaprio's Romeo first catches sight of Juliet (Claire Danes) through a fish tank (see picture of their meeting on page vi in the colour section).

Study the two pictures on this page and turn back to page 42 for activities on the first meeting of the lovers.

And palm to palm is holy palmers' kiss (*Scene 5, line 99*)

Juliet responds to Romeo's first words to her with four lines, making the second stanza of a sonnet (see p. 217).

Earlier, Lady Capulet had urged thirteen-year-old Juliet to marry. Very shortly, in the 'balcony' scene that takes place the same evening, Juliet will agree to marry Romeo the following day. In many countries today, that would be seen as inappropriate behaviour for a thirteen-year-old. What do you think of the idea of getting married at thirteen? Talk together in a group, and suggest reasons why such early marriage seems to be acceptable in Shakespeare's Verona.

Chorus reminds the audience that Romeo's infatuation with Rosaline has ended. Romeo now loves Juliet, who returns his love. But dangers beset the young lovers. Act 2 begins with Mercutio teasing the hidden Romeo.

1 Chorus speaks a sonnet (in groups of four to eight)

Sit in a circle. Read Chorus's speech, each person speaking a line in turn. Then work on several or all of the following:

a Act out the story told in the fourteen lines. The words of Chorus summarise much of the play so far and hint at the next scene. One person reads a line or two, then pauses. In that pause, other members of the group mime what is described. Two reminders: 'old desire' of line 144 is love for Rosaline; the last two lines imply that the pleasures of Romeo and Juliet's meetings make their dangers and hardships bearable.

b Choose a line which appeals to the group. Prepare and show a tableau of the line. Present it for other groups to guess your line.

c Quite often these fourteen lines are cut in performance. Imagine you are a group preparing to put on the play. Half of you want to include Chorus's fourteen lines, half don't. Debate whether they should be left in or cut.

d All companies acting Shakespeare 'double' the parts (actors play more than one role). So Chorus is spoken by someone with another role (or roles) in the play. Look at the cast list on page 1 and decide who seems most likely to 'double' Chorus.

2 'Nay, I'll conjure too' (in pairs)

Mercutio pretends to be a magician, raising up spirits. Imagine you are a director, and Mercutio has asked you what actions should accompany line 7 (all are descriptions of Romeo). Talk together about how you think Mercutio should deliver the five words.

---

young affection new love (for Juliet)
fair (line 146) Rosaline
fair (line 147) beautiful
again in return
foe supposed Juliet

complain address his love
means opportunities
Temp'ring extremities easing dangers
dull earth body
humours moody lover

[*Enter*] CHORUS.

Now old desire doth in his death-bed lie,
And young affection gapes to be his heir; 145
That fair for which love groaned for and would die,
With tender Juliet matched is now not fair.
Now Romeo is beloved, and loves again,
Alike bewitchèd by the charm of looks;
But to his foe supposed he must complain, 150
And she steal love's sweet bait from fearful hooks.
Being held a foe, he may not have access
To breathe such vows as lovers use to swear,
And she as much in love, her means much less
To meet her new-belovèd any where: 155
But passion lends them power, time means, to meet,
Temp'ring extremities with extreme sweet. [*Exit*]

Act 2 Scene 1
Outside Capulet's mansion

Enter ROMEO alone.

ROMEO Can I go forward when my heart is here?
Turn back, dull earth, and find thy centre out.
[*Romeo withdraws*]

Enter BENVOLIO *with* MERCUTIO.

BENVOLIO Romeo! my cousin Romeo! Romeo!
MERCUTIO He is wise,
And on my life hath stol'n him home to bed.
BENVOLIO He ran this way and leapt this orchard wall. 5
Call, good Mercutio.
MERCUTIO Nay, I'll conjure too.
Romeo! humours! madman! passion! lover!
Appear thou in the likeness of a sigh,

Mercutio, pretending to be a magician, uses much sexual innuendo as he mocks Romeo's love for Rosaline. Unable to get any response from Romeo, he goes off to sleep.

1 Mercutio's wordplay – very sexual

Mercutio, outrageous and imaginative as usual, teases Romeo, seizing every opportunity to make sexual puns:

> *demesnes* parklands for pleasure (or sexual parts)
> *spirit* ghost (or semen)
> *circle* magic circle (or vagina)
> *stand* ghost rising (or sexual erection)
> *down* ghost disappearing (or end of sexual intercourse)
> *honest* proper (and virginal)
> *mark* target (or sexual intercourse)
> *medlar* apple-like fruit (or female sexual organ)
> *open-arse* slang for medlar (or female sexual organ)
> *pop'rin pear* pear from Poperinghe in Flanders (shaped like a
>   penis)

As you read on, look out for more examples of Mercutio's ingenious wordplay. Why do you think Shakespeare makes Mercutio talk in this way? For example, one reason may be that his sexual joking opposes and highlights the true love of Romeo and Juliet.

'Her purblind son and heir, / Young Abraham Cupid'. Look for other mentions in the play of blind, or blindfolded, Cupid shooting his love arrows at random.

---

gossip old friend
Venus goddess of love
Abraham beggar, or old man, or famous archer
trim accurately

King Cophetua king who loved a poor girl (in an old ballad)
invocation spell
consorted with companion to
humorous moody
truckle-bed camp bed

Speak but one rhyme, and I am satisfied;
Cry but 'Ay me!', pronounce but 'love' and 'dove',   10
Speak to my gossip Venus one fair word,
One nickname for her purblind son and heir,
Young Abraham Cupid, he that shot so trim
When King Cophetua loved the beggar-maid.
He heareth not, he stirreth not, he moveth not,   15
The ape is dead, and I must conjure him.
I conjure thee by Rosaline's bright eyes,
By her high forehead and her scarlet lip,
By her fine foot, straight leg, and quivering thigh,
And the demesnes that there adjacent lie,   20
That in thy likeness thou appear to us.

BENVOLIO And if he hear thee, thou wilt anger him.

MERCUTIO This cannot anger him; 'twould anger him
To raise a spirit in his mistress' circle,
Of some strange nature, letting it there stand   25
Till she had laid it and conjured it down:
That were some spite. My invocation
Is fair and honest: in his mistress' name
I conjure only but to raise up him.

BENVOLIO Come, he hath hid himself among these trees   30
To be consorted with the humorous night:
Blind is his love, and best befits the dark.

MERCUTIO If love be blind, love cannot hit the mark.
Now will he sit under a medlar tree,
And wish his mistress were that kind of fruit   35
As maids call medlars, when they laugh alone.
O Romeo, that she were, O that she were
An open-arse, thou a pop'rin pear!
Romeo, good night, I'll to my truckle-bed,
This field-bed is too cold for me to sleep.   40
Come, shall we go?

BENVOLIO   Go then, for 'tis in vain
To seek him here that means not to be found.

                        Exit [*with Mercutio*]

Romeo, hidden from Juliet, sees her at an upstairs window. He compares her beauty to that of the sun, more bright than the stars, as glorious as an angel.

---

1 'He jests at scars that never felt a wound'

Romeo's first line is a dismissive comment on Mercutio's joking about love. Just as someone who has never been wounded can jest about a soldier's battle scars, so someone who has never been in love finds it easy to joke about the sufferings of a person deeply in love.

Suggest how Romeo might speak line 1. Is his tone bitter, or ironic, or . . . ?

2 Speak the whole scene! (in pairs)

This scene is one of the most famous in all world drama. Probably the best way into it is simply to read it straight through, one person as Romeo, the other as Juliet. If you can find an upstairs window for Juliet, so much the better. Don't pause to discuss or puzzle over words. Just go right through to line 189 on page 63. Enjoy yourselves!

3 Romeo's view of Juliet – an echoing activity (in pairs)

To help you understand how Romeo feels about Juliet, try this 'echoing' activity. Sit facing each other. One person reads lines 1–32 aloud. The other listens (or follows in the script) and quietly echoes certain words or phrases:

- to do with light (like 'sun') or brightness or eyesight
- that refer to something overhead.

As you echo each 'upward' word, point your finger upward.

Change roles and repeat. Afterwards, talk together about what those 'light-giving' words and 'upward' words tell you about Romeo's view of Juliet.

---

vestal livery virginal uniform (the moon was seen as Diana, goddess of virginity)
sick and green 'green sickness' was thought to be an illness of virgins
discourses speaks

spheres orbits (the Ptolemaic system of astronomy held that the planets circled the earth. Their orbits [paths] were believed to be crystal spheres enclosing the earth)
wingèd messenger angel

Act 2 Scene 2
Capulet's orchard

ROMEO advances.

ROMEO He jests at scars that never felt a wound.
But soft, what light through yonder window breaks?
It is the east, and Juliet is the sun.
Arise, fair sun, and kill the envious moon,
Who is already sick and pale with grief   5
That thou, her maid, art far more fair than she.
Be not her maid, since she is envious;
Her vestal livery is but sick and green,
And none but fools do wear it; cast it off.

[JULIET *appears aloft as at a window.*]

It is my lady, O it is my love: 10
O that she knew she were!
She speaks, yet she says nothing; what of that?
Her eye discourses, I will answer it.
I am too bold, 'tis not to me she speaks:
Two of the fairest stars in all the heaven,   15
Having some business, do entreat her eyes
To twinkle in their spheres till they return.
What if her eyes were there, they in her head?
The brightness of her cheek would shame those stars,
As daylight doth a lamp; her eyes in heaven   20
Would through the airy region stream so bright
That birds would sing and think it were not night.
See how she leans her cheek upon her hand!
O that I were a glove upon that hand,
That I might touch that cheek!
JULIET   Ay me!
ROMEO [*Aside*]   She speaks.   25
O speak again, bright angel, for thou art
As glorious to this night, being o'er my head,
As is a wingèd messenger of heaven
Unto the white-upturnèd wond'ring eyes

Juliet declares her love for Romeo in spite of his belonging to the hated Montagues. He is his own perfect self, whatever he is called. When Romeo reveals himself she fears for his safety.

What's in a name? When Juliet asks, 'Wherefore art thou Romeo?' she begins to question why her love should be named Romeo – a hated Montague! It's the name that is the trouble, not Romeo himself: the word, not the person. Work on the following in pairs or small groups.

1 ''Tis but thy name that is my enemy'

Make a list of some groups that are regarded by others as 'enemies', like the Montagues and the Capulets. Talk together about what would happen if a girl and boy from each opposing group fell in love.

2 'That which we call a rose
By any other word would smell as sweet'

Juliet declares that no matter what a rose is called, its essential quality would remain unchanged. She argues that the same applies to Romeo. His 'perfection' would still remain, whatever he was called. But some people (such as actors or pop stars) change their names to create what they think is a better image of themselves. What do you think? Talk together about your own names. Would changing your name make you somehow different, or would you still be essentially the same person?

3 An episode full of 'names'

One person reads aloud lines 33–61. Others echo every time 'name' is mentioned, or a proper name (e.g. Capulet) or any similar word (e.g. 'called').

Afterwards, suggest why you think Shakespeare uses so many such 'names' in this episode.

---

wherefore why	**bescreened** hidden
owes owns	**counsel** private thoughts
doff cast off	**o'erperch** fly over

Of mortals that fall back to gaze on him, 30
When he bestrides the lazy puffing clouds,
And sails upon the bosom of the air.

JULIET O Romeo, Romeo, wherefore art thou Romeo?
Deny thy father and refuse thy name;
Or if thou wilt not, be but sworn my love, 35
And I'll no longer be a Capulet.

ROMEO [*Aside*] Shall I hear more, or shall I speak at this?

JULIET 'Tis but thy name that is my enemy;
Thou art thyself, though not a Montague.
What's Montague? It is nor hand nor foot, 40
Nor arm nor face, nor any other part
Belonging to a man. O be some other name!
What's in a name? That which we call a rose
By any other word would smell as sweet;
So Romeo would, were he not Romeo called, 45
Retain that dear perfection which he owes
Without that title. Romeo, doff thy name,
And for thy name, which is no part of thee,
Take all myself.

ROMEO   I take thee at thy word:
Call me but love, and I'll be new baptised; 50
Henceforth I never will be Romeo.

JULIET What man art thou that thus bescreened in night
So stumblest on my counsel?

ROMEO   By a name
I know not how to tell thee who I am.
My name, dear saint, is hateful to myself, 55
Because it is an enemy to thee;
Had I it written, I would tear the word.

JULIET My ears have yet not drunk a hundred words
Of thy tongue's uttering, yet I know the sound.
Art thou not Romeo, and a Montague? 60

ROMEO Neither, fair maid, if either thee dislike.

JULIET How cam'st thou hither, tell me, and wherefore?
The orchard walls are high and hard to climb,
And the place death, considering who thou art,
If any of my kinsmen find thee here. 65

ROMEO With love's light wings did I o'erperch these walls,
For stony limits cannot hold love out,

Juliet warns Romeo that her family will kill him if they find him. Admitting embarrassment at being overheard telling of her love, she asks if he loves her.

---

1 Imagery: life as a hazardous voyage

In lines 82–4, Romeo uses the image of himself as a merchant adventurer who would brave any dangerous sea journey to gain Juliet ('pilot' is a sailor). The image of life as a perilous sea voyage is a tragic theme that runs through the play. But what do you think of his comparison of Juliet to 'merchandise'? Is it complimentary or condescending? Write a paragraph giving your response to this image.

2 Juliet's language – simple and true? (in small groups)

Juliet's 'Fain would I dwell on form' (line 88) suggests she would gladly stick to formality and ceremonial politeness. But her 'farewell compliment' (line 89) shows her rejecting stiff, customary ways of behaving and speaking. To find if she succeeds in her wish to speak simply and truly, without affectation, try the following activity.

Read lines 90–106. The first group member begins, but reads only to a punctuation mark (the first is a question mark). The second group member then reads to the next punctuation mark, and stops. The third does the same, and so on round the group. Read the lines several times in this way.

After the readings, talk together about Juliet's language, especially about how you think it is different from the language of all the men who have spoken in the play. Give examples of where she speaks directly and simply, without formality.

---

proof protected
proroguèd postponed
wanting of lacking
Fain gladly
perjuries lies
Jove Jupiter, god of oaths (who did not take lovers' vows seriously!)

fond foolish
light wanton, loose
coying to be strange cunning to be distant or offhand
ere I was ware before I was aware you were listening
light love false feeling

     And what love can do, that dares love attempt:
     Therefore thy kinsmen are no stop to me.

JULIET If they do see thee, they will murder thee.   70

ROMEO Alack, there lies more peril in thine eye
     Than twenty of their swords. Look thou but sweet,
     And I am proof against their enmity.

JULIET I would not for the world they saw thee here.

ROMEO I have night's cloak to hide me from their eyes,   75
     And but thou love me, let them find me here;
     My life were better ended by their hate,
     Than death proroguèd, wanting of thy love.

JULIET By whose direction found'st thou out this place?

ROMEO By Love, that first did prompt me to enquire: 80
     He lent me counsel, and I lent him eyes.
     I am no pilot, yet wert thou as far
     As that vast shore washed with the farthest sea,
     I should adventure for such merchandise.

JULIET Thou knowest the mask of night is on my face,   85
     Else would a maiden blush bepaint my cheek
     For that which thou hast heard me speak tonight.
     Fain would I dwell on form, fain, fain deny
     What I have spoke, but farewell compliment.
     Dost thou love me? I know thou wilt say 'Ay';   90
     And I will take thy word; yet if thou swear'st,
     Thou mayst prove false: at lovers' perjuries
     They say Jove laughs. O gentle Romeo,
     If thou dost love, pronounce it faithfully;
     Or if thou think'st I am too quickly won,   95
     I'll frown and be perverse, and say thee nay,
     So thou wilt woo, but else not for the world.
     In truth, fair Montague, I am too fond,
     And therefore thou mayst think my behaviour light:
     But trust me, gentleman, I'll prove more true   100
     Than those that have more coying to be strange.
     I should have been more strange, I must confess,
     But that thou overheard'st, ere I was ware,
     My true-love passion; therefore pardon me,
     And not impute this yielding to light love,   105
     Which the dark night hath so discoverèd.

Romeo and Juliet exchange vows of love, but both are fearful. Juliet fears the suddenness of their love. Romeo fears because what is happening seems dream-like and unreal.

Suggest which line is being spoken at this moment.

1 'Too like the lightning' (lines 118–20)

Shakespeare probably wrote *A Midsummer Night's Dream* at about the same time (1595) as *Romeo and Juliet*. In that play, two other young lovers are also beset with problems. Lysander uses the same image as Juliet. He compares love to the briefness of lightning:

> Swift as a shadow, short as any dream,
> Brief as the lightning in the collied night,
> That in a spleen unfolds both heaven and earth,
> And, ere a man hath power to say 'Behold!',
> The jaws of darkness do devour it up.
> So quick bright things come to confusion.

Do you feel that 'lightning' is a fitting description or image of Romeo and Juliet's love? Read lines 133–5 before you reply.

---

circled orb orbit around the earth
likewise variable similarly changing (like the moon's waxing and waning)
idolatry worship

contract exchange of lovers' vows
frank truthful, generous
bounty generosity, willingness to give
substantial real

ROMEO Lady, by yonder blessèd moon I vow,
   That tips with silver all these fruit-tree tops –
JULIET O swear not by the moon, th'inconstant moon,
   That monthly changes in her circled orb,   110
   Lest that thy love prove likewise variable.
ROMEO What shall I swear by?
JULIET   Do not swear at all;
   Or if thou wilt, swear by thy gracious self,
   Which is the god of my idolatry,
   And I'll believe thee.
ROMEO   If my heart's dear love –   115
JULIET Well, do not swear. Although I joy in thee,
   I have no joy of this contract tonight,
   It is too rash, too unadvised, too sudden,
   Too like the lightning, which doth cease to be
   Ere one can say 'It lightens'. Sweet, good night: 120
   This bud of love, by summer's ripening breath,
   May prove a beauteous flower when next we meet.
   Good night, good night! as sweet repose and rest
   Come to thy heart as that within my breast.
ROMEO O wilt thou leave me so unsatisfied?   125
JULIET What satisfaction canst thou have tonight?
ROMEO Th'exchange of thy love's faithful vow for mine.
JULIET I gave thee mine before thou didst request it;
   And yet I would it were to give again.
ROMEO Wouldst thou withdraw it? for what purpose, love?   130
JULIET But to be frank and give it thee again,
   And yet I wish but for the thing I have:
   My bounty is as boundless as the sea,
   My love as deep; the more I give to thee
   The more I have, for both are infinite.   135
         [*Nurse calls within.*]
   I hear some noise within; dear love, adieu! –
   Anon, good Nurse! – Sweet Montague, be true.
   Stay but a little, I will come again.   [*Exit above*]
ROMEO O blessèd, blessèd night! I am afeard,
   Being in night, all this is but a dream,   140
   Too flattering-sweet to be substantial.

Juliet, promising marriage, says she will send a messenger tomorrow to ask the time and place of the wedding. At the Nurse's call, Juliet goes inside the house. Returning, she calls Romeo back.

1 'O for a falc'ner's voice'

Falconry (hunting with birds of prey) was a popular sport of the Elizabethans. The falconer, or huntsman, used a lure (or bait) and a special call to bring the bird back to the captivity of his hand. Juliet likens Romeo to a 'tassel-gentle' (line 159), a male peregrine falcon, the bird of princes. Later (line 167), Romeo calls Juliet his 'niësse' (a young unfledged hawk). Some critics think the image aptly expresses Juliet's youthfulness. But does it? Decide whether you think the image is appropriate or artificial.

2 'As schoolboys from their books' (in groups of four)

Whenever Shakespeare mentions school, he seems less than enthusiastic about it. Try this one-minute activity:

Show in a tableau, what you think Shakespeare had in mind when he gave line 156 to Romeo. Freeze the tableau for thirty seconds. Try the same activity with line 157.

3 'I have forgot why I did call thee back'

Most directors of the play hope that line 170 will evoke audience laughter. Advise Juliet how to deliver the line to gain that response.

---

bent intention
cease thy strife stop your effort (of loving me)
Bondage is hoarse prisoners must whisper (Juliet has little freedom in her father's house)

Echo a cave-dwelling nymph, in love with Narcissus. She repeated the last word anyone spoke to her. Echo wasted away until only her voice remained
a'clock time

[*Enter Juliet above.*]

JULIET Three words, dear Romeo, and good night indeed.
　　　If that thy bent of love be honourable,
　　　Thy purpose marriage, send me word tomorrow,
　　　By one that I'll procure to come to thee,　　　　　　145
　　　Where and what time thou wilt perform the rite,
　　　And all my fortunes at thy foot I'll lay,
　　　And follow thee my lord throughout the world.
NURSE [*Within*] Madam!
JULIET I come, anon. – But if thou meanest not well,　　　150
　　　I do beseech thee –
NURSE [*Within*]　　　　　Madam!
JULIET　　　　　　　　　　By and by I come –
　　　To cease thy strife, and leave me to my grief.
　　　Tomorrow will I send.
ROMEO So thrive my soul –
JULIET　　　　　　　　A thousand times good night!

　　　　　　　　　　　　　　　　　　[*Exit above*]

ROMEO A thousand times the worse, to want thy light.　　155
　　　Love goes toward love as schoolboys from their books,
　　　But love from love, toward school with heavy looks.
　　　　　　　[*Retiring slowly.*]

　　　　　Enter Juliet again [*above*].

JULIET Hist, Romeo, hist! O for a falc'ner's voice,
　　　To lure this tassel-gentle back again:
　　　Bondage is hoarse, and may not speak aloud,　　　160
　　　Else would I tear the cave where Echo lies,
　　　And make her airy tongue more hoarse than mine
　　　With repetition of my Romeo's name.
ROMEO It is my soul that calls upon my name.
　　　How silver-sweet sound lovers' tongues by night,　165
　　　Like softest music to attending ears!
JULIET Romeo!
ROMEO　　　My nièsse?
JULIET　　　　　　　　What a'clock tomorrow
　　　Shall I send to thee?
ROMEO　　　　　　　　By the hour of nine.
JULIET I will not fail, 'tis twenty year till then.
　　　I have forgot why I did call thee back.　　　　　170

Romeo and Juliet reluctantly part. She compares him to a captive bird that can never escape from its owner. Romeo promises to seek Friar Lawrence's help.

1 Changing moods – and sincere speaking

a Look back over lines 1–189 and trace the changing moods of the two lovers. Find a way of illustrating those changes, for example by a graph or drawing that uses brief quotations.

b Identify several lines which you feel 'come from the heart', that is, spoken very sincerely without affectation.

c Pick out two or three images from the scene that especially appeal to you. Write why you find them particularly appealing.

2 Work out your own staging of the scene (in pairs)

Write an account of how you feel the scene could be played to maximise dramatic effect. Specify how you would set the scene, and how you think that different sections of the scene could be played. Identify several lines you think very important and write how you think they should be delivered. It is worth remembering that although this is usually called the 'balcony' scene, Shakespeare doesn't mention a balcony. So decide how you wish to act the stage direction on page 53 '*Juliet appears aloft as at a window*'.

Best of all, act out the scene in your chosen space.

3 'Parting is such sweet sorrow'

You will often hear 'Parting is such sweet sorrow' (line 184) used as an expression today. Turn to page 218 to discover many more such familiar expressions spoken in *Romeo and Juliet*.

---

wanton's bird   spoilt child's pet bird (held captive by string tied to its legs)
gyves   fetters on the legs of prisoners
kill thee . . . cherishing   kill you with kindness

ghostly sire   Friar Lawrence (Romeo's 'spiritual father')
close cell   private room
dear hap   good fortune

ROMEO Let me stand here till thou remember it.

JULIET I shall forget, to have thee still stand there,
        Rememb'ring how I love thy company.

ROMEO And I'll still stay, to have thee still forget,
        Forgetting any other home but this.   175

JULIET 'Tis almost morning, I would have thee gone:
        And yet no farther than a wanton's bird,
        That lets it hop a little from his hand,
        Like a poor prisoner in his twisted gyves,
        And with a silken thread plucks it back again,   180
        So loving-jealous of his liberty.

ROMEO I would I were thy bird.

JULIET   Sweet, so would I,
        Yet I should kill thee with much cherishing.
        Good night, good night! Parting is such sweet sorrow,
        That I shall say good night till it be morrow.   [*Exit above*]   185

ROMEO Sleep dwell upon thine eyes, peace in thy breast!
        Would I were sleep and peace, so sweet to rest!
        Hence will I to my ghostly sire's close cell,
        His help to crave, and my dear hap to tell.   *Exit*

At daybreak, Friar Lawrence is gathering flowers and herbs. He reflects that, like people, they contain both healing medicine and poison, both good and evil.

1 Friar Lawrence sees a world of oppositions

Friar Lawrence will play a vital (but unfortunate) part in what happens to Romeo and Juliet.

Read lines 1–30 to yourself, but quietly emphasise each 'opposition' (antithesis). They are: 'morn smiles' / 'frowning night', 'day' / 'night's', 'baleful weeds' / 'precious-juicèd flowers', 'mother' / 'tomb', 'grave' / 'womb', 'vile' / 'good', 'fair use' / 'abuse', 'Virtue' / 'vice', 'Poison' / 'medicine', 'cheers each part' / 'stays all senses', 'grace' / 'rude will'.

Identify an appropriate line as a caption to this picture of Friar Lawrence.

Turn to pages 209–11 to discover how Friar Lawrence's antitheses, mainly of good versus bad, reflect the various conflicts that run through the play.

2 Imagery: good kings versus bad kings

Lines 27–8 contain the image of good and evil (or virtue and vice) as 'opposèd kings' setting up their camps in both mankind and herbs. Make a sketch, or write a paragraph that shows your understanding of the image.

---

fleckled dappled
Titan Helios, the sun god, who drove his blazing chariot (the sun) across the sky
osier cage willow basket
baleful evil or poisonous
divers many, various

mickle great
ought aught, anything
strained diverted
stays kills
encamp them still always live
grace and rude will divine virtue and human passions

Act 2 Scene 3
Outside Friar Lawrence's cell

Enter FRIAR LAWRENCE alone, with a basket.

FRIAR LAWRENCE

The grey-eyed morn smiles on the frowning night,
Check'ring the eastern clouds with streaks of light;
And fleckled darkness like a drunkard reels
From forth day's path and Titan's fiery wheels:
Now ere the sun advance his burning eye,   5
The day to cheer, and night's dank dew to dry,
I must upfill this osier cage of ours
With baleful weeds and precious-juicèd flowers.
The earth that's nature's mother is her tomb;
What is her burying grave, that is her womb;   10
And from her womb children of divers kind
We sucking on her natural bosom find:
Many for many virtues excellent,
None but for some, and yet all different.
O mickle is the powerful grace that lies   15
In plants, herbs, stones, and their true qualities:
For nought so vile, that on the earth doth live,
But to the earth some special good doth give;
Nor ought so good but, strained from that fair use,
Revolts from true birth, stumbling on abuse.   20
Virtue itself turns vice, being misapplied,
And vice sometime by action dignified.

Enter ROMEO.

Within the infant rind of this weak flower
Poison hath residence, and medicine power:
For this, being smelt, with that part cheers each part,   25
Being tasted, stays all senses with the heart.
Two such opposèd kings encamp them still
In man as well as herbs, grace and rude will;
And where the worser is predominant,
Full soon the canker death eats up that plant.   30

Friar Lawrence fears that Romeo has spent the night with Rosaline. But Romeo, telling of his and Juliet's mutual love, asks the Friar to marry them.

1 Should the actors emphasise the rhymes?

Read the last word in each line aloud from line 31 ('Benedicite!', pronounced 'beneedissitee') to the end of the scene. What do you discover? Find out if the whole scene is written in this way. Then step into role as director and write a note for your actors advising them, with reasons, whether or not to strongly emphasise the rhymes.

2 Age versus youth (in pairs)

One of the themes of the play is youth versus age (see p. 211), most obviously in how the two young lovers are trapped in the web of hate of the older generation. In lines 35–8, Friar Lawrence's image identifies another contrast between young and old. Work out a physical way of illustrating what the lines say about the difference between old men and young men.

3 'Riddling confession finds but riddling shrift' (in pairs)

Friar Lawrence doesn't find Romeo's explanation in lines 48–54 at all clear. He tells Romeo that ambiguous, unclear confessions will only be given similarly unsatisfactory absolution ('riddling shrift'). As a Franciscan priest, Friar Lawrence could give absolution ('shrift' = pardon, forgiveness) to those who confessed (told him of) their sins.

To clarify Romeo's explanation, try this activity. One person reads lines 48–54. But only read up to a punctuation mark, then pause. The other person, in each pause, makes clear Romeo's veiled ('riddling') meaning. The explanations given in the glossary below will help you (and 'foe' in line 54 is Juliet – or possibly the Capulets).

Benedicite! Bless you!
unbruisèd inexperienced
unstuffed empty
distemp'rature troubled mind
ghostly spiritual (priestly)
holy physic religious medicine (the marriage ceremony)

intercession entreaty or request
steads benefits
homely direct, plain
drift meaning
rich Capulet see Act 1 Scene 5, line 116

ROMEO Good morrow, father.

FRIAR LAWRENCE   Benedicite!
　　　　　What early tongue so sweet saluteth me?
　　　　　Young son, it argues a distempered head
　　　　　So soon to bid good morrow to thy bed:
　　　　　Care keeps his watch in every old man's eye,　　　　35
　　　　　And where care lodges, sleep will never lie;
　　　　　But where unbruisèd youth with unstuffed brain
　　　　　Doth couch his limbs, there golden sleep doth reign.
　　　　　Therefore thy earliness doth me assure
　　　　　Thou art uproused with some distemp'rature;　　　　40
　　　　　Or if not so, then here I hit it right,
　　　　　Our Romeo hath not been in bed tonight.

ROMEO That last is true, the sweeter rest was mine.

FRIAR LAWRENCE God pardon sin! wast thou with Rosaline?

ROMEO With Rosaline, my ghostly father? no;　　　　45
　　　　　I have forgot that name, and that name's woe.

FRIAR LAWRENCE
　　　　　That's my good son, but where hast thou been then?

ROMEO I'll tell thee ere thou ask it me again:
　　　　　I have been feasting with mine enemy,
　　　　　Where on a sudden one hath wounded me　　　　50
　　　　　That's by me wounded; both our remedies
　　　　　Within thy help and holy physic lies.
　　　　　I bear no hatred, blessèd man; for lo,
　　　　　My intercession likewise steads my foe.

FRIAR LAWRENCE Be plain, good son, and homely in thy drift,　　　　55
　　　　　Riddling confession finds but riddling shrift.

ROMEO Then plainly know, my heart's dear love is set
　　　　　On the fair daughter of rich Capulet;
　　　　　As mine on hers, so hers is set on mine,
　　　　　And all combined, save what thou must combine　　　　60
　　　　　By holy marriage. When and where and how
　　　　　We met, we wooed, and made exchange of vow,
　　　　　I'll tell thee as we pass, but this I pray,
　　　　　That thou consent to marry us today.

After chiding Romeo for his fickleness in love, Friar Lawrence agrees to marry Romeo and Juliet because he believes their marriage will end the feuding of the Montagues and Capulets.

1 The last two lines: a guide to character (in pairs)

The final two lines (93–4) suggest much about the characters of Romeo and Friar Lawrence. Romeo is impetuous, full of urgency: he wants to rush into marriage with Juliet. Friar Lawrence, like his advice, is cautious and thoughtful, all too aware that hasty rashness can result in accidents.

Taking parts, read from line 31 to the end of the scene in the style these last two lines suggest (Romeo – hasty; Friar Lawrence – wise and slow). Afterwards, decide if you think those speaking styles are appropriate to the characters. Keep the idea of 'hasty/slow' in your mind as you read on.

2 Make the audience laugh

Many actors believe that the brief exchange between Romeo and the Friar in lines 81–4 ('Thou chid'st me . . . to have') should end with the audience laughing. Step into role as director and write notes for the actors on how to deliver the four lines so as to evoke audience laughter.

3 'Thy love did read by rote, that could not spell' (in small groups)

In line 88, Friar Lawrence says Rosaline knew that Romeo's love for her was like mere recitation memorised from a book ('by rote'), without true understanding ('could not spell'). The Friar's line is itself a roundabout way of saying that Rosaline knew well that Romeo was merely infatuated with her, rather than truly in love. Turn back to page 16 and try Activity 1 to discover if Friar Lawrence's view of Romeo's love for Rosaline is accurate.

Holy Saint Francis Friar Lawrence is a Franciscan and swears by the founder of his Order
brine salt water (tears)
sallow pale
season flavour, preserve

sentence saying, proverb
chid'st chided, rebuked
doting infatuation
bad'st ordered
grace favour
rancour hatred

FRIAR LAWRENCE Holy Saint Francis, what a change is here! 65
    Is Rosaline, that thou didst love so dear,
    So soon forsaken? Young men's love then lies
    Not truly in their hearts, but in their eyes.
    Jesu Maria, what a deal of brine
    Hath washed thy sallow cheeks for Rosaline! 70
    How much salt water thrown away in waste,
    To season love, that of it doth not taste!
    The sun not yet thy sighs from heaven clears,
    Thy old groans yet ringing in mine ancient ears;
    Lo here upon thy cheek the stain doth sit 75
    Of an old tear that is not washed off yet.
    If e'er thou wast thyself, and these woes thine,
    Thou and these woes were all for Rosaline.
    And art thou changed? Pronounce this sentence then:
    Women may fall, when there's no strength in men. 80
ROMEO Thou chid'st me oft for loving Rosaline.
FRIAR LAWRENCE For doting, not for loving, pupil mine.
ROMEO And bad'st me bury love.
FRIAR LAWRENCE   Not in a grave,
    To lay one in, another out to have.
ROMEO I pray thee chide me not. Her I love now 85
    Doth grace for grace and love for love allow;
    The other did not so.
FRIAR LAWRENCE   O she knew well
    Thy love did read by rote, that could not spell.
    But come, young waverer, come go with me,
    In one respect I'll thy assistant be: 90
    For this alliance may so happy prove
    To turn your households' rancour to pure love.
ROMEO O let us hence, I stand on sudden haste.
FRIAR LAWRENCE Wisely and slow, they stumble that run fast.

                          Exeunt

Mercutio jokes with Benvolio about Tybalt's challenge to Romeo and about Romeo's infatuation with Rosaline. He mocks Tybalt's precise style of sword-fencing and the current fashions of speaking.

These illustrations are from an Italian fencing manual published in the sixteenth century. Make your own drawings of the fencing movements that Mercutio names in line 23 ('passado' = lunge; 'punto reverso' = backhanded thrust; 'hay' = hit; 'minim rests' (line 20) = brief pauses).

the very pin . . . bow-boy's butt-shaft
  Romeo's heart has been pierced by
  Cupid's arrow
Prince of Cats   Tybalt was a popular
  name for a cat

prick-song   printed music (Mercutio
  makes an elaborate comparison
  between music and sword-fencing –
  both played precisely by the rules)
affecting phantasimes   posturing
  young men

Act 2 Scene 4
A street in Verona

MERCUTIO Where the dev'l should this Romeo be?
Came he not home tonight?

BENVOLIO Not to his father's, I spoke with his man.

MERCUTIO Why, that same pale hard-hearted wench, that Rosaline,
Torments him so, that he will sure run mad.   5

BENVOLIO Tybalt, the kinsman to old Capulet,
Hath sent a letter to his father's house.

MERCUTIO A challenge, on my life.

BENVOLIO Romeo will answer it.

MERCUTIO Any man that can write may answer a letter.   10

BENVOLIO Nay, he will answer the letter's master, how he dares, being
dared.

MERCUTIO Alas, poor Romeo, he is already dead, stabbed with a white
wench's black eye, run through the ear with a love-song, the very
pin of his heart cleft with the blind bow-boy's butt-shaft; and is   15
he a man to encounter Tybalt?

BENVOLIO Why, what is Tybalt?

MERCUTIO More than Prince of Cats. O, he's the courageous captain
of compliments: he fights as you sing prick-song, keeps time,
distance, and proportion; he rests his minim rests, one, two, and   20
the third in your bosom; the very butcher of a silk button, a duellist,
a duellist; a gentleman of the very first house, of the first and second
cause. Ah, the immortal 'passado', the 'punto reverso', the 'hay'!

BENVOLIO The what?

MERCUTIO The pox of such antic, lisping, affecting phantasimes, these 25
new tuners of accent! 'By Jesu, a very good blade! a very tall man!
a very good whore!' Why, is not this a lamentable thing, grandsire,
that we should be thus afflicted with these strange flies, these
fashion-mongers, these pardon-me's, who stand so much on the
new form, that they cannot sit at ease on the old bench? O their   30
bones, their bones!

Mercutio (thinking Romeo loves Rosaline) teases Romeo about his love, saying that many beautiful women in history cannot compare with Rosaline. The two men joke together, trying to outdo each other's puns.

1 Tragic ladies – fateful forecasts (in small groups)

'Petrarch . . . Laura . . . Dido . . . Cleopatra . . . Helen and Hero . . . Thisbe'. Mercutio teases Romeo, accusing him of writing love poetry ('numbers') to Rosaline like that of the fourteenth-century Italian poet Petrarch to his love, Laura. But the women he names ominously predict the tragic fate that will befall Romeo and Juliet:

> *Dido* queen of Carthage. When her lover Aeneas deserted her, she killed herself.
>
> *Cleopatra* queen of Egypt, loved by both Julius Caesar and Mark Antony. She and Mark Antony committed suicide.
>
> *Helen* wife of Menelaus, king of Sparta, was stolen by the Trojan, Paris. Her abduction led to the siege and destruction of Troy.
>
> *Hero*. Every night her lover Leander swam across the Hellespont (the Dardanelles) to meet her. He drowned.
>
> *Thisbe* loved Pyramus. Their families were bitter enemies. Thinking her killed by a lion, he killed himself. She then committed suicide.

Work out a mime showing all these love stories. See also page 89.

2 Puns – Mercutio's obsession

Mercutio loves puns, especially those with a sexual meaning ('roe' = sperm of fish *or* half of Romeo; 'slip' = fake coin *or* escape; 'case' = circumstance *or* genitals; 'hit it' = take the point *or* sexual intercourse; 'pink' = perfection *or* a flower *or* decoration on a shoe; 'goose' = bird *or* prostitute *or* nitwit). See page 219 for more on puns.

3 Add actions to words (in pairs)

Act out lines 33–69, one as Romeo, one as Mercutio. You'll find that actions will help you understand the meaning of the words.

---

hildings flibbertigibbets, wild women
French slop baggy trousers
hams legs
pump shoe (or penis)
solely singular threadbare

Swits and spurs urge on your wits, as if you were horse-riding, with whips and spurs
goose prostitute
cheverel leather that stretches
ell forty-five inches

Enter ROMEO.

BENVOLIO Here comes Romeo, here comes Romeo.

MERCUTIO Without his roe, like a dried herring: O flesh, flesh, how art thou fishified! Now is he for the numbers that Petrarch flowed in. Laura to his lady was a kitchen wench (marry, she had a better 35 love to berhyme her), Dido a dowdy, Cleopatra a gipsy, Helen and Hero hildings and harlots, Thisbe a grey eye or so, but not to the purpose. Signior Romeo, 'bon jour'! there's a French salutation to your French slop. You gave us the counterfeit fairly last night.

ROMEO Good morrow to you both. What counterfeit did I give you? 40

MERCUTIO The slip, sir, the slip, can you not conceive?

ROMEO Pardon, good Mercutio, my business was great, and in such a case as mine a man may strain courtesy.

MERCUTIO That's as much as to say, such a case as yours constrains a man to bow in the hams. 45

ROMEO Meaning to cur'sy.

MERCUTIO Thou hast most kindly hit it.

ROMEO A most courteous exposition.

MERCUTIO Nay, I am the very pink of courtesy.

ROMEO Pink for flower. 50

MERCUTIO Right.

ROMEO Why then is my pump well flowered.

MERCUTIO Sure wit! Follow me this jest now, till thou hast worn out thy pump, that when the single sole of it is worn, the jest may remain, after the wearing, solely singular. 55

ROMEO O single-soled jest, solely singular for the singleness!

MERCUTIO Come between us, good Benvolio, my wits faints.

ROMEO Swits and spurs, swits and spurs, or I'll cry a match.

MERCUTIO Nay, if our wits run the wild-goose chase, I am done; for thou hast more of the wild goose in one of thy wits than, I am sure, 60 I have in my whole five. Was I with you there for the goose?

ROMEO Thou wast never with me for any thing when thou wast not there for the goose.

MERCUTIO I will bite thee by the ear for that jest.

ROMEO Nay, good goose, bite not. 65

MERCUTIO Thy wit is a very bitter sweeting, it is a most sharp sauce.

ROMEO And is it not then well served in to a sweet goose?

MERCUTIO O here's a wit of cheverel, that stretches from an inch narrow to an ell broad!

Mercutio's joking becomes more and more sexual. When the Nurse appears, seeking Romeo, Mercutio directs his sexual teasing at her. Romeo identifies himself.

1 Should Mercutio add actions to words?

Mercutio relishes his sexual puns. After his fairly conventional use of 'art' five times in lines 73–4 (meaning 'are' or 'skill'), his sexual imagination takes over. Here are just some of his puns: 'bauble' = stick carried by professional fool, *or* penis; 'hole' = hole *or* vagina; 'tale' = story *or* penis. In Elizabethan times, even the word 'occupy' (line 80) had a sexual double meaning.

How actively do you think Mercutio should bring out the sexual meanings in a stage performance? Write a paragraph explaining whether you feel that adding actions to the 'sexual' words opposite would add to an audience's enjoyment and understanding, or whether you think such actions are unnecessary. Give reasons for your preference.

2 'A sail, a sail!' (in pairs)

What is the Nurse wearing that provokes Romeo's cry in line 83? Design a costume for the Nurse that justifies Romeo's cry.

3 What's in a name?

Characters' names sometimes contain a clue to their personalities. Mercutio, for example, is like 'mercurial': lively, effervescent, quickly changing, bouncy. It also is a reminder of Mercury, messenger of the gods, who was a trickster, renowned for eloquence, luck, word-magic and dreams.

See page 30 to remind yourself of what Benvolio's name means. Then think about Prince Escales. How might his name suggest his personality or status? (See p. 156 for a note on the Nurse's name.)

---

broad   indecent ('a broad goose' probably means 'dirty-minded')
natural   idiot
gear   stuff (joking), or clothes (the Nurse), or sexual organs

good den   good evening (Elizabethans used this greeting anytime in the afternoon)
bawd   someone who profits by prostitution. A brothel-keeper
So ho!   Tallyho!

ROMEO I stretch it out for that word 'broad', which, added to the goose,   70
proves thee far and wide a broad goose.

MERCUTIO Why, is not this better now than groaning for love? Now
art thou sociable, now art thou Romeo; now art thou what thou
art, by art as well as by nature, for this drivelling love is like a great
natural that runs lolling up and down to hide his bauble in a hole.   75

BENVOLIO Stop there, stop there.

MERCUTIO Thou desirest me to stop in my tale against the hair.

BENVOLIO Thou wouldst else have made thy tale large.

MERCUTIO O thou art deceived; I would have made it short, for I was
come to the whole depth of my tale, and meant indeed to occupy   80
the argument no longer.

ROMEO Here's goodly gear!

Enter NURSE *and her man* [PETER].

A sail, a sail!

MERCUTIO Two, two: a shirt and a smock.

NURSE Peter!   85

PETER Anon.

NURSE My fan, Peter.

MERCUTIO Good Peter, to hide her face, for her fan's the fairer face.

NURSE God ye good morrow, gentlemen.

MERCUTIO God ye good den, fair gentlewoman.   90

NURSE Is it good den?

MERCUTIO 'Tis no less, I tell ye, for the bawdy hand of the dial is now
upon the prick of noon.

NURSE Out upon you, what a man are you?

ROMEO One, gentlewoman, that God hath made, himself to mar.   95

NURSE By my troth, it is well said: 'for himself to mar', quoth'a?
Gentlemen, can any of you tell me where I may find the young
Romeo?

ROMEO I can tell you, but young Romeo will be older when you have
found him than he was when you sought him: I am the youngest   100
of that name, for fault of a worse.

NURSE You say well.

MERCUTIO Yea, is the worst well? Very well took, i'faith, wisely,
wisely.

NURSE If you be he, sir, I desire some confidence with you.   105

BENVOLIO She will indite him to some supper.

MERCUTIO A bawd, a bawd, a bawd! So ho!

Mercutio sings a song full of indecent meaning. He leaves, continuing to mock the Nurse. She protests against his sauciness to her, then cautions Romeo not to deceive Juliet.

---

1 Mercutio's song – obscene (but obscure) humour

In his song, lines 111–16, Mercutio is playing his usual language game, seizing every opportunity for sexual punning. His 'So ho!' (line 107) sets him off on a hunting metaphor: chasing the hare. In his song, 'stale', 'hare' and 'hoar' can mean or sound like 'whore': a prostitute. The song has the surface meaning that any old dish is good to eat when you're hungry, but if it goes mouldy, it's not worth paying for ('too much for a score').

Modern audiences and readers are often puzzled by the song, because both its surface meaning and its indecent meaning are obscure. If you were directing the play, would you cut it from the performance? Why, or why not?

2 More mockery of the Nurse? (in small groups)

The actor playing Mercutio often adds 'business' (stage action) to his farewell, usually playing some trick on the Nurse. Work out several ideas of your own for how Mercutio might leave the stage (lines 119–20). Act out the one that you think would most amuse the audience.

3 But is it fair? (in pairs)

Talk together about what you think of the way in which the young men treat the Nurse (who is probably much older than them). Look at how she talks with Romeo from line 136 onwards, warning him that he should not seduce Juliet ('lead her in a fool's paradise'). Do you think that someone who is so concerned for Juliet's wellbeing deserves such mockery?

---

lenten pie a pie without meat (to be eaten in Lent – when Christians abstained from meat)
score bill for food
hoars goes mouldy
ropery indecent jokes

stand to listen to (but Romeo might also be making a sexual pun)
flirt-gills flirts
skains-mates cut-throats, rascals
weapon sword or penis (Peter makes a sexual pun)

ROMEO What hast thou found?

MERCUTIO No hare, sir, unless a hare, sir, in a lenten pie, that is
something stale and hoar ere it be spent.   110

                [*He walks by them and sings.*]

             An old hare hoar,

             And an old hare hoar,

         Is very good meat in Lent;

            But a hare that is hoar

            Is too much for a score,   115

        When it hoars ere it be spent.

    Romeo, will you come to your father's? We'll to dinner thither.

ROMEO I will follow you.

MERCUTIO Farewell, ancient lady, farewell, lady, [*Singing.*] 'lady,
lady'.   120

                   Exeunt [*Mercutio and Benvolio*]

NURSE I pray you, sir, what saucy merchant was this that was so full
of his ropery?

ROMEO A gentleman, Nurse, that loves to hear himself talk, and will
speak more in a minute than he will stand to in a month.

NURSE And 'a speak any thing against me, I'll take him down, and 'a   125
were lustier than he is, and twenty such Jacks; and if I cannot, I'll
find those that shall. Scurvy knave, I am none of his flirt-gills, I
am none of his skains-mates. [*She turns to Peter, her man.*] And thou
must stand by too and suffer every knave to use me at his pleasure!

PETER I saw no man use you at his pleasure; if I had, my weapon should 130
quickly have been out. I warrant you, I dare draw as soon as another
man, if I see occasion in a good quarrel, and the law on my side.

NURSE Now afore God, I am so vexed that every part about me quivers.
Scurvy knave! Pray you, sir, a word: and as I told you, my young
lady bid me enquire you out; what she bid me say, I will keep to   135
myself. But first let me tell ye, if ye should lead her in a fool's
paradise, as they say, it were a very gross kind of behaviour, as they
say; for the gentlewoman is young; and therefore, if you should deal
double with her, truly it were an ill thing to be offered to any
gentlewoman, and very weak dealing.   140

ROMEO Nurse, commend me to thy lady and mistress. I protest unto
thee –

NURSE Good heart, and i'faith I will tell her as much. Lord, Lord, she
will be a joyful woman.

Romeo arranges to marry Juliet that afternoon at Friar Lawrence's cell. He will send a rope ladder to the Nurse so that he may climb to Juliet's room in Capulet's house.

1 Decisions about the Nurse (in pairs)

a **Does the Nurse take the money?** In lines 151–3, Romeo offers money to the Nurse. The episode can be made very funny on stage, and can add to the audience's understanding of the Nurse's character. Work out a staging of the three lines that you feel will amuse the audience.

b **'As pale as any clout in the versal world'** In lines 168–72, the Nurse says that when she tells Juliet that Paris is a handsomer ('properer') man than Romeo, Juliet looks as white as a sheet ('clout' = washed-out rag, 'versal' = universal). But is she just making up a story she thinks Romeo wishes to hear? From all your experience of the play so far, suggest whether or not you think she is telling the truth.

c **'R is for the –'** Was the Nurse about to say 'arse' in line 175? Talk together about what you think she had in mind when she suddenly stopped. What word or phrase do you think fits her character?

2 Enjoy the Nurse's language (in small groups)

Go back to where the Nurse first speaks in this scene (line 85). Speak all her lines aloud, each person reading to a full stop before handing over. Then talk together about how you would play her on stage to make her contribution to the scene as funny as possible.

3 Verse and prose

Most of the scene is in prose, but a few short sections are in verse. Identify the verse sections, then turn to page 218. From what you read there, suggest why Shakespeare switched between prose and verse in this scene.

---

shrift confession (see p. 66)
shrived given absolution (pardon) for the sins she has confessed
tackled stair rope ladder
top-gallant summit (topmost mast of ship)
quit reward

would fain lay knife aboard would claim Juliet as his (guests in Elizabethan times brought their own knives to claim a place at table)
dog-name 'R' was called the dog's letter because it sounded like a dog growling

ROMEO What wilt thou tell her, Nurse? thou dost not mark me. 145

NURSE I will tell her, sir, that you do protest, which, as I take it, is a gentleman-like offer.

ROMEO Bid her devise
    Some means to come to shrift this afternoon,
    And there she shall at Friar Lawrence' cell 150
    Be shrived and married. Here is for thy pains.

NURSE No truly, sir, not a penny.

ROMEO Go to, I say you shall.

NURSE This afternoon, sir? Well, she shall be there.

ROMEO And stay, good Nurse, behind the abbey wall: 155
    Within this hour my man shall be with thee,
    And bring thee cords made like a tackled stair,
    Which to the high top-gallant of my joy
    Must be my convoy in the secret night.
    Farewell, be trusty, and I'll quit thy pains. 160
    Farewell, commend me to thy mistress.

NURSE Now God in heaven bless thee! Hark you, sir.

ROMEO What say'st thou, my dear Nurse?

NURSE Is your man secret? Did you ne'er hear say,
    'Two may keep counsel, putting one away'? 165

ROMEO 'Warrant thee, my man's as true as steel.

NURSE Well, sir, my mistress is the sweetest lady – Lord, Lord! when 'twas a little prating thing – O, there is a nobleman in town, one Paris, that would fain lay knife aboard; but she, good soul, had as lieve see a toad, a very toad, as see him. I anger her sometimes, 170 and tell her that Paris is the properer man, but I'll warrant you, when I say so, she looks as pale as any clout in the versal world. Doth not rosemary and Romeo begin both with a letter?

ROMEO Ay, Nurse, what of that? Both with an R.

NURSE Ah, mocker, that's the dog-name. R is for the – no, I know it 175 begins with some other letter – and she hath the prettiest sententious of it, of you and rosemary, that it would do you good to hear it.

ROMEO Commend me to thy lady.

NURSE Ay, a thousand times.

                                    [Exit Romeo]

              Peter!

PETER Anon.

NURSE [*Handing him her fan.*] Before and apace. 180

                          Exit [*after Peter*]

Juliet is impatient for the Nurse's return. She compares the speed of love and young people with the slowness of the old. The Nurse finally arrives, grumbling of her aches and pains.

---

1 Juliet's impatience (in pairs)

Juliet is eagerly awaiting the Nurse's return with a message from Romeo. She cannot wait to hear the news. Take turns to read Juliet's lines 1–19 to each other, speaking them with Juliet's impatience in mind. After your readings, work together to write a set of notes for the actor playing Juliet, advising her how to deliver different sections of the soliloquy.

2 Feel the movement in Juliet's language (in pairs)

Take Juliet's lines 1–19. From each line, say out loud just one word connected with movement (for example, line 1 – 'send', line 2 – 'return'). How many of these 'movement' words can you find? Talk together about how they create a sense of urgency.

3 Write your own rhyming couplet

Lines 16–17 are a rhyming couplet (two consecutive lines that rhyme), a favourite language device of Shakespeare and his con-temporaries. Make up your own rhyming couplet in the same style, and which might be a suitable ending to Juliet's soliloquy.

4 Delaying tactics

Juliet sent the Nurse at nine o'clock, but she met Romeo at twelve (see the previous scene, lines 92–3). No one knows what the Nurse was doing during that time, but it has served to increase Juliet's eagerness for news. In this scene, Shakespeare builds up a sense of urgency in Juliet's soliloquy. He then creates dramatic tension and humour by having the Nurse use all kinds of delaying tricks that frustrate Juliet and increase her impatience.

Perchance perhaps
heralds messengers
low'ring louring, threatening
nimble-pinioned doves swift-winged doves pulling the chariot of Venus, goddess of love

bandy strike to and fro (like a tennis ball)
feign pretend, appear
jaunce exhausting, bumpy journey

Act 2 Scene 5
Capulet's mansion

Enter JULIET.

JULIET The clock struck nine when I did send the Nurse;
    In half an hour she promised to return.
    Perchance she cannot meet him: that's not so.
    O, she is lame! Love's heralds should be thoughts,
    Which ten times faster glides than the sun's beams,   5
    Driving back shadows over low'ring hills;
    Therefore do nimble-pinioned doves draw Love,
    And therefore hath the wind-swift Cupid wings.
    Now is the sun upon the highmost hill
    Of this day's journey, and from nine till twelve   10
    Is three long hours, yet she is not come.
    Had she affections and warm youthful blood,
    She would be as swift in motion as a ball;
    My words would bandy her to my sweet love,
    And his to me.   15
    But old folks, many feign as they were dead,
    Unwieldy, slow, heavy, and pale as lead.

Enter NURSE [*with* PETER].

    O God, she comes! O honey Nurse, what news?
    Hast thou met with him? Send thy man away.
NURSE Peter, stay at the gate.   20

[Exit Peter]

JULIET Now, good sweet Nurse – O Lord, why look'st thou sad?
    Though news be sad, yet tell them merrily;
    If good, thou shamest the music of sweet news
    By playing it to me with so sour a face.
NURSE I am a-weary, give me leave a while.   25
    Fie, how my bones ache! What a jaunce have I!
JULIET I would thou hadst my bones, and I thy news.
    Nay, come, I pray thee speak, good, good Nurse, speak.
NURSE Jesu, what haste! can you not stay a while?
    Do you not see that I am out of breath?   30

Juliet is increasingly frustrated by the Nurse's irrelevant replies. At last, Juliet hears the longed-for news: Romeo waits to marry her at Friar Lawrence's cell.

1 Stage the scene (in pairs)

Read through the whole scene, one person as Juliet, the other as the Nurse. Just enjoy how the Nurse keeps Juliet waiting, until she finally tells the news of Romeo. After reading it, work out how to stage the scene. Write notes for the actors, suggesting how to show the changing moods of Juliet and the Nurse.

Best of all – act it out!

Juliet and the Nurse. In most productions there is a good deal of action. For instance, the Nurse struggles repeatedly to get comfortable; Juliet massages her back, neck and shoulders. At lines 56–7, Juliet sometimes explodes in exasperation, much to the audience's amusement.

Which line do you think is being spoken at this moment?

---

stay the circumstance wait for the details
warrant guarantee
Beshrew curse, shame on
Marry come up, I trow expressions of impatience ('by the Virgin Mary, hang on, I trust')

poultice comforting treatment
coil fuss
leave permission
hie hasten

JULIET How art thou out of breath, when thou hast breath
　　　　To say to me that thou art out of breath?
　　　　The excuse that thou dost make in this delay
　　　　Is longer than the tale thou dost excuse.
　　　　Is thy news good or bad? Answer to that. 35
　　　　Say either, and I'll stay the circumstance:
　　　　Let me be satisfied, is't good or bad?
NURSE Well, you have made a simple choice, you know not how to
choose a man: Romeo? no, not he; though his face be better than
any man's, yet his leg excels all men's, and for a hand and a foot 40
and a body, though they be not to be talked on, yet they are past
compare. He is not the flower of courtesy, but I'll warrant him, as
gentle as a lamb. Go thy ways, wench, serve God. What, have you
dined at home?
JULIET No, no! But all this did I know before. 45
　　　　What says he of our marriage, what of that?
NURSE Lord, how my head aches! what a head have I!
　　　　It beats as it would fall in twenty pieces.
　　　　My back a't'other side – ah, my back, my back!
　　　　Beshrew your heart for sending me about 50
　　　　To catch my death with jauncing up and down!
JULIET I'faith, I am sorry that thou art not well.
　　　　Sweet, sweet, sweet Nurse, tell me, what says my love?
NURSE Your love says, like an honest gentleman,
　　　　And a courteous, and a kind, and a handsome, 55
　　　　And I warrant a virtuous – Where is your mother?
JULIET Where is my mother? why, she is within,
　　　　Where should she be? How oddly thou repliest:
　　　　'Your love says, like an honest gentleman,
　　　　"Where is your mother?" '
NURSE 　　　　　　　　　O God's lady dear, 60
　　　　Are you so hot? Marry come up, I trow;
　　　　Is this the poultice for my aching bones?
　　　　Henceforward do your messages yourself.
JULIET Here's such a coil! Come, what says Romeo?
NURSE Have you got leave to go to shrift today? 65
JULIET I have.
NURSE Then hie you hence to Friar Lawrence' cell,
　　　　There stays a husband to make you a wife.

The Nurse, with a sexual joke, sends Juliet off to her marriage with Romeo. In Scene 6, Friar Lawrence and Romeo await Juliet. Romeo longs for marriage, but his words have an ominous ring.

---

1 Embarrassed responses?

'Now comes the wanton blood up in your cheeks'. The Nurse's vivid image is a way of saying 'You're blushing!' In Act 2 Scene 2, lines 85–6, there is another example of Juliet blushing. She appears to be quickly embarrassed, so how does she respond to the sexual jokes in the Nurse's lines 72–5? Suggest what movements and expressions Juliet might use as she hears the Nurse talk of 'bird's nest' and 'bear the burden'.

2 Appropriate exits (in pairs)

Work out how Juliet and the Nurse would leave the stage at the end of this scene. The way they leave should match their feelings and language.

3 Scene change

Write a paragraph, perhaps accompanied by a sketch, showing how you would effect a swift scene change from Scene 5 to Scene 6.

4 'Love-devouring Death' (in small groups)

'Love-devouring Death' is a personification, a type of imagery that turns death into a person and gives it human feelings and actions (see p. 215). Friar Lawrence also personifies 'the heavens' (Scene 6, line 1) where he imagines the heavens smiling. In the next line he imagines 'after-hours' (the future) sorrowfully rebuking himself and Romeo.

Make a tableau (a frozen picture) entitled 'Love-devouring Death'. Let your imaginations run to produce as dramatic a picture as possible.

---

wanton uncontrolled, passionate
bird's nest Juliet's bedroom (or the Nurse's sexual joke about Juliet's pubic hair)
the burden the weight of Romeo's body

That after-hours ... not so that we are not rebuked or punished with sadness later
countervail outweigh

Now comes the wanton blood up in your cheeks,
They'll be in scarlet straight at any news. 70
Hie you to church, I must another way,
To fetch a ladder, by the which your love
Must climb a bird's nest soon when it is dark.
I am the drudge, and toil in your delight;
But you shall bear the burden soon at night. 75
Go, I'll to dinner, hie you to the cell.
JULIET Hie to high fortune! Honest Nurse, farewell.

Exeunt

Act 2 Scene 6
Friar Lawrence's cell

Enter FRIAR LAWRENCE and ROMEO.

FRIAR LAWRENCE So smile the heavens upon this holy act,
That after-hours with sorrow chide us not.
ROMEO Amen, amen! but come what sorrow can,
It cannot countervail the exchange of joy
That one short minute gives me in her sight. 5
Do thou but close our hands with holy words,
Then love-devouring Death do what he dare,
It is enough I may but call her mine.

The Friar advises moderation in love, not violent excess. In reply to Romeo's elaborate language asking her to give an ornate description of their happiness, Juliet speaks of her true love. They leave to be married.

1 Imagery – the Friar warns and praises

Friar Lawrence's first speech opposite is rich in imagery. He begins with an image of joyous love as fire and gunpowder, which destroy ('consume') at the very moment ('triumph') of meeting ('kiss'). His next image is of how over-sweet honey can become revolting and can destroy the appetite. His image of Juliet is of how someone in love seems to float on air.

Match these images with the lines opposite. Then write a paragraph on each, telling how Friar Lawrence feels each of the three images applies to Romeo and Juliet's love.

2 Can true love be measured? (in pairs)

Romeo, in elaborate language, invites Juliet to tell of their love like a rich description ('blazon') of a coat of arms. But Juliet argues ('Conceit, more rich in matter than in words', line 30) that true love doesn't need words. It is so rich, it cannot be measured, nor can it ever be fully described. Talk together about what you think of Juliet's argument. Is she right?

In a later play, *Antony and Cleopatra*, Shakespeare expressed the same idea: 'There's beggary in the love that can be reckoned'.

3 Show the marriage ceremony? (in small groups)

Shakespeare does not show the wedding of Romeo and Juliet. Talk together about whether you think the dramatic effect of the play would be increased by adding a wedding scene.

To help your thinking, rehearse and perform a scene showing the wedding to see how well it 'works'.

---

powder gunpowder
confounds destroys
tardy late
bestride the gossamers walk on
 threads of a spider's web
vanity love's pleasure

ghostly confessor spiritual adviser
blazon describe or portray
Conceit imagination
Till Holy Church . . . one until you are
 joined in marriage by proper religious
 ceremony

FRIAR LAWRENCE These violent delights have violent ends,
   And in their triumph die like fire and powder,   10
   Which as they kiss consume. The sweetest honey
   Is loathsome in his own deliciousness,
   And in the taste confounds the appetite.
   Therefore love moderately, long love doth so;
   Too swift arrives as tardy as too slow.   15

    Enter JULIET.

   Here comes the lady. O, so light a foot
   Will ne'er wear out the everlasting flint;
   A lover may bestride the gossamers
   That idles in the wanton summer air,
   And yet not fall, so light is vanity.   20
JULIET Good even to my ghostly confessor.
FRIAR LAWRENCE Romeo shall thank thee, daughter, for us both.
    [*Romeo kisses Juliet.*]
JULIET As much to him, else is his thanks too much.
    [*Juliet returns his kiss.*]
ROMEO Ah, Juliet, if the measure of thy joy
   Be heaped like mine, and that thy skill be more   25
   To blazon it, then sweeten with thy breath
   This neighbour air, and let rich music's tongue
   Unfold the imagined happiness that both
   Receive in either by this dear encounter.
JULIET Conceit, more rich in matter than in words,   30
   Brags of his substance, not of ornament;
   They are but beggars that can count their worth,
   But my true love is grown to such excess
   I cannot sum up sum of half my wealth.
FRIAR LAWRENCE
   Come, come with me, and we will make short work,   35
   For by your leaves, you shall not stay alone
   Till Holy Church incorporate two in one.
        [*Exeunt*]

Looking back at Act 2
Activities for groups or individuals

1 Headlines: what's happened in Act 2?

Imagine you are a newspaper sub-editor. Is your paper a tabloid or a 'heavy'? Your job is to write brief, memorable headlines for each of the six scenes of Act 1. Make your six headlines as accurate as possible. Try to use some of Shakespeare's own words.

2 What is your image of Juliet?

Throughout this edition there are many photographs of different portrayals of Juliet on stage and film. Look first at the illustrations in the colour section, then at all the other pictures of Juliet. Which comes closest to your imagining of what Juliet is like? Write a paragraph giving reasons why you have chosen that picture – and why some others do not match your impression.

3 Cast the play

You are a director about to film the play. Who would you sign up to play some of the characters you've met so far? Choose anyone you like: film or television actors, singers or other public figures. Say why you think each is suitable. You might try casting the play from the teachers and students in your school or college. Remember, Juliet is only thirteen!

4 What kind of balcony?

Study the pictures of the 'balcony' on pages vii, 58, 222 and 225. Think about how different each presentation of the 'balcony' is – and how 'realistic' you think it should be in a stage production. Afterwards, put your ideas into practice and design your own balcony.

5 Burlesque or parody – an improvisation

The 'balcony' scene (Act 2 Scene 2) is a favourite of comedians, who 'send it up something rotten'. Try your own improvisation on Shakespeare's setting. A boy in love talks with a young girl at an upstairs window; or a girl, downstairs, talks to a boy who is on an upstairs landing; or . . . make up your own situation!

6 Two topics for research

a Malapropisms The Nurse uses malapropisms. 'Confidence' (Act 2 Scene 4, line 105) is her mistake for 'conference'. Benvolio, replying, uses 'indite' (line 106) for 'invite' (presumably mockingly). Malapropisms are named after Mrs Malaprop, who muddled up her language, in Sheridan's play *The Rivals*. Find out more about her in the library or on the Internet. Shakespeare would have known malapropisms as 'cacozelia'.

b Tragic females Mercutio speaks of Dido, Cleopatra, Helen, Hero and Thisbe (Act 2 Scene 4, lines 36–7). Find out more about them in the library or on the Internet. Write an assignment on how they add to your understanding of *Romeo and Juliet*.

7 Verse, prose and rhyme

Glance through Scenes 1–6. Five are written in verse, one in prose. Why do you think Shakespeare changed his style from verse to prose in that one particular scene? Page 218 will help you.

Next, read aloud the last word only of each line in Scene 3. What do you discover? Finally, how many rhyming couplets (two consecutive lines that rhyme) can you find in Scene 2? Suggest why Shakespeare used rhymes at those moments.

'Come, come with me, and we will make short work'. At the end of Act 2, Romeo and Juliet leave to marry. Work out how you would stage the closing moments of Act 2 (and see Activity 3 on p. 86).

Benvolio fears meeting the Capulets, knowing a fight will surely follow. Mercutio laughs at his fears, accusing Benvolio of being a quick-tempered quarreller.

Mercutio, in Zeffirelli's thirteenth-century setting of the play.

Tybalt, in the Royal Shakespeare Company's twentieth-century setting.

1 Picking five quarrels (in pairs)

Mercutio, who is probably describing himself, gives five examples of Benvolio's quarrels (lines 15–25). Every quarrel was caused by a trivial incident. Work out actions Mercutio might use to accompany each. For example, does he pat Benvolio's chin for the first?

claps me throws
operation effect
drawer barman
moody angry
doublet tight jacket (like Mercutio's above)

riband ribbon
fee-simple legal ownership. Benvolio's statement that if he were as quick to pick a quarrel as Mercutio, he wouldn't last long, ominously forecasts Mercutio's death

Act 3 Scene 1
Verona, a public place

Enter MERCUTIO *and his* PAGE, BENVOLIO, *and men.*

BENVOLIO I pray thee, good Mercutio, let's retire:
    The day is hot, the Capels are abroad,
    And if we meet we shall not scape a brawl,
    For now, these hot days, is the mad blood stirring.

MERCUTIO Thou art like one of these fellows that, when he enters the 5
confines of a tavern, claps me his sword upon the table, and says
'God send me no need of thee!'; and by the operation of the second
cup draws him on the drawer, when indeed there is no need.

BENVOLIO Am I like such a fellow?

MERCUTIO Come, come, thou art as hot a Jack in thy mood as any in 10
Italy, and as soon moved to be moody, and as soon moody to be
moved.

BENVOLIO And what to?

MERCUTIO Nay, and there were two such, we should have none shortly,
for one would kill the other. Thou? why, thou wilt quarrel with 15
a man that hath a hair more or a hair less in his beard than thou
hast; thou wilt quarrel with a man for cracking nuts, having no other
reason but because thou hast hazel eyes. What eye but such an eye
would spy out such a quarrel? Thy head is as full of quarrels as
an egg is full of meat, and yet thy head hath been beaten as addle 20
as an egg for quarrelling. Thou hast quarrelled with a man for
coughing in the street, because he hath wakened thy dog that hath
lain asleep in the sun. Didst thou not fall out with a tailor for
wearing his new doublet before Easter? with another for tying his
new shoes with old riband? and yet thou wilt tutor me from 25
quarrelling?

BENVOLIO And I were so apt to quarrel as thou art, any man should
buy the fee-simple of my life for an hour and a quarter.

MERCUTIO The fee-simple? O simple!

Mercutio taunts Tybalt, but Tybalt ignores his insults, because he is seeking Romeo. However, Romeo refuses to accept Tybalt's challenge to fight and tries to placate him, much to Mercutio's disgust.

1 Picking – or avoiding – a quarrel (in groups of four)

Each person takes a part: Benvolio, Mercutio, Tybalt, Romeo. Two are out to pick a fight; two wish to avoid one (Benvolio, always the peacekeeper, and Romeo).

Read through lines 30–65 to gain a feeling of what's happening. Next, read the lines again, but pause at the end of each line or sentence. In the pause, whoever has just spoken explains the motivation behind what their character said. For example, after his first line, Benvolio might say, 'Be careful, let's avoid a fight.'

2 Mercutio's wordplay on 'man'

At line 49, Tybalt says Romeo is the man he intends to fight. But Mercutio, who has already made double meanings out of Tybalt's 'consortest', now pretends that 'man' means servant or 'follower'. He says Romeo will never wear the uniform of Tybalt's servants. Only if Tybalt invites Romeo to meet at a duelling place ('field') will Romeo be Tybalt's 'man'. As you will soon see at line 90, even at the point of death Mercutio revels in the joy of playing with language.

3 'Be satisfied' (in groups of four or more)

Line 65 is an electric moment in the play. Tybalt has deeply insulted Romeo ('villain', 'boy'). But because he is now married to Juliet, Romeo wishes to make peace with Tybalt, who is now his kinsman. Everyone on stage will react dramatically to Romeo's two words.

Prepare a tableau to show all characters at the moment when Romeo says 'be satisfied'. Hold the frozen moment for thirty seconds. Other groups identify who's who in your 'still picture'.

---

good den   good evening
occasion   cause
Consort   associate with, play with
minstrels   hired musicians (insulting to high-born Mercutio)
fiddlestick   sword

'Zounds   by Christ's wounds (an oath)
livery   servants' uniform
appertaining   appropriate
devise   guess
tender   value

Enter TYBALT, PETRUCHIO, *and others.*

BENVOLIO By my head, here comes the Capulets.   30
MERCUTIO By my heel, I care not.
TYBALT Follow me close, for I will speak to them.
   Gentlemen, good den, a word with one of you.
MERCUTIO And but one word with one of us? couple it with something,
   make it a word and a blow.   35
TYBALT You shall find me apt enough to that, sir, and you will give
   me occasion.
MERCUTIO Could you not take some occasion without giving?
TYBALT Mercutio, thou consortest with Romeo.
MERCUTIO Consort? what, dost thou make us minstrels? And thou   40
   make minstrels of us, look to hear nothing but discords. Here's my
   fiddlestick, here's that shall make you dance. 'Zounds, consort!
BENVOLIO We talk here in the public haunt of men:
   Either withdraw unto some private place,
   Or reason coldly of your grievances,   45
   Or else depart; here all eyes gaze on us.
MERCUTIO Men's eyes were made to look, and let them gaze;
   I will not budge for no man's pleasure, I.

Enter ROMEO.

TYBALT Well, peace be with you, sir, here comes my man.
MERCUTIO But I'll be hanged, sir, if he wear your livery.   50
   Marry, go before to field, he'll be your follower;
   Your worship in that sense may call him man.
TYBALT Romeo, the love I bear thee can afford
   No better term than this: thou art a villain.
ROMEO Tybalt, the reason that I have to love thee   55
   Doth much excuse the appertaining rage
   To such a greeting. Villain am I none;
   Therefore farewell, I see thou knowest me not.
TYBALT Boy, this shall not excuse the injuries
   That thou hast done me, therefore turn and draw.   60
ROMEO I do protest I never injuried thee,
   But love thee better than thou canst devise,
   Till thou shalt know the reason of my love;
   And so, good Capulet, which name I tender
   As dearly as mine own, be satisfied.   65
MERCUTIO O calm, dishonourable, vile submission!

Mercutio, angered by Romeo's refusal to fight, challenges Tybalt. Romeo tries to make peace, but his intervention is fatal for Mercutio, who, mortally wounded, curses Montagues and Capulets alike.

1 Always joking? (in pairs)

Even though he knows he will shortly die, Mercutio continues to pun jokingly: 'Ask for me tomorrow, and you shall find me a grave man.'

One person reads all of Mercutio's lines on the opposite page, but stops at the end of each sentence. The other person says to whom the sentence is probably spoken, and describes Mercutio's tone of voice (e.g. mocking, angry, serious, and so on). (See page viii in the colour section for depictions of the fight.) Note: 'A plague a'both your houses!' = curses upon Montagues and Capulets alike.

2 Performing Mercutio's final moments (in small groups)

In every production, the director and actors decide how to play lines 82–99. For example, just when do Mercutio's friends realise that he isn't joking, merely scratched, but mortally wounded?

Take roles (as director, Mercutio, Benvolio, Romeo, and others). Talk together about how you think this part of the scene should be played. What kind of performance will have the greatest effect on the audience? Stage your version, showing how each person behaves from moment to moment.

3 Why does Mercutio die so early in the play?

Many people think that Shakespeare kills off Mercutio before the play reaches its halfway point because he thought Mercutio was such an attractive character that he would 'steal the play' from Romeo and Juliet. But as you read on, think of other dramatic reasons for Mercutio's early death.

'Alla stoccata' rapier thrust (Tybalt's nickname?)
dry-beat thrash without drawing blood
pilcher scabbard
'passado' thrust
bandying fighting

sped done for, killed
villain fellow (Elizabethans often used 'villain' to address servants. It was not a term of abuse – unlike the use in lines 54, 57 and 92)
book of arithmetic rule book (see p. 70)

'Alla stoccata' carries it away. [*Draws.*]
Tybalt, you rat-catcher, will you walk?

TYBALT What wouldst thou have with me?

MERCUTIO Good King of Cats, nothing but one of your nine lives that   70
I mean to make bold withal, and as you shall use me hereafter,
dry-beat the rest of the eight. Will you pluck your sword out of
his pilcher by the ears? Make haste, lest mine be about your ears
ere it be out.

TYBALT I am for you. [*Drawing.*]   75

ROMEO Gentle Mercutio, put thy rapier up.

MERCUTIO Come, sir, your 'passado'.
                        [*They fight.*]

ROMEO Draw, Benvolio, beat down their weapons.
            Gentlemen, for shame forbear this outrage!
            Tybalt, Mercutio, the Prince expressly hath   80
            Forbid this bandying in Verona streets.
                    [*Romeo steps between them.*]
            Hold, Tybalt! Good Mercutio!
            [*Tybalt under Romeo's arm thrusts Mercutio in.*]
                                Away Tybalt [*with his followers*]

MERCUTIO   I am hurt.
            A plague a'both houses! I am sped.
            Is he gone and hath nothing?

BENVOLIO   What, art thou hurt?

MERCUTIO Ay, ay, a scratch, a scratch, marry, 'tis enough.   85
            Where is my page? Go, villain, fetch a surgeon.
                                            [*Exit Page*]

ROMEO Courage, man, the hurt cannot be much.

MERCUTIO No, 'tis not so deep as a well, nor so wide as a church-door,
but 'tis enough, 'twill serve. Ask for me tomorrow, and you shall
find me a grave man. I am peppered, I warrant, for this world. A   90
plague a'both your houses! 'Zounds, a dog, a rat, a mouse, a cat,
to scratch a man to death! a braggart, a rogue, a villain, that fights
by the book of arithmetic. Why the dev'l came you between us?
I was hurt under your arm.

ROMEO I thought all for the best.   95

MERCUTIO Help me into some house, Benvolio,
            Or I shall faint. A plague a'both your houses!
            They have made worms' meat of me. I have it,
            And soundly too. Your houses!
                                Exit [*with Benvolio*]

Romeo, blaming himself for Mercutio's wound, and resentful of Tybalt's insults, fears that his love for Juliet has weakened his courage. Learning that Mercutio is dead, he vows to kill Tybalt, slays him, then flees.

1 'This day's black fate on moe days doth depend'

At line 110, Romeo fears that the evil outcomes ('black fate') of today's violence lie in the future ('moe [more] days'). Some critics argue that this is the point in the play where the tragedy really begins.

In lines 107–15, Shakespeare uses the language of **Revenge Tragedy**. This type of play was very popular in the 1590s when he was writing *Romeo and Juliet*. In Revenge Tragedy, the main character is a 'revenger', and his language is high sounding and portentous. So should these lines be spoken in a declamatory way, or is it possible to speak them in an ordinary, conversational tone? Try saying them in different styles and then write a paragraph advising the actors how to speak here. (Also advise Romeo how to deliver line 127, 'O, I am fortune's fool'.)

2 How to stage the fight? (in pairs)

In Zeffirelli's film of *Romeo and Juliet*, Romeo pursues Tybalt and kills him in a savage brawl. There is a similarly vicious struggle in Baz Luhrmann's film. Both versions were intended to show that violence lies just below Verona's glamorous surface appearance.

Should the fight be staged as a dignified, formal fencing match, rather like the illustrations on pages viii and 70, or as brutal, dirty and painful? Talk together about how Tybalt's death (lines 121–2) might be staged, and decide on your version. Arrange the movements of the fight, but be very careful. The first rule of all stage-fighting is that no one must be hurt. Try everything out in slow motion first.

---

ally relative
temper character
softened valour's steel weakened my bravery
respective lenity respectful mildness

above our heads on the way to heaven
doom thee death sentence you to death
fortune's fool the plaything of mere chance

ROMEO This gentleman, the Prince's near ally,   100
     My very friend, hath got this mortal hurt
     In my behalf; my reputation stained
     With Tybalt's slander – Tybalt, that an hour
     Hath been my cousin. O sweet Juliet,
     Thy beauty hath made me effeminate,   105
     And in my temper softened valour's steel!

Enter Benvolio.

BENVOLIO O Romeo, Romeo, brave Mercutio is dead.
     That gallant spirit hath aspired the clouds,
     Which too untimely here did scorn the earth.
ROMEO This day's black fate on moe days doth depend,   110
     This but begins the woe others must end.

[Enter Tybalt.]

BENVOLIO Here comes the furious Tybalt back again.
ROMEO Again, in triumph, and Mercutio slain?
     Away to heaven, respective lenity,
     And fire-eyed fury be my conduct now!   115
     Now, Tybalt, take the 'villain' back again
     That late thou gavest me, for Mercutio's soul
     Is but a little way above our heads,
     Staying for thine to keep him company:
     Either thou or I, or both, must go with him.   120
TYBALT Thou wretched boy, that didst consort him here,
     Shalt with him hence.
ROMEO   This shall determine that.
     They fight; Tybalt falls.
BENVOLIO Romeo, away, be gone!
     The citizens are up, and Tybalt slain.
     Stand not amazed, the Prince will doom thee death   125
     If thou art taken. Hence be gone, away!
ROMEO O, I am fortune's fool.
BENVOLIO   Why dost thou stay?
                                 Exit Romeo

Enter Citizens [as OFFICERS of the Watch].

OFFICER Which way ran he that killed Mercutio?
     Tybalt, that murderer, which way ran he?

Lady Capulet demands that Romeo must die. Her demand for Montague blood reveals the depth of hatred between the two families. Benvolio tells the story of how Mercutio and Tybalt died.

1 Lady Capulet grieves for Tybalt

Lady Capulet's words suggest extreme emotion as she mourns over Tybalt and calls for Romeo's death. Some productions have presented an intimate, even sexual relationship between her and Tybalt (see p. 38). Would such a relationship add dramatic power to her grief? Write, giving reasons, how you would advise Lady Capulet to deliver her five lines opposite (think about tone, expressions, actions, etc.).

2 How truthful is Benvolio's story? (in small groups)

Does Benvolio give Prince Escales an accurate and unbiased account of the brawl? Or does he tell it from a Montague's viewpoint?

One person reads Benvolio's lines 133–66, pausing after every couple of lines. At each pause, the others question him, for example:

- Why did you say 'unlucky'? (line 134)
- Why remind the Prince that Mercutio was his kinsman? (line 136)
- Why do you call Mercutio 'brave'? (line 136)
- Why do you imply Tybalt started the quarrel? (line 143)

3 Imagery: a sword by any other name

Benvolio uses metaphors in place of 'swords' and 'sword-fighting': 'piercing steel' (line 150); 'deadly point to point' (line 151); 'Cold death' (line 153); 'fatal points' (line 157); 'envious thrust' (line 159).

Suggest a few other such images for a sword. Or take any everyday object (e.g. a bicycle or a pen) and make up similarly vivid metaphors to represent it. See pages 214–15 for more on metaphors.

---

discover reveal
manage progress
spoke him fair was courteous to Tybalt
nice trivial

unruly spleen fiery anger (Elizabethans thought anger came from the spleen)
martial warlike
Retorts returns
stout brave

BENVOLIO There lies that Tybalt.
OFFICER   Up, sir, go with me;   130
       I charge thee in the Prince's name obey.

      Enter PRINCE, *old* MONTAGUE, CAPULET, *their* WIVES,
                      and all.

PRINCE Where are the vile beginners of this fray?
BENVOLIO O noble Prince, I can discover all
       The unlucky manage of this fatal brawl;
       There lies the man, slain by young Romeo,   135
       That slew thy kinsman, brave Mercutio.
LADY CAPULET Tybalt, my cousin! O my brother's child!
       O Prince! O husband! O, the blood is spilled
       Of my dear kinsman. Prince, as thou art true,
       For blood of ours, shed blood of Montague.   140
       O cousin, cousin!
PRINCE Benvolio, who began this bloody fray?
BENVOLIO Tybalt, here slain, whom Romeo's hand did slay.
       Romeo, that spoke him fair, bid him bethink
       How nice the quarrel was, and urged withal   145
       Your high displeasure; all this, utterèd
       With gentle breath, calm look, knees humbly bowed,
       Could not take truce with the unruly spleen
       Of Tybalt deaf to peace, but that he tilts
       With piercing steel at bold Mercutio's breast,   150
       Who, all as hot, turns deadly point to point,
       And with a martial scorn, with one hand beats
       Cold death aside, and with the other sends
       It back to Tybalt, whose dexterity
       Retorts it. Romeo he cries aloud,   155
       'Hold, friends! friends, part!' and swifter than his tongue,
       His agile arm beats down their fatal points,
       And 'twixt them rushes; underneath whose arm
       An envious thrust from Tybalt hit the life
       Of stout Mercutio, and then Tybalt fled;   160
       But by and by comes back to Romeo,
       Who had but newly entertained revenge,
       And to't they go like lightning, for, ere I
       Could draw to part them, was stout Tybalt slain;

Lady Capulet, accusing Benvolio of lying, again demands Romeo's death. But Prince Escales orders that, for killing Tybalt, Romeo will be banished from Verona.

1 Ending in rhyme

The scene ends with all the speeches opposite spoken in rhyme. Do you think the actors should emphasise the rhymes? Decide by thinking about what that would contribute to the closing dramatic atmosphere of the scene.

2 Report the action!

Imagine you are a reporter for *The Verona Mail* (or make up your own newspaper title). Write an account of the events in this scene. Include interviews with those who saw what happened.

The death of Tybalt. Identify Tybalt, Romeo and Benvolio. Choose a line from Scene 1 as a suitable caption.

Affection love (for Romeo)

interest (because Mercutio was my kinsman)

hearts' proceeding emotional actions (bloody brawling)

amerce punish

purchase out make amends for, excuse

Mercy but . . . kill showing mercy to murderers results in further murders

And as he fell, did Romeo turn and fly.   165
This is the truth, or let Benvolio die.
LADY CAPULET He is a kinsman to the Montague,
Affection makes him false, he speaks not true:
Some twenty of them fought in this black strife,
And all those twenty could but kill one life.   170
I beg for justice, which thou, Prince, must give:
Romeo slew Tybalt, Romeo must not live.
PRINCE Romeo slew him, he slew Mercutio;
Who now the price of his dear blood doth owe?
MONTAGUE Not Romeo, Prince, he was Mercutio's friend;   175
His fault concludes but what the law should end,
The life of Tybalt.
PRINCE   And for that offence
Immediately we do exile him hence.
I have an interest in your hearts' proceeding:
My blood for your rude brawls doth lie a-bleeding;   180
But I'll amerce you with so strong a fine
That you shall all repent the loss of mine.
I will be deaf to pleading and excuses,
Nor tears nor prayers shall purchase out abuses:
Therefore use none. Let Romeo hence in haste,   185
Else, when he is found, that hour is his last.
Bear hence this body, and attend our will:
Mercy but murders, pardoning those that kill.

Exeunt

Juliet, unaware of the murderous events of the day, and filled with love for Romeo, longs for the night to come. She thinks of Romeo, after her death, as like a star in the night sky.

1 Juliet longs for night and Romeo (in small groups)

Juliet passionately reveals the depth of her longing for Romeo. Critics call her thirty-one lines an *epithalamium* or wedding song. Use the following activities to help you experience and understand her feelings.

a **Haste and commands** Sit closely together. One person quietly reads the speech. The others echo aloud all words that seem to be commands or concerned with speed or haste (e.g. 'Gallop', 'fiery-footed', 'whip', and so on). Try the activity again, adding actions. Afterwards, talk together about how such words convey the intensity of Juliet's feelings.

b **'Such a waggoner . . .'** In Greek mythology, Phaëton was the son of Phoebus (the sun god). He drove the horses pulling his father's chariot (the sun) so recklessly that Zeus, king of the gods, killed him with a thunderbolt.

   Prepare a tableau to show Phaëton's fate. Make your still picture as vivid and dramatic as possible. Afterwards, talk together about how this image of the youthful, rash Phaëton is an ominous prediction of what will happen in *Romeo and Juliet*.

c **Embarrassing?** The soliloquy has erotic elements, and in Victorian times, some readers found Juliet's speech embarrassingly sexual (and some productions cut the speech). Which lines and words do you think they thought embarrassing? Remember, the lines are spoken by a thirteen-year-old girl.

d **Favourite lines and images** Each group member picks out a line or image they find especially appealing. Talk together about them, then write why you enjoy your chosen line or image.

Phoebus' lodging the west (where the sun sets)

That runaways' eyes may wink No one can be certain what this means. Over forty different meanings have been suggested. What do you think?

stainless innocent

Hood my unmanned blood, bating in my cheeks an untrained hawk, unused to men ('unmanned'), fluttered its wings ('bating') until it was 'hooded' with a black cap (or 'mantle') (see p. 60)

Act 3 Scene 2
Juliet's room in Capulet's mansion

Enter JULIET *alone.*

JULIET Gallop apace, you fiery-footed steeds,
     Towards Phoebus' lodging; such a waggoner
     As Phaëton would whip you to the west,
     And bring in cloudy night immediately.
     Spread thy close curtain, love-performing Night, 5
     That runaways' eyes may wink, and Romeo
     Leap to these arms, untalked of and unseen:
     Lovers can see to do their amorous rites
     By their own beauties, or if love be blind,
     It best agrees with night. Come, civil Night, 10
     Thou sober-suited matron all in black,
     And learn me how to lose a winning match,
     Played for a pair of stainless maidenhoods.
     Hood my unmanned blood, bating in my cheeks,
     With thy black mantle, till strange love grow bold, 15
     Think true love acted simple modesty.
     Come, Night, come, Romeo, come, thou day in night,
     For thou wilt lie upon the wings of night,
     Whiter than new snow upon a raven's back.
     Come, gentle Night, come, loving, black-browed Night, 20
     Give me my Romeo, and when I shall die,
     Take him and cut him out in little stars,
     And he will make the face of heaven so fine
     That all the world will be in love with night,
     And pay no worship to the garish sun. 25
     O, I have bought the mansion of a love,
     But not possessed it, and though I am sold,
     Not yet enjoyed. So tedious is this day
     As is the night before some festival
     To an impatient child that hath new robes 30
     And may not wear them. O, here comes my Nurse,

Juliet, alarmed by the Nurse's mourning for Tybalt's death, thinks that Romeo has died. She wishes that she too could die, and lie beside Romeo in death.

---

1 'I', 'ay' and 'eyes' (in pairs)

Elizabethans not only enjoyed joking puns (of which Mercutio was a master), but also appreciated punning in tragic situations. In lines 45–52, Juliet and the Nurse repeatedly use one vowel sound: 'I'. This repetitive wordplay can sound strange or artificial to a modern audience at such a serious moment in the play.

Read the lines aloud to each other, in any manner you think appropriate. Then imagine you are directing the play. Write the advice you would give your two actors as to how they could deliver these eight lines to maximise dramatic effect.

2 'Vile earth, to earth resign, end motion here' (in pairs)

In line 59 Juliet wishes that her body ('Vile earth') should be buried ('to earth resign'), ending her life ('end motion here'). Shakespeare uses words between lines 36 and 60 to emphasise that his subject is death and suffering.

Catch the mood of this part of the scene by reading to your partner just one word from each line that emphasises death or disaster. How many lines lack such words? Talk together about how your chosen words create the atmosphere of this passage.

3 Changing moods

Identify the different moods Juliet experiences in the episode opposite. Write the line numbers for each mood change, and what she feels (for example, lines 32–3, elation; lines 34–5, puzzlement; line 36, fear . . .).

4 Why does the Nurse mislead Juliet?

Why doesn't the Nurse immediately tell Juliet that it's Tybalt, not Romeo, who is dead? Suggest one or two possible reasons.

---

cords rope ladder
weraday alas!
envious spiteful
cockatrice the basilisk, a legendary beast. Half snake, half cockerel, its stare could kill

weal welfare, joy
corse corpse
sounded swooned
bankrout bankrupt (Juliet has lost her 'investment of love' in Romeo)
press . . . bier lie together in death

Enter NURSE, *with* [*the ladder of*] *cords* [*in her lap*].

And she brings news, and every tongue that speaks
But Romeo's name speaks heavenly eloquence.
Now, Nurse, what news? What hast thou there? the cords
That Romeo bid thee fetch?

NURSE   Ay, ay, the cords.   35

[*Throws them down.*]

JULIET Ay me, what news? Why dost thou wring thy hands?
NURSE Ah weraday, he's dead, he's dead, he's dead!
        We are undone, lady, we are undone.
        Alack the day, he's gone, he's killed, he's dead!
JULIET Can heaven be so envious?
NURSE   Romeo can,   40
        Though heaven cannot. O Romeo, Romeo!
        Who ever would have thought it? Romeo!
JULIET What devil art thou that dost torment me thus?
        This torture should be roared in dismal hell.
        Hath Romeo slain himself? Say thou but 'ay',   45
        And that bare vowel 'I' shall poison more
        Than the death-darting eye of cockatrice.
        I am not I, if there be such an 'ay',
        Or those eyes shut, that makes thee answer 'ay'.
        If he be slain, say 'ay', or if not, 'no':   50
        Brief sounds determine my weal or woe.
NURSE I saw the wound, I saw it with mine eyes
        (God save the mark!), here on his manly breast:
        A piteous corse, a bloody piteous corse,
        Pale, pale as ashes, all bedaubed in blood,   55
        All in gore blood; I sounded at the sight.
JULIET O break, my heart, poor bankrout, break at once!
        To prison, eyes, ne'er look on liberty!
        Vile earth, to earth resign, end motion here,
        And thou and Romeo press one heavy bier!   60
NURSE O Tybalt, Tybalt, the best friend I had!
        O courteous Tybalt, honest gentleman,
        That ever I should live to see thee dead!
JULIET What storm is this that blows so contrary?
        Is Romeo slaughtered? and is Tybalt dead?   65
        My dearest cousin, and my dearer lord?

Juliet learns that Tybalt is dead and Romeo banished. She begins to accuse Romeo of seeming beautiful but acting vilely, but then rebukes the Nurse for wishing shame on Romeo.

1 Appearance and reality (in small groups)

The theme of the difference between appearance and reality is important in every Shakespeare play. Juliet, hearing of Romeo's killing of Tybalt, laments that a beautiful appearance can hide an evil reality ('beautiful tyrant', 'damnèd saint', and so on). Phrases composed of 'opposite' words directly placed next to each other are called oxymorons. Romeo has used them earlier (see pp. 14 and 216). Where the 'opposites' are not immediately adjacent it is an antithesis (e.g. 'O serpent heart, hid with a flow'ring face!').

How many oxymorons and antitheses can you count in lines 73–85? Choose one of them and prepare a tableau involving every member of the group. Each group shows its tableau. The other groups guess which oxymorons or antitheses are portrayed.

2 The Nurse's negative view of men (in pairs)

Identify the seven things the Nurse says about men in lines 85–7. Talk together about possible reasons why she sets out such a list. Is it because of what she has experienced in Verona? Don't be afraid to speculate about her reasons. You'll find it helpful to talk about each characteristic in turn ('no trust', 'No faith', and so on).

3 Juliet's abrupt mood change

Juliet switches very abruptly from harsh criticism of Romeo (lines 73–85) to high praise (from line 91). Every actor playing Juliet has to make that mood change convincing. Step into role as director and write notes on ways in which she could make the shift of her feelings believable to an audience.

---

the general doom doomsday, the end of the world (sounded by the last trumpet)

Despisèd . . . show loathsome reality of heavenly appearance

bower enclose

perjured liars

forsworn promise breakers

naught wicked, vicious

aqua-vitae brandy

chide at criticise

tributary drops tears of tribute

Then, dreadful trumpet, sound the general doom,
For who is living, if those two are gone?

NURSE Tybalt is gone and Romeo banishèd,
Romeo that killed him, he is banishèd.

JULIET O God, did Romeo's hand shed Tybalt's blood?

NURSE It did, it did, alas the day, it did!

JULIET O serpent heart, hid with a flow'ring face!
Did ever dragon keep so fair a cave?
Beautiful tyrant, fiend angelical!
Dove-feathered raven, wolvish-ravening lamb!
Despisèd substance of divinest show!
Just opposite to what thou justly seem'st,
A damnèd saint, an honourable villain!
O nature, what hadst thou to do in hell
When thou didst bower the spirit of a fiend
In mortal paradise of such sweet flesh?
Was ever book containing such vile matter
So fairly bound? O that deceit should dwell
In such a gorgeous palace!

NURSE There's no trust,
No faith, no honesty in men, all perjured,
All forsworn, all naught, all dissemblers.
Ah, where's my man? Give me some aqua-vitae;
These griefs, these woes, these sorrows make me old.
Shame come to Romeo!

JULIET Blistered be thy tongue
For such a wish! he was not born to shame:
Upon his brow shame is ashamed to sit;
For 'tis a throne where honour may be crowned
Sole monarch of the universal earth.
O what a beast was I to chide at him!

NURSE Will you speak well of him that killed your cousin?

JULIET Shall I speak ill of him that is my husband?
Ah, poor my lord, what tongue shall smooth thy name,
When I, thy three-hours wife, have mangled it?
But wherefore, villain, didst thou kill my cousin?
That villain cousin would have killed my husband.
Back, foolish tears, back to your native spring,
Your tributary drops belong to woe,
Which you mistaking offer up to joy.

Juliet is devastated by the thought of Romeo's banishment. She threatens to kill herself. But she is cheered by the Nurse's promise to find Romeo and send him to her bedchamber that night.

1 More on Juliet's changing moods (in pairs)

Throughout this scene, Juliet's feelings fluctuate rapidly. Activities on pages 104 and 106 have already invited you to work on some of those mood swings. Now consider the whole scene. Devise a way of showing her changing moods: it might be a graph, or a series of words, or a sequence of pictures, or a mime, or . . .

2 How does the Nurse speak line 138?

Find four quite different ways of speaking 'Hie to your chamber.' Which do you prefer?

3 'His last farewell'

In her final couplet, Juliet first uses the language of chivalry ('my true knight'). But her last line is both simple and ominous, seeming to mean she will be parted from Romeo for ever. Write how you think the two lines could be most effectively spoken as Juliet's exit lines.

fain gladly
fellowship company (misfortune never comes alone)
needly of necessity
modern lamentation ordinary or usual grief

rear-ward final word
beguiled deceived, cheated
Hie go at once
wot well know well

My husband lives that Tybalt would have slain,   105
And Tybalt's dead that would have slain my husband:
All this is comfort, wherefore weep I then?
Some word there was, worser than Tybalt's death,
That murdered me; I would forget it fain,
But O, it presses to my memory,   110
Like damnèd guilty deeds to sinners' minds:
'Tybalt is dead, and Romeo banishèd.'
That 'banishèd', that one word 'banishèd',
Hath slain ten thousand Tybalts. Tybalt's death
Was woe enough if it had ended there;   115
Or if sour woe delights in fellowship,
And needly will be ranked with other griefs,
Why followed not, when she said 'Tybalt's dead',
'Thy father' or 'thy mother', nay, or both,
Which modern lamentation might have moved?   120
But with a rear-ward following Tybalt's death,
'Romeo is banishèd': to speak that word,
Is father, mother, Tybalt, Romeo, Juliet,
All slain, all dead. 'Romeo is banishèd!'
There is no end, no limit, measure, bound,   125
In that word's death, no words can that woe sound.
Where is my father and my mother, Nurse?

NURSE Weeping and wailing over Tybalt's corse.
Will you go to them? I will bring you thither.

JULIET Wash they his wounds with tears? mine shall be spent,   130
When theirs are dry, for Romeo's banishment.
Take up those cords. Poor ropes, you are beguiled,
Both you and I, for Romeo is exiled.
He made you for a highway to my bed,
But I, a maid, die maiden-widowèd.   135
Come, cords, come, Nurse, I'll to my wedding bed,
And death, not Romeo, take my maidenhead!

NURSE Hie to your chamber. I'll find Romeo
To comfort you, I wot well where he is.
Hark ye, your Romeo will be here at night.   140
I'll to him, he is hid at Lawrence' cell.

JULIET O find him! Give this ring to my true knight,
And bid him come to take his last farewell.

                                                    Exeunt

Friar Lawrence tells Romeo of the Prince's sentence: he is to be banished. The news appals Romeo. Life, for him, exists only in Verona with Juliet. Exile is the same as death.

1 Romeo enters (in pairs)

Romeo is in hiding, having fled after killing Tybalt. One production showed him cowering under a table. The audience laughed as Friar Lawrence dragged him out. Do you think that was an appropriate 'entrance' for Romeo? How would you stage his entry?

A twentieth-century Romeo and Juliet? In 1948, Seretse Khama, king of the British Protectorate of Bechuanaland (later Botswana), married Ruth Williams. His family rejected the match. The British Government sent Seretse into exile for five years because of the marriage. But the story of Seretse and Ruth ended happily, unlike the play.

---

fearful   for Elizabethans, 'fearful' meant 'full of fear', 'terrible' or 'fatal'. Do you think each meaning applies to Romeo?
enamoured of thy parts   in love with every aspect of you

doom   sentence
sour company   sorrow
without   outside
purgatory   where the dead suffered torment
mistermed   wrongly named

Act 3 Scene 3
Friar Lawrence's cell

Enter FRIAR LAWRENCE.

FRIAR LAWRENCE
    Romeo, come forth, come forth, thou fearful man:
    Affliction is enamoured of thy parts,
    And thou art wedded to calamity.

[*Enter*] ROMEO.

ROMEO Father, what news? What is the Prince's doom?
    What sorrow craves acquaintance at my hand,   5
    That I yet know not?
FRIAR LAWRENCE   Too familiar
    Is my dear son with such sour company!
    I bring thee tidings of the Prince's doom.
ROMEO What less than doomsday is the Prince's doom?
FRIAR LAWRENCE A gentler judgement vanished from his lips: 10
    Not body's death, but body's banishment.
ROMEO Ha, banishment? be merciful, say 'death':
    For exile hath more terror in his look,
    Much more than death. Do not say 'banishment'!
FRIAR LAWRENCE Here from Verona art thou banishèd.   15
    Be patient, for the world is broad and wide.
ROMEO There is no world without Verona walls,
    But purgatory, torture, hell itself:
    Hence 'banishèd' is banished from the world,
    And world's exile is death; then 'banishèd'   20
    Is death mistermed. Calling death 'banishèd',
    Thou cut'st my head off with a golden axe,
    And smilest upon the stroke that murders me.

Friar Lawrence condemns Romeo's ingratitude, and claims that the Prince is merciful. Romeo, distraught because banishment will mean he can no longer be with Juliet, refuses to be comforted.

1 Audiences – then and now

Once again, Shakespeare has written lines that his Elizabethan audiences enjoyed, but modern audiences find strange or artificial: when Romeo talks of 'every cat and dog / And little mouse' being able to look on Juliet (lines 30–1), and flies being able to kiss her (lines 35–7), his words can sound bizarre today. But Elizabethans relished the comparisons, and liked the punning ('Flies may do this, but I from this must fly'). Perhaps Shakespeare wrote the lines to bring out Romeo's immaturity. Or he may have written them to emphasise the depth of Romeo's grief, in which even the smallest, most trivial things are hugely important.

The speech presents a challenge to the actor. So help Romeo by writing your advice on how he might speak lines 29–51.

2 Two issues to argue over (in small groups)

a 'Adversity's sweet milk, philosophy'. Friar Lawrence argues that philosophy (thinking, reasoning) will comfort someone in adversity (beset by problems). Romeo angrily dismisses that advice ('Hang up philosophy!') because thinking without action is no help.

Do you favour the Friar's argument or Romeo's? Take sides and argue your case. Use Romeo's situation, or examples from your own experience.

b Death or banishment? Romeo believes that banishment is far worse than death. Do you? Talk together about whether you think he is right.

---

validity values
courtship courtly behaviour
  (or 'wooing')
vestal virginal
sudden mean violent method
ghostly confessor spiritual adviser

sin-absolver someone who forgives
  sins
fond foolish
Displant uproot
doom death sentence

FRIAR LAWRENCE O deadly sin! O rude unthankfulness!
    Thy fault our law calls death, but the kind Prince,   25
    Taking thy part, hath rushed aside the law,
    And turned that black word 'death' to 'banishment'.
    This is dear mercy, and thou seest it not.
ROMEO 'Tis torture, and not mercy. Heaven is here
    Where Juliet lives, and every cat and dog   30
    And little mouse, every unworthy thing,
    Live here in heaven, and may look on her,
    But Romeo may not. More validity,
    More honourable state, more courtship lives
    In carrion flies than Romeo; they may seize   35
    On the white wonder of dear Juliet's hand,
    And steal immortal blessing from her lips,
    Who even in pure and vestal modesty
    Still blush, as thinking their own kisses sin;
    But Romeo may not, he is banishèd.   40
    Flies may do this, but I from this must fly;
    They are free men, but I am banishèd:
    And sayest thou yet that exile is not death?
    Hadst thou no poison mixed, no sharp-ground knife,
    No sudden mean of death, though ne'er so mean,   45
    But 'banishèd' to kill me? 'Banishèd'?
    O Friar, the damnèd use that word in hell;
    Howling attends it. How hast thou the heart,
    Being a divine, a ghostly confessor,
    A sin-absolver, and my friend professed,   50
    To mangle me with that word 'banishèd'?
FRIAR LAWRENCE Thou fond mad man, hear me a little speak.
ROMEO O thou wilt speak again of banishment.
FRIAR LAWRENCE I'll give thee armour to keep off that word:
    Adversity's sweet milk, philosophy,   55
    To comfort thee though thou art banishèd.
ROMEO Yet 'banishèd'? Hang up philosophy!
    Unless philosophy can make a Juliet,
    Displant a town, reverse a prince's doom,
    It helps not, it prevails not; talk no more.   60
FRIAR LAWRENCE O then I see that mad men have no ears.
ROMEO How should they when that wise men have no eyes?

Romeo, bewailing all that's happened, falls weeping to the ground and ignores the Friar's pleas to stand up. The Nurse arrives and also begs him to stand.

1 Suit the actions to the words (in pairs)

Shakespeare builds his stage directions into his language. One person reads Romeo's lines 64–70. The other accompanies them with gestures and actions. Change roles and repeat the exercise. Then write the advice you would give to an actor on how to deliver these seven lines.

2 More action-packed language (in pairs)

Friar Lawrence's lines 74–80 show his agitation as he responds to the repeated knocking. Work together, as in Activity 1 above. First, try out some actions as your partner reads. Again, write the advice you would give the actor.

3 Can adults understand? (in groups of four)

Romeo accuses the Friar (who has taken a vow of celibacy) of not being able to understand how a young person in love feels: 'Thou canst not speak of that thou dost not feel' (line 64). Do you agree with Romeo that a celibate priest (or person) is incapable of understanding adolescent passion? Take sides and present your arguments for and against.

4 Is the Nurse using sexual language?

Some people feel uncomfortable because even at this serious moment the Nurse uses words with sexual double meanings ('case', 'stand', 'rise', 'O'). Do you think the Nurse is aware of the double meanings of her words? Give a reason for your answer.

---

dispute talk calmly
estate situation
Doting loving madly
Taking the measure . . . grave
 measuring out my future grave

taken arrested
case condition (or genitals)
so deep an O such moaning

FRIAR LAWRENCE Let me dispute with thee of thy estate.
ROMEO Thou canst not speak of that thou dost not feel.
       Wert thou as young as I, Juliet thy love,   65
       An hour but married, Tybalt murderèd,
       Doting like me, and like me banishèd,
       Then mightst thou speak, then mightst thou tear thy hair,
       And fall upon the ground as I do now,
       Taking the measure of an unmade grave.   70

Enter Nurse [within] and knock.

FRIAR LAWRENCE Arise, one knocks. Good Romeo, hide thyself.
ROMEO Not I, unless the breath of heart-sick groans
       Mist-like infold me from the search of eyes.
*   Knock.*

FRIAR LAWRENCE
       Hark how they knock! – Who's there? – Romeo, arise,
       Thou wilt be taken. – Stay a while! – Stand up;   75
*   Loud knock.*
       Run to my study. – By and by! – God's will,
       What simpleness is this? – I come, I come!
*   Knock.*
       Who knocks so hard? whence come you? what's your will?
NURSE [*Within*] Let me come in, and you shall know my errand:
       I come from Lady Juliet.
FRIAR LAWRENCE   Welcome then. [*Unlocks the door.*]   80

Enter NURSE.

NURSE O holy Friar, O tell me, holy Friar,
       Where's my lady's lord? where's Romeo?
FRIAR LAWRENCE
       There on the ground, with his own tears made drunk.
NURSE O he is even in my mistress' case,
       Just in her case. O woeful sympathy!   85
       Piteous predicament! even so lies she,
       Blubb'ring and weeping, weeping and blubb'ring.
       Stand up, stand up, stand, and you be a man;
       For Juliet's sake, for her sake, rise and stand;
       Why should you fall into so deep an O?   90

On hearing the Nurse tell of Juliet's sorrow, Romeo tries to stab himself. The Nurse seizes his dagger and Friar Lawrence rebukes him for his suicide attempt.

1 More problems with a 'name'

Hearing of Juliet's sorrow, Romeo angrily condemns his own name, and threatens to cut it from his body. His lines 102–7 echo those of Juliet in Act 2 Scene 2, lines 38–49. Turn back to that earlier speech and explore the relationships of these two sets of lines on 'names'.

2 Stage 'business' – who snatches the dagger?

Some people believe Shakespeare did not include the stage direction (line 108), but that the actor playing the Nurse added it. Would it make any difference if the Friar, rather than the Nurse, snatches the dagger from Romeo? For example, does being disarmed by a woman increase Romeo's sense of self-loathing? Decide how you would stage the 'snatch'.

3 The Friar rebukes Romeo (in pairs)

Sharing the lines between you, speak the Friar's lines 108–34. They are a long condemnation of Romeo's attempt at suicide. Afterwards, speak only one or two words from each line – words you think will have most effect on Romeo. Are there 'key' words in each line?

4 'Thou sham'st thy shape, thy love, thy wit'

The Friar says Romeo shames his good looks ('shape'), his declarations of love ('love') and his intelligence ('wit'). He's like a stingy money-lender ('usurer') because, although he possesses those excellent qualities in abundance, he doesn't use them properly. Read what the Friar says about each quality (lines 126–34), and then describe them in your own language.

blood removed . . . own (Tybalt)
concealed lady secret wife
level aim
sack destroy
rail'st complain

bedeck decorate
form of wax waxwork, easily melted
Digressing deviating, or taking away from

ROMEO Nurse! [*He rises.*]

NURSE Ah, sir, ah, sir, death's the end of all.

ROMEO Spakest thou of Juliet? how is it with her?
   Doth not she think me an old murderer,
   Now I have stained the childhood of our joy   95
   With blood removed but little from her own?
   Where is she? and how doth she? and what says
   My concealed lady to our cancelled love?

NURSE O she says nothing, sir, but weeps and weeps,
   And now falls on her bed, and then starts up,   100
   And Tybalt calls, and then on Romeo cries,
   And then down falls again.

ROMEO   As if that name,
   Shot from the deadly level of a gun,
   Did murder her, as that name's cursèd hand
   Murdered her kinsman. O tell me, Friar, tell me,   105
   In what vile part of this anatomy
   Doth my name lodge? Tell me, that I may sack
   The hateful mansion.

[*He offers to stab himself, and Nurse snatches the dagger away.*]

FRIAR LAWRENCE   Hold thy desperate hand!
   Art thou a man? thy form cries out thou art;
   Thy tears are womanish, thy wild acts denote   110
   The unreasonable fury of a beast.
   Unseemly woman in a seeming man,
   And ill-beseeming beast in seeming both,
   Thou hast amazed me. By my holy order,
   I thought thy disposition better tempered.   115
   Hast thou slain Tybalt? wilt thou slay thyself,
   And slay thy lady that in thy life lives,
   By doing damnèd hate upon thyself?
   Why rail'st thou on thy birth? the heaven and earth?
   Since birth, and heaven, and earth, all three do meet 120
   In thee at once, which thou at once wouldst lose.
   Fie, fie, thou sham'st thy shape, thy love, thy wit,
   Which like a usurer abound'st in all,
   And usest none in that true use indeed
   Which should bedeck thy shape, thy love, thy wit: 125
   Thy noble shape is but a form of wax,
   Digressing from the valour of a man;

Friar Lawrence rebukes Romeo for his lack of love and intelligence. He reminds Romeo of his good fortune and plans how he can eventually be recalled from exile.

1 The Friar's long speech (in small groups)

The Friar's long speech (lines 108–58) has three sections. He first rebukes Romeo, then seeks to cheer him, then sets out a plan of action. The following activities will help your understanding of the speech.

a One person reads the Friar's lines aloud, pausing frequently. In each pause, everyone else mimes appropriate expressions and movements for what they have heard. Freeze occasionally for everyone to compare each other's actions. (You will find it fascinating to see the different ways of representing the same line or image.)

b The condemnation (lines 108–34). Take turns to speak this section, using a critical, disparaging tone of voice.

c Cheering up Romeo (lines 135–45). Speak the section in a good-humoured, positive tone. Emphasise the repetitions of 'there art thou happy'. But notice the section ends with three lines of rebuke.

d The Friar's plan (lines 146–58). One person slowly speaks the lines; the others act out what the Friar advises. Try to show every action he describes. Might the Friar hesitate as he thinks up different parts of his plan?

e Using the group's experience of the activities above, each group member takes responsibility for one of the three sections of the speech. Each steps into the role of director and writes advice to the three actors (the Friar, Romeo, the Nurse). Your advice should suggest how the Friar delivers his lines, and how Romeo and the Nurse react to them.

2 'O, what learning is!'

How can the Nurse speak line 160 to make the audience laugh?

---

perjury oath-breaking, false promising
flask a container for gunpowder (the Friar compares Romeo's misused intelligence to a clumsy soldier accidentally killing himself)
mishavèd misbehaved

Watch be set police come on duty (see gloss of 'Watch' on p. 182)
blaze announce
lamentation sorrow
apt unto liable to

Thy dear love sworn but hollow perjury,
Killing that love which thou hast vowed to cherish;
Thy wit, that ornament to shape and love, 130
Misshapen in the conduct of them both,
Like powder in a skilless soldier's flask,
Is set afire by thine own ignorance,
And thou dismembered with thine own defence.
What, rouse thee, man! thy Juliet is alive, 135
For whose dear sake thou wast but lately dead:
There art thou happy. Tybalt would kill thee,
But thou slewest Tybalt: there art thou happy.
The law that threatened death becomes thy friend,
And turns it to exile: there art thou happy. 140
A pack of blessings light upon thy back,
Happiness courts thee in her best array,
But like a mishavèd and sullen wench,
Thou pouts upon thy fortune and thy love:
Take heed, take heed, for such die miserable. 145
Go get thee to thy love as was decreed,
Ascend her chamber, hence and comfort her;
But look thou stay not till the Watch be set,
For then thou canst not pass to Mantua,
Where thou shalt live till we can find a time 150
To blaze your marriage, reconcile your friends,
Beg pardon of the Prince, and call thee back
With twenty hundred thousand times more joy
Than thou went'st forth in lamentation.
Go before, Nurse, commend me to thy lady, 155
And bid her hasten all the house to bed,
Which heavy sorrow makes them apt unto.
Romeo is coming.
NURSE O Lord, I could have stayed here all the night
To hear good counsel. O, what learning is! 160
My lord, I'll tell my lady you will come.
ROMEO Do so, and bid my sweet prepare to chide.
[*Nurse offers to go in, and turns again.*]
NURSE Here, sir, a ring she bid me give you, sir.
Hie you, make haste, for it grows very late.
ROMEO How well my comfort is revived by this. 165
[*Exit Nurse*]

119

Friar Lawrence sends Romeo to Juliet, warning him to leave early for Mantua and await news. In Scene 4, Capulet tells Paris that because of Tybalt's death, he has not yet talked with Juliet about marriage.

1 Romeo: from misery to joy (in pairs)

Romeo leaves, expressing his infinite desire to be with Juliet tonight ('a joy past joy'). His mood has been very different for most of the scene. He expresses anguish and dejection until he finally sees hope in Friar Lawrence's plan. Some people think his emotions are too extreme and that he doesn't think about Juliet, only his own despair.

Look back through Scene 3 and identify where you think Romeo's feelings and language are genuine and where they are 'over the top'. Work out a way of representing Romeo's mood through most of the scene, and the change at the end. A few quotations, plotted on a graph or diagram, might be one method to consider.

2 Focus on Paris (in pairs)

In Baz Luhrmann's film, Paris was a bland but likeable character who appeared in a spacesuit at Capulet's party in Act 1 Scene 5. Talk together about your view of him, for example his age and appearance. Then consider how you think he might behave in Scene 4. Write your advice to the actor playing Paris: think about movements, tone of voice, and so on.

3 Fathers and daughters – something to find out

Capulet is certain that Juliet will obey him ('I think she will be ruled / In all respects by me; nay more, I doubt it not'). Shakespeare often wrote about fathers who wished to dominate their daughters' lives. Here are some of the daughters' names: Cordelia, Hero, Imogen, Desdemona, Portia, Ophelia, Miranda, Celia, Hermia, Jessica. Do some research to identify the plays in which each daughter appears.

---

here stands all your state here is your future
Sojourn stay, wait
hap happening
fall'n out worked out

move persuade
mewed up to her heaviness caged up in her sorrow (falcons were kept caged in mews)
desperate tender bold offer

FRIAR LAWRENCE
    Go hence, good night, and here stands all your state:
    Either be gone before the Watch be set,
    Or by the break of day disguised from hence.
    Sojourn in Mantua; I'll find out your man,
    And he shall signify from time to time   170
    Every good hap to you that chances here.
    Give me thy hand, 'tis late. Farewell, good night.
ROMEO But that a joy past joy calls out on me,
    It were a grief, so brief to part with thee:
    Farewell.   175

Exeunt

Act 3 Scene 4
Capulet's mansion

Enter old CAPULET, his WIFE, and PARIS.

CAPULET Things have fall'n out, sir, so unluckily
    That we have had no time to move our daughter.
    Look you, she loved her kinsman Tybalt dearly,
    And so did I. Well, we were born to die.
    'Tis very late, she'll not come down tonight.   5
    I promise you, but for your company,
    I would have been abed an hour ago.
PARIS These times of woe afford no times to woo.
    Madam, good night, commend me to your daughter.
LADY CAPULET I will, and know her mind early tomorrow;   10
    Tonight she's mewed up to her heaviness.
    [*Paris offers to go in, and Capulet calls him again.*]
CAPULET Sir Paris, I will make a desperate tender
    Of my child's love: I think she will be ruled
    In all respects by me; nay more, I doubt it not.

Capulet instructs his wife to tell Juliet that she is to be married to Paris. He decides the wedding will be in three days' time with only a few invited guests.

1 Husband and wife (in groups of three)

Every production of the play must address the question of how Juliet's parents feel about each other. Do they love each other? Did they love each other when they married?

Act out the whole scene, but with Lady Capulet commenting quietly on everything her husband says. Try out different styles, such as: she finds him tiresome and boring; she is afraid of him; she still loves him. Did she have a father like her husband (see Act 1 Scene 3, line 73)? Can you agree on which interpretation you prefer?

And what does Capulet think of his wife?

2 Time begins to run faster (in pairs)

Read the scene aloud, emphasising all the words to do with time. There are well over thirty; how many can you count? Notice how these words add to the impression of fast-moving events.

Then read Capulet's lines 19–35 in a jerky, hasty manner. Talk together about whether such a way of reading helps the audience gain a sense of the gathering momentum of events.

3 Dramatic irony (in pairs)

The scene is full of **dramatic irony** (when the audience knows something the character does not know). Even as Capulet plans Juliet's marriage, she is eagerly awaiting her husband Romeo in her bedroom. Identify four or five examples of dramatic irony in the lines and suggest what makes each ironic (see also pp. 128, 132 and 150).

---

my son   Capulet already sees Paris as his son-in-law

keep no great ado   it will be a simple affair

so late   so recently

held him carelessly   had little regard for him

Afore me   indeed

by and by   soon

Wife, go you to her ere you go to bed,   15
Acquaint her here of my son Paris' love,
And bid her – mark you me? – on Wednesday next –
But soft, what day is this?
PARIS   Monday, my lord.
CAPULET Monday, ha, ha! Well, Wednesday is too soon,
A'Thursday let it be – a'Thursday, tell her,   20
She shall be married to this noble earl.
Will you be ready? do you like this haste?
Well, keep no great ado – a friend or two,
For hark you, Tybalt being slain so late,
It may be thought we held him carelessly,   25
Being our kinsman, if we revel much:
Therefore we'll have some half a dozen friends,
And there an end. But what say you to Thursday?
PARIS My lord, I would that Thursday were tomorrow.
CAPULET Well, get you gone, a'Thursday be it then. –   30
Go you to Juliet ere you go to bed,
Prepare her, wife, against this wedding day.
Farewell, my lord. Light to my chamber, ho!
Afore me, it is so very late that we
May call it early by and by. Good night.   35

                                                    Exeunt

After their wedding night together, Juliet tries to persuade Romeo that it is not yet dawn, not yet time for him to leave her. At first he says he must go, but then resolves to stay and face capture and death.

1 A bed, or no bed?

Most modern productions have a bed on stage. Earlier productions did not. Would you include a bed? Why, or why not?

2 How should the lines be spoken? (in pairs)

Take parts and try different ways of speaking lines 1–25 (for example, Juliet as loving, or impatient, or bossy or sleepy, or . . . ; Romeo as loving, or afraid, or secretly desiring to go . . .). Can you agree on how you think the lines should be delivered? In particular, how should lines 11 and 12 be spoken? Pick one or two favourite lines. Talk with your partner about why you enjoy them.

3 Imagery

Suggest why Shakespeare uses the images 'Night's candles' and 'vaulty heaven' rather than 'stars' and 'sky'.

The moment of parting as staged in 1858 and 1973. Compare these illustrations with the pictures of Romeo and Juliet's first meeting on page vi in the colour section and on page 47.

---

envious   malicious
jocund   cheerful
some meteor that the sun exhaled
  meteors were thought to be caused by
  the sun drawing up vapours from the
  earth and igniting them

tane   captured (taken)
reflex of Cynthia's brow   reflection of
  the edge of the moon (Cynthia is the
  moon goddess)

Act 3 Scene 5
Juliet's bedroom

Enter ROMEO *and* JULIET *aloft at the window.*

JULIET Wilt thou be gone? It is not yet near day:
    It was the nightingale, and not the lark,
    That pierced the fearful hollow of thine ear;
    Nightly she sings on yond pomegranate tree.
    Believe me, love, it was the nightingale.   5
ROMEO It was the lark, the herald of the morn,
    No nightingale. Look, love, what envious streaks
    Do lace the severing clouds in yonder east:
    Night's candles are burnt out, and jocund day
    Stands tiptoe on the misty mountain tops.   10
    I must be gone and live, or stay and die.
JULIET Yond light is not daylight, I know it, I:
    It is some meteor that the sun exhaled
    To be to thee this night a torch-bearer,
    And light thee on thy way to Mantua.   15
    Therefore stay yet, thou need'st not to be gone.
ROMEO Let me be tane, let me be put to death,
    I am content, so thou wilt have it so.
    I'll say yon grey is not the morning's eye,
    'Tis but the pale reflex of Cynthia's brow;   20
    Nor that is not the lark whose notes do beat
    The vaulty heaven so high above our heads.
    I have more care to stay than will to go:
    Come, death, and welcome! Juliet wills it so.
    How is't, my soul? Let's talk, it is not day.   25

Juliet accepts that it is morning and time to part. The Nurse warns the lovers that Lady Capulet is coming. As Romeo leaves, Juliet's words are filled with foreboding.

1 'Some say the lark and loathèd toad changed eyes'

There was an old belief that skylarks and toads had exchanged eyes. This explained why toads' eyes were thought more beautiful than larks' eyes. Juliet wishes they had exchanged voices too, because the harsh voice of the toad is more suitable to the lovers' sad parting. If you were making a film of the play and wanted to 'dub in' (add) a sad or ominous sound as background here, what sound would it be?

2 'He goeth down' – stage direction, line 42

As you turn the page you'll see on page 129 that Juliet also 'goeth down' (stage direction, line 67). Work out how you would stage the scene to make these 'goeth down' movements by Romeo and Juliet as convincing as possible. Sketch a design for your stage set.

3 Doom-laden visions (in groups of four)

The final words that the lovers ever speak together are filled with apprehension (lines 54–9). Prepare an enactment of these six lines, two of you as Romeo, two as Juliet. One pair delivers the lines, the others present the vision each partner 'sees'.

Show your versions to the class. As you read to the end of the play, you will see how these sombre forebodings work out.

4 Last time together

Lines 1–59 are the last time Romeo and Juliet will see each other alive. Write how you would stage this episode to bring out its poignancy and dramatic impact.

---

division music (see how Juliet puns on 'divideth' in the next line. Notice too how Romeo puns on 'light' and 'dark' in line 36)

affray frighten (from each other's arms)

hunt's-up hunters' morning song

much in years much older

ill-divining evil-expecting

Dry sorrow Elizabethans thought that each sigh cost a drop of blood

JULIET It is, it is, hie hence, be gone, away!
       It is the lark that sings so out of tune,
       Straining harsh discords and unpleasing sharps.
       Some say the lark makes sweet division:
       This doth not so, for she divideth us.   30
       Some say the lark and loathèd toad changed eyes;
       O now I would they had changed voices too,
       Since arm from arm that voice doth us affray,
       Hunting thee hence with hunt's-up to the day.
       O now be gone, more light and light it grows.   35
ROMEO More light and light, more dark and dark our woes!

Enter NURSE [*hastily*].

NURSE Madam!
JULIET Nurse?
NURSE Your lady mother is coming to your chamber.
       The day is broke, be wary, look about.   [*Exit*]   40
JULIET Then, window, let day in, and let life out.
ROMEO Farewell, farewell! one kiss, and I'll descend.
             [*He goeth down.*]
JULIET Art thou gone so, love, lord, ay husband, friend?
       I must hear from thee every day in the hour,
       For in a minute there are many days.   45
       O, by this count I shall be much in years
       Ere I again behold my Romeo!
ROMEO [*From below*] Farewell!
       I will omit no opportunity
       That may convey my greetings, love, to thee.   50
JULIET O think'st thou we shall ever meet again?
ROMEO I doubt it not, and all these woes shall serve
       For sweet discourses in our times to come.
JULIET O God, I have an ill-divining soul!
       Methinks I see thee now, thou art so low,   55
       As one dead in the bottom of a tomb.
       Either my eyesight fails, or thou look'st pale.
ROMEO And trust me, love, in my eye so do you:
       Dry sorrow drinks our blood. Adieu, adieu!   *Exit*

Lady Capulet mistakes Juliet's tears for Romeo as grief for Tybalt's death. Juliet's replies strengthen her mother's mistaken belief, and she threatens vengeance, promising to have Romeo poisoned in Mantua.

1 Fortune (individually or in pairs)

Juliet turns fortune into a person in lines 60–4 (see pp. 44, 84 and 215 for more on personification). Imagine you are the designer for a production of the play. The director tells you that he wants an image or a statue of Fortune to be on stage throughout the play. Make drawings of your suggestions for that statue.

Talk with others about whether you think the director's request for such an always-present image is a good idea.

2 Double meanings (in groups of four)

Lady Capulet thinks that Juliet is agreeing with her. But Juliet's replies to her mother are filled with double meaning as she responds equivocally each time. It is another example of dramatic irony (see pp. 122 and 150), because the audience, like Juliet, knows what Lady Capulet does not.

Here is a way to bring out the double meanings: one person reads Lady Capulet and one reads Juliet (lines 68–102); the other two are Juliet's *alter ego*. They comment as many times as possible on what Juliet is really thinking as she speaks. Juliet reads slowly, a line or two at a time. For example:

Juliet: Madam, I am not well.
Alter ego: Because I've just parted from my husband and my heart is full of sorrow.
Juliet: Yet let me weep for such a feeling loss.
Alter ego: But let me weep for Romeo, who I love.

Try the exercise several times, changing roles. Discuss what these double meanings tell you about Juliet's character, and how they add to the dramatic impact of the play. Notice that in line 81 Juliet speaks without double meaning. Her line is an Aside, not spoken to Lady Capulet.

---

fickle changeable, faithless
unaccustomed cause unexpected event
procures brings
And if even if

asunder apart
runagate runaway
unaccustomed dram unexpected dose of poison

JULIET O Fortune, Fortune, all men call thee fickle;   60
       If thou art fickle, what dost thou with him
       That is renowned for faith? Be fickle, Fortune:
       For then I hope thou wilt not keep him long,
       But send him back.

          Enter Mother [LADY CAPULET *below*].

LADY CAPULET   Ho, daughter, are you up?
JULIET Who is't that calls? It is my lady mother.   65
       Is she not down so late, or up so early?
       What unaccustomed cause procures her hither?
       [*She goeth down from the window and enters below.*]
LADY CAPULET Why how now, Juliet?
JULIET   Madam, I am not well.
LADY CAPULET Evermore weeping for your cousin's death?
       What, wilt thou wash him from his grave with tears?   70
       And if thou couldst, thou couldst not make him live;
       Therefore have done. Some grief shows much of love,
       But much of grief shows still some want of wit.
JULIET Yet let me weep for such a feeling loss.
LADY CAPULET So shall you feel the loss, but not the friend   75
       Which you weep for.
JULIET   Feeling so the loss,
       I cannot choose but ever weep the friend.
LADY CAPULET Well, girl, thou weep'st not so much for his death
       As that the villain lives which slaughtered him.
JULIET What villain, madam?
LADY CAPULET   That same villain Romeo.   80
JULIET [*Aside*] Villain and he be many miles asunder. –
       God pardon him, I do with all my heart:
       And yet no man like he doth grieve my heart.
LADY CAPULET That is because the traitor murderer lives.
JULIET Ay, madam, from the reach of these my hands.   85
       Would none but I might venge my cousin's death!
LADY CAPULET We will have vengeance for it, fear thou not:
       Then weep no more. I'll send to one in Mantua,
       Where that same banished runagate doth live,
       Shall give him such an unaccustomed dram   90
       That he shall soon keep Tybalt company;
       And then I hope thou wilt be satisfied.

Juliet continues to mislead her mother. Lady Capulet tells her she must marry Paris on Thursday. Juliet, appalled, refuses to do so. Capulet comes in and mistakes Juliet's tears for sorrow for Tybalt.

1 How to speak the words? (in pairs)

Read through lines 104–25, one person as Juliet, one as Lady Capulet.

a Consider Juliet's 'in happy time' (line 111) and her mother's 'tell him so yourself' (line 124). How do you think those lines should be delivered? Is Juliet being sarcastic? Is her mother being callous and cruel?

b Notice how Juliet echoes her mother in the exchange in lines 114–17: 'by Saint Peter's Church and Peter too', 'not make', 'joyful bride'. Is her tone defiant, or . . . ?

2 Fathers' control over daughters (in small groups)

What does this arranged marriage suggest to you about male–female relationships in Verona?

If you are female, what would you do if you were suddenly told that your father had arranged a marriage for you to a man you barely know?

If you are male, do you think fathers should decide whom their daughters should marry?

3 Capulet: from comforting to furious father

As you read what Capulet says in this scene, you will find that the tone and style of his language change. He begins (lines 126–38) confidently offering fatherly comfort to Juliet. But then, as he learns of Juliet's refusal to marry Paris, his language changes, and in lines 141–5, he speaks of her in the third person ('she', 'her'). It signals that he is distancing himself from his daughter, and in his speeches that follow he explodes in fury, heaping all his rage on Juliet.

vexed troubled
temper mix (but Juliet also means weaken the poison to give Romeo peaceful sleep)
wreak avenge or bestow

beseech 'may I ask'
heaviness sadness
Ere before
conduit water-pipe or fountain

JULIET Indeed I never shall be satisfied
　　　　With Romeo, till I behold him – dead –
　　　　Is my poor heart, so for a kinsman vexed.　　　　95
　　　　Madam, if you could find out but a man
　　　　To bear a poison, I would temper it,
　　　　That Romeo should upon receipt thereof
　　　　Soon sleep in quiet. O how my heart abhors
　　　　To hear him named and cannot come to him,　　　100
　　　　To wreak the love I bore my cousin
　　　　Upon his body that hath slaughtered him!
LADY CAPULET Find thou the means, and I'll find such a man.
　　　　But now I'll tell thee joyful tidings, girl.
JULIET And joy comes well in such a needy time.　　　　105
　　　　What are they, beseech your ladyship?
LADY CAPULET Well, well, thou hast a careful father, child,
　　　　One who, to put thee from thy heaviness,
　　　　Hath sorted out a sudden day of joy,
　　　　That thou expects not, nor I looked not for.　　　110
JULIET Madam, in happy time, what day is that?
LADY CAPULET Marry, my child, early next Thursday morn,
　　　　The gallant, young, and noble gentleman,
　　　　The County Paris, at Saint Peter's Church,
　　　　Shall happily make thee there a joyful bride.　　　115
JULIET Now by Saint Peter's Church and Peter too,
　　　　He shall not make me there a joyful bride.
　　　　I wonder at this haste, that I must wed
　　　　Ere he that should be husband comes to woo.
　　　　I pray you tell my lord and father, madam,　　　120
　　　　I will not marry yet, and when I do, I swear
　　　　It shall be Romeo, whom you know I hate,
　　　　Rather than Paris. These are news indeed!
LADY CAPULET Here comes your father, tell him so yourself;
　　　　And see how he will take it at your hands.　　　125

Enter CAPULET *and Nurse.*

CAPULET When the sun sets, the earth doth drizzle dew,
　　　　But for the sunset of my brother's son
　　　　It rains downright.
　　　　How now, a conduit, girl? What, still in tears?

Capulet elaborately compares Juliet's tears to a shipwrecking storm. But he then flies into a towering rage on hearing of Juliet's refusal to marry Paris. He threatens and insults her.

1 Capulet's rage – experiencing Juliet's feelings (in large groups)

This is an activity for the hall or drama studio, but it can also be adapted for the classroom.

One person is Juliet; all the others are Capulet. Juliet sits still in the middle of a circle, the others all round her. Those reading Capulet will speak everything in lines 149–57, 160–8 and 176–95. They walk around Juliet and hurl their language at her. Each Capulet speaks just a phrase or a line or two before the next Capulet carries on. For example: first Capulet, 'How how, how how, chopt-logic?'; second Capulet, 'What is this?'; third Capulet, '"Proud" and "I thank you", and "I thank you not"', and so on (it becomes far worse!).

Juliet replies to every Capulet with her lines 158–9 ('Good father, I beseech you on my knees, / Hear me with patience but to speak a word').

Work through the activity several times, with a different Juliet each time. Remember that it's a difficult thing for Juliet to endure because she's on the receiving end of a terrifying tongue-lashing by her father. So don't force anyone into playing Juliet; only use volunteers!

When you've tried this activity a number of times, talk together about the language. What's it like to undergo this verbal abuse? How does it feel to be delivering it? What does it tell you about Capulet's character?

2 Does Lady Capulet mean it?

'I would the fool were married to her grave', says Lady Capulet (line 140). Do you think she really means it? Does this become another example of dramatic irony (see pp. 122, 128 and 150) as the play unfolds and the audience sees what finally happens to Juliet?

---

counterfeits make an image of
bark ship
chopt-logic riddles
minion spoilt brat
fettle your fine joints get ready (the expression comes from grooming a horse)

hurdle frame on which prisoners were dragged to execution
green-sickness carrion pale-faced rotting meat
tallow pale, waxy
hilding useless person

Evermore show'ring? In one little body   130
Thou counterfeits a bark, a sea, a wind:
For still thy eyes, which I may call the sea,
Do ebb and flow with tears; the bark thy body is,
Sailing in this salt flood; the winds, thy sighs,
Who, raging with thy tears and they with them,   135
Without a sudden calm, will overset
Thy tempest-tossèd body. How now, wife,
Have you delivered to her our decree?
LADY CAPULET Ay, sir, but she will none, she gives you thanks.
I would the fool were married to her grave.   140
CAPULET Soft, take me with you, take me with you, wife.
How, will she none? doth she not give us thanks?
Is she not proud? doth she not count her blest,
Unworthy as she is, that we have wrought
So worthy a gentleman to be her bride?   145
JULIET Not proud you have, but thankful that you have:
Proud can I never be of what I hate,
But thankful even for hate that is meant love.
CAPULET How how, how how, chopt-logic? What is this?
'Proud', and 'I thank you', and 'I thank you not',   150
And yet 'not proud', mistress minion you?
Thank me no thankings, nor proud me no prouds,
But fettle your fine joints 'gainst Thursday next,
To go with Paris to Saint Peter's Church,
Or I will drag thee on a hurdle thither.   155
Out, you green-sickness carrion! out, you baggage!
You tallow-face!
LADY CAPULET   Fie, fie, what, are you mad?
JULIET Good father, I beseech you on my knees,
Hear me with patience but to speak a word.
                    [*She kneels down.*]
CAPULET Hang thee, young baggage, disobedient wretch!   160
I tell thee what: get thee to church a'Thursday,
Or never after look me in the face.
Speak not, reply not, do not answer me!
My fingers itch. Wife, we scarce thought us blest
That God had lent us but this only child,   165
But now I see this one is one too much,
And that we have a curse in having her.
Out on her, hilding!

Capulet, further enraged by the Nurse's defence of Juliet, continues to storm at Juliet, threatening to disown her if she will not obey him and marry Paris. Lady Capulet refuses to help her daughter.

1 The power of fathers

But and you will not wed, I'll pardon you (*line 187*)

And you be mine, I'll give you to my friend (*line 191*)

'If you don't wed Paris, get out!' is what Capulet says, using 'pardon' (forgive) ironically. He then asserts his absolute possession of Juliet: she is like an object he can give away to anyone he pleases (see the pictures on pp. ix and 139).

Do some research into what power fathers had over their daughters in Shakespeare's time. Write up your findings, and add a paragraph on what power you think they have today.

2 Hard hearted? Or fearful of her husband? Or . . . ?

In line 198, Juliet pleads:

O sweet my mother, cast me not away!

Why do you think Lady Capulet replies as she does in lines 202–3?

3 Improvise the Capulets' conversation (in pairs)

Imagine that Lady Capulet catches up with her husband shortly after leaving Juliet. What do they say to each other? Improvise their conversation.

4 Imagery: Juliet's ominous prediction

Make a drawing to illustrate Juliet's prophecy in lines 200–1:

make the bridal bed
In that dim monument where Tybalt lies.

---

rate scold
God-i-goden! clear off! (mockingly: 'good evening')
gossip's bowl drinks at a hen party
God's bread the sacred bread served at Mass (an oath)

demesnes lands
ligned descended
puling crying
mammet puppet
be forsworn be denied, break my oath

NURSE   God in heaven bless her!
        You are to blame, my lord, to rate her so.
CAPULET And why, my Lady Wisdom? Hold your tongue,   170
        Good Prudence, smatter with your gossips, go.
NURSE I speak no treason.
CAPULET   O God-i-goden!
NURSE May not one speak?
CAPULET   Peace, you mumbling fool!
        Utter your gravity o'er a gossip's bowl,
        For here we need it not.
LADY CAPULET   You are too hot.   175
CAPULET God's bread, it makes me mad! Day, night, work, play,
        Alone, in company, still my care hath been
        To have her matched; and having now provided
        A gentleman of noble parentage,
        Of fair demesnes, youthful and nobly ligned,   180
        Stuffed, as they say, with honourable parts,
        Proportioned as one's thought would wish a man,
        And then to have a wretched puling fool,
        A whining mammet, in her fortune's tender,
        To answer 'I'll not wed, I cannot love;   185
        I am too young, I pray you pardon me.'
        But and you will not wed, I'll pardon you:
        Graze where you will, you shall not house with me.
        Look to't, think on't, I do not use to jest.
        Thursday is near, lay hand on heart, advise: 190
        And you be mine, I'll give you to my friend;
        And you be not, hang, beg, starve, die in the streets,
        For by my soul, I'll ne'er acknowledge thee,
        Nor what is mine shall never do thee good.
        Trust to't, bethink you, I'll not be forsworn.   *Exit*   195
JULIET Is there no pity sitting in the clouds
        That sees into the bottom of my grief?
        O sweet my mother, cast me not away!
        Delay this marriage for a month, a week,
        Or if you do not, make the bridal bed   200
        In that dim monument where Tybalt lies.
LADY CAPULET Talk not to me, for I'll not speak a word.
        Do as thou wilt, for I have done with thee.   *Exit*

Juliet seeks comfort from the Nurse, who urges her to marry Paris. Feeling betrayed, Juliet sends the Nurse away, vowing never to trust her again. Juliet resolves to seek Friar Lawrence's aid.

1 Juliet feels betrayed by the Nurse (in pairs)

Read or act out lines 204–42, one person as Juliet, one as the Nurse. Afterwards, work together to write a paragraph on each of the following:

- what you think of the Nurse's advice
- whether you think the Nurse recognises Juliet's irony or sarcasm when she says 'Amen' and 'Well, thou hast comforted me marvellous much'
- what the Nurse's advice adds to your knowledge of her character
- how your understanding of Juliet has grown in this scene
- what you think would be the most dramatically effective way of staging these lines.

2 The Nurse meets her 'gossips' (in groups of four)

Imagine the Nurse meets three of her friends. They are eager to know what happened in the Capulet household that day. Improvise their conversation. Remember that this group is probably what Capulet had in mind when he spoke dismissively of 'a gossip's bowl' (line 174).

3 Juliet's sense of isolation

Juliet increasingly feels trapped. Her father has threatened her, her mother has abandoned her, and she feels the Nurse has proved a false friend. She also feels her religion adds to her desolation. In lines 205–8, she recognises that only by Romeo's death can she sincerely take a faithful (religious) vow to marry Paris. So how might she deliver her final line 242 as she leaves to visit the Friar?

---

stratagems tricks
challenge claim
dishclout dishcloth, rag
green green eyes were thought to be especially admirable
Beshrew curse

absolved forgiven
wish me thus forsworn make me a promise-breaker
bosom secret thoughts
twain two (separated)

JULIET O God! – O Nurse, how shall this be prevented?
My husband is on earth, my faith in heaven;   205
How shall that faith return again to earth,
Unless that husband send it me from heaven
By leaving earth? Comfort me, counsel me.
Alack, alack, that heaven should practise stratagems
Upon so soft a subject as myself!   210
What say'st thou? hast thou not a word of joy?
Some comfort, Nurse.
NURSE   Faith, here it is:
Romeo is banished, and all the world to nothing
That he dares ne'er come back to challenge you;
Or if he do, it needs must be by stealth.   215
Then since the case so stands as now it doth,
I think it best you married with the County.
O, he's a lovely gentleman!
Romeo's a dishclout to him. An eagle, madam,
Hath not so green, so quick, so fair an eye   220
As Paris hath. Beshrew my very heart,
I think you are happy in this second match,
For it excels your first, or if it did not,
Your first is dead, or 'twere as good he were
As living here and you no use of him.   225
JULIET Speak'st thou from thy heart?
NURSE And from my soul too, else beshrew them both.
JULIET Amen.
NURSE What?
JULIET Well, thou hast comforted me marvellous much.   230
Go in, and tell my lady I am gone,
Having displeased my father, to Lawrence' cell,
To make confession and to be absolved.
NURSE Marry, I will, and this is wisely done.   [*Exit*]
JULIET [*She looks after Nurse.*]
Ancient damnation! O most wicked fiend!   235
Is it more sin to wish me thus forsworn,
Or to dispraise my lord with that same tongue
Which she hath praised him with above compare
So many thousand times? Go, counsellor,
Thou and my bosom henceforth shall be twain.   240
I'll to the Friar to know his remedy;
If all else fail, myself have power to die.   *Exit*

Looking back at Act 3
Activities for groups or individuals

1 Shakespeare's stagecraft – contrasts

One reason why Shakespeare's plays work so well on stage is because he ensured that every scene contrasts in some way with the scene that precedes or follows it. These contrasts (or 'juxtapositions') are often ironic. For example, Act 3 Scene 1 ends with Mercutio and Tybalt killed and Romeo banished on pain of death. But Scene 2 opens with Juliet in an ecstatic mood, longing for Romeo to come to her. The audience knows, but she is unaware of the disasters that have happened. This dramatic irony adds to the emotional impact of the play on the audience as they watch a joyful Juliet, knowing her happiness will shortly be shattered.

Work through Act 3 and write a paragraph (like the explanation given above) of how each scene contrasts with the one that precedes it.

2 Characters' motives?

List each character who appears in this act. Write a single sentence for each which begins 'What I want most is . . .'. How much agreement is there in the class on each character's major motive?

3 Banishment – three questions for discussion

- Is there a modern equivalent of the punishment of banishment?
- Is banishment really worse than death, as Romeo imagines?
- Why doesn't Juliet simply decide to join Romeo in Mantua?

4 Soundbites

Soundbites are very short clips of what someone has said, broadcast on television or radio. Make up soundbites for each scene. Remember, they should be pithy and attention-grabbing, rather like headlines.

5 Design a 'wanted' poster

Romeo is banished on pain of death. Design the poster that is pasted up on the walls of Verona to announce his sentence.

6 Why did Mercutio have to die?

Many reasons have been suggested for why Shakespeare kills off Mercutio so early in the play, for instance that it serves to:

- increase Romeo's anguish and despair
- spur Romeo to revenge
- help establish the play as a tragedy
- intensify the feud between the Montagues and Capulets
- deepen the contrast between 'love' and 'hate' in the play.

Use these suggestions and the information on pages 94 and 207 to help you write an assignment on Mercutio's character and his 'early' death. You may also find it helpful to refer to the pictures on page viii in the colour section.

7 Guess the incident – or the line

Select an incident or line from the act and prepare a short mime or a tableau. Tell the class from which scene you have chosen the event or line. Then show your mime or tableau. If the other groups can guess the incident or line correctly, that's a compliment to their perception and to your ability in performance!

'Hang thee, young baggage, disobedient wretch!', Capulet rages at Juliet. Choose a different line from Scene 5 as a suitable caption to this picture.

Paris tells Friar Lawrence that Capulet, believing Juliet is grieving for Tybalt, wishes to have her married soon. Capulet thinks an early marriage will ease her sorrow.

Paris is related to Prince Escales and therefore has very high status in Verona. If he marries Juliet, the standing of the Capulet family will rise, giving them more social prestige than the Montagues. It is understandable why Capulet wants him as a son-in-law.

In Baz Luhrmann's 1996 film, Paris was played as an amiable but insignificant character who appeared at the Capulet festivities in Act 1 Scene 5 as an astronaut. His costume for this later scene would of course be different, but it would be both fashionable and expensive.

You will find an activity on page 142 inviting you to explore ways in which Paris might speak to Juliet. Here, consider the tone he might adopt towards Friar Lawrence. For example, does he consider the Friar to be socially inferior, and therefore resent having to explain the reason for a hasty marriage?

1 'What must be shall be'

What does Juliet mean in line 21? Her remark echoes a major theme running through the play (see p. 209, 'Fate versus free will').

My father Capulet Paris already thinks of Capulet as his father-in-law to be

nothing slow to slack unwilling to argue against

Uneven is the course this is very irregular

Venus goddess of love

sway influence, power

inundation flood

too much minded . . . alone brooding in her solitude

society company, companionship

Act 4 Scene 1
Friar Lawrence's cell

Enter FRIAR LAWRENCE *and* COUNTY PARIS.

FRIAR LAWRENCE On Thursday, sir? the time is very short.
PARIS My father Capulet will have it so,
    And I am nothing slow to slack his haste.
FRIAR LAWRENCE You say you do not know the lady's mind?
    Uneven is the course, I like it not.   5
PARIS Immoderately she weeps for Tybalt's death,
    And therefore have I little talked of love,
    For Venus smiles not in a house of tears.
    Now, sir, her father counts it dangerous
    That she do give her sorrow so much sway;   10
    And in his wisdom hastes our marriage
    To stop the inundation of her tears,
    Which too much minded by herself alone
    May be put from her by society.
    Now do you know the reason of this haste.   15
FRIAR LAWRENCE [*Aside*]
    I would I knew not why it should be slowed. –
    Look, sir, here comes the lady toward my cell.

Enter JULIET.

PARIS Happily met, my lady and my wife!
JULIET That may be, sir, when I may be a wife.
PARIS That 'may be' must be, love, on Thursday next.   20
JULIET What must be shall be.
FRIAR LAWRENCE   That's a certain text.

Juliet's replies to Paris are filled with double meaning. After Paris leaves, Juliet asks Friar Lawrence for help, threatening to kill herself if she is forced to marry Paris.

---

1 How do Paris and Juliet talk to each other? (in pairs)

Juliet is in an appallingly difficult position. She knows (as does the Friar) what Paris does not: that she is already married to Romeo. So her responses to Paris are full of meanings that Paris does not understand.

Take parts as Paris and Juliet and speak lines 18–43 (leaving out Friar Lawrence's lines). Experiment with different ways of speaking your characters' lines. For example, first read Paris's lines tenderly and courteously. Then speak his lines as if he were officious, having no regard for Juliet's feelings, but treating her as a mere possession (e.g. 'Thy face is mine', line 35). Also explore different ways Juliet might speak.

Talk together about your different styles of speaking. Can you agree which tones and attitudes are most appropriate for each character?

2 'Keep this holy kiss'

Step into role as director and advise Paris just how to kiss Juliet at line 43. And how does she receive the kiss?

3 'Come weep with me, past hope, past cure, past help!'

Write a poem using line 45 as the opening line. Your poem may express Juliet's plight, or you may prefer to write a free-ranging poem. If you wish to write your poem as a sonnet, see page 217.

4 Actions and words

What does Juliet *do* with the knife as she speaks lines 50–9?

---

pensive sad (but the Friar's knowledge of the reason for Juliet's sadness is different from that of Paris)
entreat request
shield forbid

the compass of my wits the range of my understanding
prorogue delay
resolution determination
presently immediately
label seal (on a legal document)

PARIS Come you to make confession to this father?
JULIET To answer that, I should confess to you.
PARIS Do not deny to him that you love me.
JULIET I will confess to you that I love him. 25
PARIS So will ye, I am sure, that you love me.
JULIET If I do so, it will be of more price,
     Being spoke behind your back, than to your face.
PARIS Poor soul, thy face is much abused with tears.
JULIET The tears have got small victory by that, 30
     For it was bad enough before their spite.
PARIS Thou wrong'st it more than tears with that report.
JULIET That is no slander, sir, which is a truth,
     And what I spake, I spake it to my face.
PARIS Thy face is mine, and thou hast slandered it. 35
JULIET It may be so, for it is not mine own.
     Are you at leisure, holy father, now,
     Or shall I come to you at evening mass?
FRIAR LAWRENCE My leisure serves me, pensive daughter, now.
     My lord, we must entreat the time alone. 40
PARIS God shield I should disturb devotion!
     Juliet, on Thursday early will I rouse ye;
     Till then adieu, and keep this holy kiss. *Exit*
JULIET O shut the door, and when thou hast done so,
     Come weep with me, past hope, past cure, past help! 45
FRIAR LAWRENCE O Juliet, I already know thy grief,
     It strains me past the compass of my wits.
     I hear thou must, and nothing may prorogue it,
     On Thursday next be married to this County.
JULIET Tell me not, Friar, that thou hearest of this, 50
     Unless thou tell me how I may prevent it.
     If in thy wisdom thou canst give no help,
     Do thou but call my resolution wise,
     And with this knife I'll help it presently.
     God joined my heart and Romeo's, thou our hands, 55
     And ere this hand, by thee to Romeo's sealed,
     Shall be the label to another deed,
     Or my true heart with treacherous revolt
     Turn to another, this shall slay them both:

Juliet pleads for the Friar's advice, and again threatens to kill herself. Friar Lawrence begins to devise a plan to prevent Juliet's marriage to Paris. Juliet declares that she will do anything to escape the wedding.

---

1 'Rather than marry Paris' (in groups of any size)

Shakespeare enjoyed compiling 'lists': piling up item on item, and so enabling the character to give different emphasis to each to increase dramatic effect.

Lines 77–86 list six things Juliet says she would do rather than marry Paris. Work out a mime showing all six actions.

Afterwards, each person compiles a list of the things they would rather do than marry someone not of their own choice. Compare your lists. You may hear some surprising things!

2 The charnel-house (line 81)

Most Elizabethan graveyards had a charnel-house. It was a building where bones and skulls were stacked after they were dug up when fresh graves were being prepared for new burials. In Shakespeare's time, Stratford-upon-Avon churchyard possessed a large charnel-house. Write a poem or a short story with the title 'The Charnel-house'. You may wish to use some of Juliet's language.

---

extremes perilous situation	**cop'st with** meets and struggles with
arbitrating judging	
commission authority	**reeky shanks** stinking leg bones
issue outcome	**chapless** without a jawbone

Therefore, out of thy long-experienced time,   60
Give me some present counsel, or, behold,
'Twixt my extremes and me this bloody knife
Shall play the umpire, arbitrating that
Which the commission of thy years and art
Could to no issue of true honour bring.   65
Be not so long to speak, I long to die,
If what thou speak'st speak not of remedy.

FRIAR LAWRENCE Hold, daughter, I do spy a kind of hope,
Which craves as desperate an execution
As that is desperate which we would prevent.   70
If, rather than to marry County Paris,
Thou hast the strength of will to slay thyself,
Then is it likely thou wilt undertake
A thing like death to chide away this shame,
That cop'st with Death himself to scape from it;   75
And if thou dar'st, I'll give thee remedy.

JULIET O bid me leap, rather than marry Paris,
From off the battlements of any tower,
Or walk in thievish ways, or bid me lurk
Where serpents are; chain me with roaring bears,   80
Or hide me nightly in a charnel-house,
O'ercovered quite with dead men's rattling bones,
With reeky shanks and yellow chapless skulls;
Or bid me go into a new-made grave,
And hide me with a dead man in his shroud –   85
Things that to hear them told have made me tremble –
And I will do it without fear or doubt,
To live an unstained wife to my sweet love.

FRIAR LAWRENCE Hold then, go home, be merry, give consent
To marry Paris. Wednesday is tomorrow;   90
Tomorrow night look that thou lie alone,
Let not the Nurse lie with thee in thy chamber.

Friar Lawrence explains his plan. He will give Juliet a potion to make her seem dead. She will be placed in the Capulet vault and Romeo will be with her when she awakens to take her to Mantua.

---

1 Mime the Friar's plan – is it sensible? (in pairs)

Friar Lawrence sees that Juliet's willingness to kill herself means that she will endure any danger rather than marry Paris. So he invents a hazardous and gruesome plan to reunite her with Romeo. One person reads the Friar's plan (lines 89–117) in sections, one small part at a time, like this: 'Hold then', 'go home', 'be merry', . . . 'Take thou this vial', 'being then in bed', 'And this distilling liquor drink thou off', and so on.

As each small section is spoken, the other mimes the actions. It will help you understand what the Friar is proposing. Afterwards, talk together about what you think of his scheme.

2 Juliet's reactions

Juliet listens to Friar Lawrence's long explanation of his plan, but does not speak. How does she react to each part of the scheme? Write notes to guide her actions and expressions as she listens to lines 89–117.

3 What are the Friar's motives? (in groups of four)

From all your knowledge of him so far, talk together about what you think of Friar Lawrence. Explore why he works out such a complicated and perilous plan. What are his motives? Juliet trusts him – do you think she is wise to take the risk?

4 Juliet: character development

Juliet is only thirteen, but her fearlessness now shows how much she has gained in maturity. Look back to where she first appeared in the play. Write a paragraph on how different she is now.

---

vial small bottle
humour fluid, feeling
no pulse . . . surcease your pulse will stop beating
wanny pale
Death (notice the personification)

supple government easy movement
against before
drift purpose or plan
toy whim, trifle
Abate reduce

Take thou this vial, being then in bed,
And this distilling liquor drink thou off,
When presently through all thy veins shall run   95
A cold and drowsy humour; for no pulse
Shall keep his native progress, but surcease;
No warmth, no breath shall testify thou livest;
The roses in thy lips and cheeks shall fade
To wanny ashes, thy eyes' windows fall,   100
Like Death when he shuts up the day of life;
Each part, deprived of supple government,
Shall stiff and stark and cold appear like death,
And in this borrowed likeness of shrunk death
Thou shalt continue two and forty hours,   105
And then awake as from a pleasant sleep.
Now when the bridegroom in the morning comes
To rouse thee from thy bed, there art thou dead.
Then as the manner of our country is,
In thy best robes, uncovered on the bier,   110
Thou shall be borne to that same ancient vault
Where all the kindred of the Capulets lie.
In the mean time, against thou shalt awake,
Shall Romeo by my letters know our drift,
And hither shall he come, and he and I   115
Will watch thy waking, and that very night
Shall Romeo bear thee hence to Mantua.
And this shall free thee from this present shame,
If no inconstant toy, nor womanish fear,
Abate thy valour in the acting it.   120
JULIET Give me, give me! O tell not me of fear.
FRIAR LAWRENCE Hold, get you gone, be strong and prosperous
        In this resolve; I'll send a friar with speed
        To Mantua, with my letters to thy lord.
JULIET Love give me strength, and strength shall help afford. 125
        Farewell, dear father.
                                                    Exeunt

Capulet is busy with the wedding preparations. The Servingman jokes about cooking. Juliet enters and begs forgiveness. She promises to obey her father in future.

---

1 Relationships – and another insight into character

What do lines 1–9 suggest about master–servant relationships in Capulet's household – and about Capulet's character?

2 'How now, my headstrong . . .' (in pairs)

Speak line 15 in as many different ways as you can. Talk together about how you think it should be spoken on stage. What more does it tell you about Capulet's character?

Capulet is planning a grand wedding feast. He seems to have forgotten his earlier intention to have 'no great ado' (Act 3 Scene 4, line 23).

The last time Capulet appeared he was an unreasonable, enraged father. In this scene he shows a more genial side of his character as he talks with his servants. His attitude to Juliet also seems to change (but see p. 150).

---

cunning skilful
none ill no bad cooks
try test
unfurnished unprepared
forsooth in truth, indeed
harlotry hussy, good-for-nothing

shrift confession
gadding wandering
behests commands
enjoined commanded
beseech beg

Act 4 Scene 2
Capulet's mansion

Enter Father CAPULET, *Mother* [LADY CAPULET], NURSE, *and*
SERVINGMEN, *two or three.*

CAPULET So many guests invite as here are writ.

[*Exit Servingman*]

Sirrah, go hire me twenty cunning cooks.

SERVINGMAN You shall have none ill, sir, for I'll try if they can lick
their fingers.

CAPULET How canst thou try them so?   5

SERVINGMAN Marry, sir, 'tis an ill cook that cannot lick his own
fingers; therefore he that cannot lick his fingers goes not with me.

CAPULET Go, be gone.

[*Exit Servingman*]

We shall be much unfurnished for this time.
What, is my daughter gone to Friar Lawrence?   10

NURSE Ay forsooth.

CAPULET Well, he may chance to do some good on her.
A peevish self-willed harlotry it is.

Enter JULIET.

NURSE See where she comes from shrift with merry look.

CAPULET How now, my headstrong, where have you been gadding?   15

JULIET Where I have learnt me to repent the sin
Of disobedient opposition
To you and your behests, and am enjoined
By holy Lawrence to fall prostrate here
To beg your pardon.

[*She kneels down.*]

Pardon, I beseech you!   20
Henceforward I am ever ruled by you.

Capulet is delighted by Juliet's submission. He decides she shall be married tomorrow, and he will manage all the wedding arrangements himself.

---

1 Capulet's self-centredness?

Juliet has begged forgiveness, but Capulet's first words are not to her, but to a servant. He orders that the wedding be brought forward to tomorrow (from Thursday to Wednesday: 'tomorrow morning'). This puts more pressure on Juliet, who had expected a longer time before putting Friar Lawrence's dangerous plan into action. Capulet's impetuous decision is an important factor in accelerating the tragedy (see p. 211). Do you think that Capulet's two lines 22–3 suggest he is less interested in Juliet than in ensuring a prestigious marriage?

2 True, false or double meaning? (in small groups)

Look at everything Juliet says between lines 16 and 33. Judge whether you think each thing she says is 'true', 'false' or 'double meaning'.

One person speaks Juliet's words. The others say 'true' or 'false' or 'double meaning' for each small section.

Talk together about what you think of Juliet's behaviour here. Does it alter your feelings about her in any way?

3 More dramatic irony (in pairs)

'Dramatic irony' (see pp. 122, 128 and 132) is when the audience knows something that at least one of the characters on stage does not know, and when what is said contrasts with what happens elsewhere in the play. There are many examples of dramatic irony in the lines opposite. Write down as many as you can find. Compare your list with those of other pairs.

---

this knot knit up the wedding carried out

becomèd proper or appropriate

marry by Saint Mary

bound to him indebted to the Friar

closet private room

needful ornaments necessary clothes

short in our provision lacking in food and drink

deck up dress

CAPULET Send for the County, go tell him of this.
　　　　I'll have this knot knit up tomorrow morning.
JULIET I met the youthful lord at Lawrence' cell,
　　　　And gave him what becomèd love I might,　　　　　　25
　　　　Not stepping o'er the bounds of modesty.
CAPULET Why, I am glad on't, this is well, stand up.
　　　　This is as't should be. Let me see the County;
　　　　Ay, marry, go, I say, and fetch him hither.
　　　　Now afore God, this reverend holy Friar,　　　　　　30
　　　　All our whole city is much bound to him.
JULIET Nurse, will you go with me into my closet,
　　　　To help me sort such needful ornaments
　　　　As you think fit to furnish me tomorrow?
LADY CAPULET No, not till Thursday, there is time enough.　　35
CAPULET Go, Nurse, go with her, we'll to church tomorrow.
　　　　　　　　　　　　　　Exeunt [Juliet and Nurse]

LADY CAPULET We shall be short in our provision,
　　　　'Tis now near night.
CAPULET　　　　　　　　Tush, I will stir about,
　　　　And all things shall be well, I warrant thee, wife:
　　　　Go thou to Juliet, help to deck up her;　　　　　　40
　　　　I'll not to bed tonight; let me alone,
　　　　I'll play the huswife for this once. What ho!
　　　　They are all forth. Well, I will walk myself
　　　　To County Paris, to prepare up him
　　　　Against tomorrow. My heart is wondrous light,　　　45
　　　　Since this same wayward girl is so reclaimed.
　　　　　　　　　　　　　　　　　　　　Exeunt

Juliet sends her Nurse and mother away. Alone, she fights her fears, plucking up courage to drink the 'poison'. If it does not work she will kill herself with a dagger rather than be married.

1 Juliet's double meanings (in pairs)

Juliet deliberately deceives her mother and the Nurse. In lines 1–12, she once again uses language rich in double meanings and dramatic irony. This short activity explores what is in her mind. One person speaks everything Juliet says up to line 12, pausing after each short section. In each pause, your partner says aloud what Juliet is really thinking.

Talk together about how this adds to your understanding of Juliet's character, and of her feelings about her mother and the Nurse.

2 Shakespeare's imagination at work

Lines 1–12 are Shakespeare's rewriting of a section of a long poem by Arthur Brooke, *The Tragicall Historye of Romeus and Juliet* (1562). What differences can you find between Shakespeare's version and the original below?

> Unto her chamber doth the pensive wight repair
> And in her hand a percher light the Nurse bears up the stair.
> In Juliet's chamber was her wonted use to lie,
> Wherefore her mistress dreading that she should her work descry
> As soon as she began her pallet to unfold
> Thinking to lie that night, where she was wont to lie of old,
> Doth gently pray her seek her lodging somewhere else.

Find a copy of Brooke's poem (e.g. in the New Cambridge Shakespeare edition of the play). Compare it with *Romeo and Juliet*. You'll be surprised at how closely Shakespeare follows many passages. But see how his language and imagination transform them! (There's more about this on p. 219.)

---

attires clothes
orisons prayers
smile upon my state look kindly on
 my condition

culled picked out
behoveful appropriate

Act 4 Scene 3
Juliet's bedroom

Enter JULIET *and* NURSE.

JULIET Ay, those attires are best, but, gentle Nurse,
     I pray thee leave me to myself tonight:
     For I have need of many orisons
     To move the heavens to smile upon my state,
     Which, well thou knowest, is cross and full of sin.   5

Enter Mother [LADY CAPULET].

LADY CAPULET What, are you busy, ho? need you my help?
JULIET No, madam, we have culled such necessaries
     As are behoveful for our state tomorrow.
     So please you, let me now be left alone,
     And let the Nurse this night sit up with you,   10
     For I am sure you have your hands full all,
     In this so sudden business.
LADY CAPULET   Good night.
     Get thee to bed and rest, for thou hast need.
Exeunt [*Lady Capulet and Nurse*]
JULIET Farewell! God knows when we shall meet again.
     I have a faint cold fear thrills through my veins   15
     That almost freezes up the heat of life:
     I'll call them back again to comfort me.
     Nurse! – What should she do here?
     My dismal scene I needs must act alone.
     Come, vial.   20
     What if this mixture do not work at all?
     Shall I be married then tomorrow morning?
     No, no, this shall forbid it; lie thou there.
[*Laying down her dagger.*]

Juliet is filled with fearful thoughts. Is the Friar honest? Will she awake in the tomb before Romeo comes? Will she go mad with dread? She drinks the potion.

1 Juliet's fearful imagination (lines 15–58)

Try some of the following to express Juliet's thoughts and fears (see the picture on p. x in the colour section):

a **Echo the ominous words** (in pairs)   Take lines 30–57. One person reads the lines. The other echoes every word to do with fear or death. You will find that Shakespeare loads the speech with such words to express Juliet's fears.

b **Whispering** (in small groups)   Put your heads as close together as you can bear. Speak lines 15–58 around the group as a whispered, fearful conversation, with each person speaking a short section then handing on.

c **Act out the sections** (in small groups)   Break the speech into sections, for example lines 15–19, 20–3, 24–9, 30–5, 36–54, 55–7 and 58. As a different person speaks each section, the others find a way of acting out the words (e.g. for the first section: shivering, calling back the Nurse, rejecting her, taking out the vial and holding it at arm's length, miming marriage, taking out the dagger and laying it down, and so on).

d **Learn the lines** (an activity for individuals)   Why not learn the whole speech and act it out? Learn the lines, or a section. Rehearse and present your performance.

e **Staging**   Step into role as director. Write notes for Juliet, advising her how to deliver lines 15–58. Suggest actions, expressions, tone of voice and pauses. The stage direction '*within the curtains*' was written for the Elizabethan theatre, which had a curtained alcove at the back of the stage.

Subtly craftily
ministered administered, given
still been tried always proved
conceit thought
green in earth freshly buried

mandrakes plants that were believed to grow beneath gallows and to shriek as they were pulled up
Environèd surrounded
spit pierce

What if it be a poison which the Friar
Subtly hath ministered to have me dead,   25
Lest in this marriage he should be dishonoured,
Because he married me before to Romeo?
I fear it is, and yet methinks it should not,
For he hath still been tried a holy man.
How if, when I am laid into the tomb,   30
I wake before the time that Romeo
Come to redeem me? There's a fearful point!
Shall I not then be stifled in the vault,
To whose foul mouth no healthsome air breathes in,
And there die strangled ere my Romeo comes?   35
Or if I live, is it not very like
The horrible conceit of death and night,
Together with the terror of the place –
As in a vault, an ancient receptacle,
Where for this many hundred years the bones   40
Of all my buried ancestors are packed,
Where bloody Tybalt, yet but green in earth,
Lies fest'ring in his shroud, where, as they say,
At some hours in the night spirits resort –
Alack, alack, is it not like that I,   45
So early waking – what with loathsome smells,
And shrieks like mandrakes' torn out of the earth,
That living mortals hearing them run mad –
O, if I wake, shall I not be distraught,
Environèd with all these hideous fears,   50
And madly play with my forefathers' joints,
And pluck the mangled Tybalt from his shroud,
And in this rage, with some great kinsman's bone,
As with a club, dash out my desp'rate brains?
O look! methinks I see my cousin's ghost   55
Seeking out Romeo that did spit his body
Upon a rapier's point. Stay, Tybalt, stay!
Romeo, Romeo, Romeo! Here's drink – I drink to thee.
    [*She falls upon her bed, within the curtains.*]

It is early morning and the wedding preparations are well under way. Lady
Capulet hints that Capulet has been an unfaithful husband in the past.

1 Angelica – is that the Nurse's name? (in pairs)

No one is quite sure whether Angelica is the Nurse's name or Lady
Capulet's. In the 1992 production by the Royal Shakespeare Company, Angelica was a young serving-woman with whom Capulet was
obviously having an affair. Talk together about who you think Capulet
is calling Angelica. It may be helpful to know that for Shakespeare
and his contemporaries, Angelica probably meant 'beautiful princess'.

2 Who speaks the lines?

Some people think that it should be Lady Capulet, rather than the
Nurse, who speaks lines 6–8. This edition gives the lines to the
Nurse, and so implies that she can be very familiar with her master
when she wishes. Who do you think is most likely to speak the lines?

3 Husband and wife – a distrustful relationship? (in pairs)

Talk together about why you think Lady Capulet says lines 11–12
to her husband. They seem to suggest that Capulet has chased after
other women, but that Lady Capulet will now keep a close eye on
him. In response, Capulet accuses her of being jealous. What is her
tone of voice? Improvise a conversation between two servants in
which they talk about the past and present relationship of Capulet
and his wife.

4 Watching

Notice how all three characters play on the word 'watch' (lines 7–12).
Can you work out the various meanings in their punning?

---

pastry part of the kitchen where
pastry was made
second . . . crowed it's past 3 a.m.
curfew bell bell announcing daylight

cot-quean man who does woman's
work
mouse-hunt woman-chaser
hood woman

Act 4 Scene 4
A room in Capulet's mansion

Enter lady of the house LADY CAPULET *and* NURSE *with herbs.*

LADY CAPULET Hold, take these keys and fetch more spices, Nurse.
NURSE They call for dates and quinces in the pastry.

Enter old CAPULET.

CAPULET Come, stir, stir, stir! the second cock hath crowed,
    The curfew bell hath rung, 'tis three a'clock.
    Look to the baked meats, good Angelica,   5
    Spare not for cost.
NURSE   Go, you cot-quean, go,
    Get you to bed. Faith, you'll be sick tomorrow
    For this night's watching.
CAPULET No, not a whit. What, I have watched ere now
    All night for lesser cause, and ne'er been sick.   10
LADY CAPULET Ay, you have been a mouse-hunt in your time,
    But I will watch you from such watching now.
                  Exeunt Lady [Capulet] and Nurse
CAPULET A jealous hood, a jealous hood!

*Enter three or four [*SERVINGMEN*] with spits and logs and
baskets.*

                  Now, fellow,
    What is there?
FIRST SERVINGMAN Things for the cook, sir, but I know not what.   15

Capulet fusses busily with the wedding arrangements. He tells the Nurse to wake Juliet. The next scene opens with the Nurse attempting to rouse Juliet.

1 Master and servants

a What action do you think the servant makes when he says, 'I have a head, sir, that will find out logs'?

b On page 148 you were asked about master and servant relationships in Capulet's household. What does Scene 4 add to your understanding of those relationships?

2 Make the scene flow (in pairs)

Scenes 3, 4 and 5 are set in Capulet's mansion (in Juliet's bedroom and another room). How could you ensure that the stage action flows smoothly throughout these scenes?

Work out how that 'flow' can be achieved in these three scenes. Design a stage set and write how it enables the action to move swiftly from one place to another without delay for elaborate scene-shifting. (On Shakespeare's own stage, Juliet almost certainly lay in an alcove concealed by a curtain at the back of the stage.)

3 Dramatic construction

Scene 4, with its bustle, humour, and much talk of 'haste', sharply contrasts with the mood of Scenes 3 and 5.

This technique of contrasting scenes is typical of Shakespeare's stagecraft (see p. 138). He knew that he could increase dramatic effect by such juxtapositions. In this case, give two or three reasons for why you think Shakespeare places Scene 4 between the serious ones that precede and follow it.

Mass by the Mass (a mild oath)
whoreson bastard (Do you think Capulet says this seriously or jokingly?)

loggerhead blockhead (but 'loggerheads' also means 'quarrel' or 'dispute', one of the themes of the play. See pp. 209–11.)
set up his rest decided

CAPULET Make haste, make haste.

[*Exit First Servingman*]

Sirrah, fetch drier logs.
Call Peter, he will show thee where they are.

SECOND SERVINGMAN I have a head, sir, that will find out logs,
And never trouble Peter for the matter.

CAPULET Mass, and well said, a merry whoreson, ha!   20
Thou shalt be loggerhead.

[*Exeunt Second Servingman and any others*]

Good faith, 'tis day.
The County will be here with music straight,
For so he said he would.

(*Play music* [*within*].)

I hear him near.
Nurse! Wife! What ho! What, Nurse, I say!

Enter Nurse.

Go waken Juliet, go and trim her up,   25
I'll go and chat with Paris. Hie, make haste,
Make haste, the bridegroom he is come already,
Make haste, I say.   [*Exit*]

Act 4 Scene 5
Juliet's bedroom

NURSE Mistress, what mistress! Juliet! Fast, I warrant her, she.
Why, lamb! why, lady! fie, you slug-a-bed!
Why, love, I say! madam! sweet heart! why, bride!
What, not a word? You take your pennyworths now;
Sleep for a week, for the next night I warrant   5
The County Paris hath set up his rest
That you shall rest but little. God forgive me!

The Nurse, thinking Juliet to be dead, raises the house with her cries. Lady Capulet and her husband express their grief. Paris, unaware, enters to take Juliet to church.

1 The Nurse's changing mood (in pairs)

The Nurse begins the scene trying to wake Juliet. Her language in lines 4–11 jokingly contains sexual double meanings about Juliet's wedding night. But the Nurse's mood changes as she comes to believe that Juliet is dead. Her language now is full of alarmed, brief exclamations and cries.

Read lines 1–16 to each other, trying out different ways of saying each line. Can you agree on a version you prefer? Work out the actions and movements you would use to accompany the Nurse's words. Decide whether your version includes a 'sudden' or 'gradual' realisation by the Nurse of Juliet's death.

2 Lady Capulet's anguish

Lady Capulet's attitude towards her daughter has swung dramatically through the play. When Juliet refused to marry Paris, her mother showed no sympathy or affection. But now, thinking Juliet dead, she seems broken-hearted. As you read on, you will find she becomes even more grief-stricken.

3 Friar Lawrence's private thoughts

Friar Lawrence enters with Paris and the musicians. He alone knows that Juliet is not dead. Write what he is probably thinking as he enters, and how he speaks his question at line 33 (to which he already knows the answer).

4 'Death lies on her like an untimely frost
Upon the sweetest flower of all the field'

Make a drawing, or write a poem or story to show what these lines mean to you.

weraday	alas	**heavy**	sorrowful
aqua-vitae	brandy	**settled**	congealed

Marry and amen! How sound is she asleep!
I needs must wake her. Madam, madam, madam!
Ay, let the County take you in your bed,   10
He'll fright you up, i'faith. Will it not be?
    [*Draws back the curtains.*]
What, dressed, and in your clothes, and down again?
I must needs wake you. Lady, lady, lady!
Alas, alas! Help, help! my lady's dead!
O weraday that ever I was born!   15
Some aqua-vitae, ho! My lord! My lady!

    [*Enter Mother,* LADY CAPULET.]

LADY CAPULET What noise is here?
NURSE   O lamentable day!
LADY CAPULET What is the matter?
NURSE   Look, look! O heavy day!
LADY CAPULET O me, O me, my child, my only life!
    Revive, look up, or I will die with thee.   20
    Help, help! Call help.

    Enter Father [CAPULET].

CAPULET For shame, bring Juliet forth, her lord is come.
NURSE She's dead, deceased, she's dead, alack the day!
LADY CAPULET Alack the day, she's dead, she's dead, she's dead!
CAPULET Hah, let me see her. Out alas, she's cold,   25
    Her blood is settled, and her joints are stiff:
    Life and these lips have long been separated;
    Death lies on her like an untimely frost
    Upon the sweetest flower of all the field.
NURSE O lamentable day!
LADY CAPULET   O woeful time!   30
CAPULET Death that hath tane her hence to make me wail
    Ties up my tongue and will not let me speak.

    Enter FRIAR [LAWRENCE] *and the* COUNTY [PARIS *with the*
        MUSICIANS].

FRIAR LAWRENCE Come, is the bride ready to go to church?

The Capulets, the Nurse and Paris mourn for Juliet. The Friar attempts to offer consolation, saying that Juliet is now in a better state because she is in heaven.

1 Mourning for Juliet (in groups of four)

Each person takes a part: Capulet, Paris, Lady Capulet, the Nurse. Read aloud lines 35–64. Change parts and read again. Change again until everyone has read all four parts.

Talk together about the different ways in which the four characters express their grief over the 'dead' Juliet.

Critics of the play have said that this mourning is selfish, artificial and self-indulgent – even absurd (and in some productions this episode is cut). Other critics defend the language, saying it is sincere, and typical of the characters and the occasion (and it was a familiar convention in the tragic plays of the time). What are your views? Work together to write a statement about each character, explaining whether you think that the way in which the character mourns matches their personality.

2 What do you think the audience should feel?

If you were directing the play, what effect on an audience would you hope to achieve in your staging of this scene of mourning? After all, the audience knows that Juliet is alive, not dead.

3 'In lasting labour of his pilgrimage!' (in pairs)

In lines 44–5, Lady Capulet personifies time. She turns 'time' into a pilgrim toiling unceasingly through each day. But the major personification throughout this mourning scene is that of Death. How many of such personifications can you find? Choose one and make a sketch of the image it suggests to you.

---

deflowerèd seduced
thought long been impatient
solace take comfort
Beguiled cheated
solemnity celebrations

Confusion/confusions
  calamity/sorrowings
Your part in her (Juliet's body)
his part (Juliet's soul)

CAPULET Ready to go, but never to return. –
        O son, the night before thy wedding day   35
        Hath Death lain with thy wife. There she lies,
        Flower as she was, deflowerèd by him.
        Death is my son-in-law, Death is my heir,
        My daughter he hath wedded. I will die,
        And leave him all; life, living, all is Death's.   40
PARIS Have I thought long to see this morning's face,
        And doth it give me such a sight as this?
LADY CAPULET Accursed, unhappy, wretched, hateful day!
        Most miserable hour that e'er time saw
        In lasting labour of his pilgrimage!   45
        But one, poor one, one poor and loving child,
        But one thing to rejoice and solace in,
        And cruel Death hath catched it from my sight!
NURSE O woe! O woeful, woeful, woeful day!
        Most lamentable day, most woeful day   50
        That ever, ever, I did yet behold!
        O day, O day, O day, O hateful day!
        Never was seen so black a day as this.
        O woeful day, O woeful day!
PARIS Beguiled, divorcèd, wrongèd, spited, slain!   55
        Most detestable Death, by thee beguiled,
        By cruel, cruel thee quite overthrown!
        O love! O life! not life, but love in death!
CAPULET Despised, distressèd, hated, martyred, killed!
        Uncomfortable time, why cam'st thou now   60
        To murder, murder our solemnity?
        O child, O child! my soul, and not my child!
        Dead art thou. Alack, my child is dead,
        And with my child my joys are burièd.
FRIAR LAWRENCE Peace ho, for shame! Confusion's cure lives not 65
        In these confusions. Heaven and yourself
        Had part in this fair maid, now heaven hath all,
        And all the better is it for the maid:
        Your part in her you could not keep from death,
        But heaven keeps his part in eternal life.   70

Friar Lawrence rebukes the family for their grief. They should stop crying because Juliet is now in heaven. He tells them to prepare her funeral. Everyone leaves except Peter and the musicians.

---

1 More of the Friar's secret thoughts (in pairs)

The Friar knows Juliet is not dead, but he talks to the family as though she were.

One person reads aloud Friar Lawrence's lines 65–83. Pause frequently. In each pause, the other person says aloud what the Friar is really thinking at that moment.

2 'Black funeral' – make the antitheses physical

You will need an empty space for this activity. It will help you identify the antitheses in Capulet's speech.

Capulet's lines 84–90 have a rhythm all of their own. Walk around the room reading the lines aloud. Every time you come to a 'turning' word such as 'turn', 'to' or 'serve', change direction in your walking. Invent different ways of physically expressing the movement of his speech (e.g. sitting down but turning your hand or body from side to side as the language 'turns').

Is there a 'natural' way in which these lines might be spoken? That is, where the speech is spoken without the formal, declamatory style it seems to require.

You will find another activity based on Capulet's lines 84–90 (and Juliet's funeral) on page 168.

3 The ballad of Juliet

Make up a ballad telling the story of what happened to Juliet in Act 4. You might use one of the musicians' songs in Scene 5 as a title.

---

rosemary a herb for remembrance at funerals (and weddings)
corse corpse
fond foolish
office proper purposes
dirges sad songs

low'r lour, frown
put up put away
by my troth in truth
dump sad tune (so 'merry dump' is yet another oxymoron – see p. 216)

The most you sought was her promotion,
For 'twas your heaven she should be advanced,
And weep ye now, seeing she is advanced
Above the clouds, as high as heaven itself?
O, in this love, you love your child so ill   75
That you run mad, seeing that she is well.
She's not well married that lives married long,
But she's best married that dies married young.
Dry up your tears, and stick your rosemary
On this fair corse, and as the custom is,   80
And in her best array, bear her to church;
For though fond nature bids us all lament,
Yet nature's tears are reason's merriment.
CAPULET   All things that we ordainèd festival,
Turn from their office to black funeral: 85
Our instruments to melancholy bells,
Our wedding cheer to a sad burial feast;
Our solemn hymns to sullen dirges change;
Our bridal flowers serve for a buried corse;
And all things change them to the contrary.   90
FRIAR LAWRENCE   Sir, go you in, and, madam, go with him,
And go, Sir Paris. Every one prepare
To follow this fair corse unto her grave.
The heavens do low'r upon you for some ill;
Move them no more by crossing their high will.   95
              [*They all, but the Nurse and the Musicians, go forth,*
                        casting rosemary on her, and shutting the curtains]
FIRST MUSICIAN   Faith, we may put up our pipes and be gone.
NURSE   Honest good fellows, ah put up, put up,
For well you know this is a pitiful case.   [*Exit*]
FIRST MUSICIAN   Ay, by my troth, the case may be amended.

                    Enter PETER.

PETER   Musicians, O musicians, 'Heart's ease', 'Heart's ease'! O,   100
and you will have me live, play 'Heart's ease'.
FIRST MUSICIAN   Why 'Heart's ease'?
PETER   O musicians, because my heart itself plays 'My heart is full'.
O play me some merry dump to comfort me.

Peter talks with the musicians. He variously insults, threatens and mocks them. They do not care for his humour.

---

1 Staging the musicians (in groups of four)

Each person takes a part (Peter, musicians). Read through lines 100–38. Work out how you would stage them. Would the scene work if you changed the musicians into modern rock or pop stars?

2 To cut or not to cut? (in groups of four)

The musicians' episode changes the mood of the scene. It descends into bathos (anti-climax). So what is the purpose of bringing them on?

Sometimes lines 100–38 are cut from performances. Talk together about whether you would cut the musicians and Peter from your production. Two argue for leaving out this part of the play. Two argue against cutting. Share your verdict and reasons with the rest of the class.

3 The musician's tale

Write the story one of the three musicians later tells a friend. He was hired to play at the wedding of Juliet and Paris. But unexpected things happened . . .

4 Create the music or write the song (in pairs)

Either set Peter's three lines 'When griping griefs the heart doth wound . . . her silver sound' (lines 120–2) to your own music.

Or, in lines 100–4, you will find the titles of two popular songs of Shakespeare's day: 'Heart's ease' and 'My heart is full'. Their words are now lost. Make up a song using one or both titles.

---

the gleek an insult. Today Peter would probably accompany his words with a two-fingered gesture!

the minstrel good-for-nothing (another insult)

Catling, Rebeck, Soundpost Peter calls the musicians by the names of parts of their instruments. Do you think these are their actual names or is Peter once more insulting them?

Prates! Nonsensical chatter!

MUSICIANS Not a dump we, 'tis no time to play now. 105
PETER You will not then?
FIRST MUSICIAN No.
PETER I will then give it you soundly.
FIRST MUSICIAN What will you give us?
PETER No money, on my faith, but the gleek; I will give you the 110
  minstrel.
FIRST MUSICIAN Then will I give you the serving-creature.
PETER Then will I lay the serving-creature's dagger on your pate. I will
  carry no crotchets, I'll re you, I'll fa you. Do you note me?
FIRST MUSICIAN And you re us and fa us, you note us. 115
SECOND MUSICIAN Pray you put up your dagger, and put out your
  wit.
PETER Then have at you with my wit! I will dry-beat you with an iron
  wit, and put up my iron dagger. Answer me like men:
      'When griping griefs the heart doth wound, 120
      And doleful dumps the mind oppress,
      Then music with her silver sound –'
  Why 'silver sound'? why 'music with her silver sound'? What say
  you, Simon Catling?
FIRST MUSICIAN Marry, sir, because silver hath a sweet sound. 125
PETER Prates! What say you, Hugh Rebeck?
SECOND MUSICIAN I say 'silver sound' because musicians sound for
  silver.
PETER Prates too! What say you, James Soundpost?
THIRD MUSICIAN Faith, I know not what to say. 130
PETER O, I cry you mercy, you are the singer; I will say for you: It
  is 'music with her silver sound' because musicians have no gold
  for sounding.
      'Then music with her silver sound
      With speedy help doth lend redress.' *Exit* 135
FIRST MUSICIAN What a pestilent knave is this same!
SECOND MUSICIAN Hang him, Jack! Come, we'll in here, tarry for the
  mourners, and stay dinner.
                                          Exeunt

Looking back at Act 4
Activities for groups or individuals

---

1 Juliet's funeral procession

> Every one prepare
> To follow this fair corse unto her grave. (*Scene 5, lines 92–3*)

In the eighteenth and nineteenth centuries, theatre productions often added a scene to show the funeral of Juliet. The playbill opposite advertises a production at Drury Lane in 1756. It advertises the funeral procession as a highlight of the production.

In groups of eight to twelve, work out how you could stage Juliet's funeral. Use Capulet's lines 84–90 from Scene 5. Make your presentation as dramatically striking as possible. You could speak or sing or chant the words. Each group member can choose to be a character and use some of that character's mourning language (lines 34–64 in Scene 5) in the funeral march.

Try to find some music to accompany your group's actions, such as 'The Dead March' from Handel's *Saul*, or Fauré's *Requiem*.

2 Design a poster

Theatre posters advertising plays have changed greatly since the playbill shown opposite. Collect some examples of recent posters or advertisements for plays. Design your own poster for a production of *Romeo and Juliet*.

3 Focus on Juliet – Romeo's absence

Romeo does not appear in Act 4. Shakespeare keeps the dramatic focus tightly on Juliet throughout. Even in 'death' in Scene 5 she remains the centre of other characters' attention. Consider each scene in turn and write a sentence or paragraph on each identifying how Juliet is central to the scene.

4 Telling lies – is it always wrong?

Juliet talks ambiguously to Paris in Scene 1. She deceives her father in Scene 2, and speaks with double meaning to her mother and the Nurse in Scene 3. Talk together about whether you think it's right to lie to your parents. Are there occasions when you might deceive your parents, and if so, why?

AT THE

TheatreRoyal in *Drury-Lane*,

This prefent *Tuefday*, being the 16th of *November*, 1756
Will be prefented a PLAY, call'd

ROMEO and JULIET.

Romeo by Mr. GARRICK,

Efcalus by Mr. BRANSBY,

Capulet by Mr. BERRY,

Paris by Mr. JEFFERSON,
Benvolio by Mr. USHER,
Mountague by Mr. BURTON,
Tibalt by Mr. BLAKES,

Fryar *Lawrence* by Mr. HAVARD,

Mercutio by Mr. WOODWARD,

Lady *Capulet* by Mrs. PRITCHARD,

Nurfe by Mrs. MACKLIN,

Juliet by Mifs PRITCHARD.

With the ADDITIONAL SCENE Reprefenting

TheFuneralPROCESSION

To the MONUMENT of the *CAPULETS*.

The VOCAL PARTS by
Mr. *Beard*, Mr. *Champnefs* and *Others*.
In Act I. a *Mafquerade Dance* proper to the Play.
To which will be added a FARCE, call'd

The ANATOMIST.

Monf. *Le Medecin* by Mr. BLAKES,
Crifpin by Mr. YATES,
Beatrice by Mrs. BENNET.

Boxes 5s. Pit 3s. Firft Gallery 2s. Upper Gallery 1s.
Places for the Boxes to be had of Mr. VARNEY, at the Stage-
door of the *Theatre*.
✝ *No Perfons to be admitted behind the Scenes, nor any Money to be returned
after the* Curtain *is drawn up.* Vivat REX.

To-morrow, the MOURNING BRIDE. *Ofmyn* by Mr. MOSSOP,
(*Being the Firft Time of his appearing in that Character.*)

Romeo, in Mantua, talks joyfully of his strange dream: he dreamt that he died, but Juliet revived him with kisses. But Balthasar brings him dreadful news.

1 Romeo's dream – fill in the details (in pairs)

Romeo tells only the bare outline of his dream (lines 6–9). He gives none of the details. Imagine some further details of his dream and discuss its possible interpretations. Then work together to write an account of it under the title 'Romeo's dream'. Try to ensure that your account includes both sombre and joyful elements.

2 Balthasar's predicament – how to tell Romeo?

a Imagine you are Balthasar, riding from Verona to Mantua to tell Romeo of Juliet's death. What are your thoughts as you ride – just how are you to tell Romeo the dreadful news? Think of different ways you might recount the story, and your fears about each. Write down your thoughts as a kind of dialogue with yourself.

b When Balthasar arrives, Romeo bombards him with questions. If you were Balthasar, how would you behave throughout lines 12–16?

3 Change the scene to Mantua

The previous scene is set in Juliet's bedroom in Verona. Act 5 begins in Mantua, twenty-five miles away. Work out how you would carry out the scene change swiftly and effectively. Remember, the location suggested here ('A street in Mantua') has been made up for this edition (see p. 4). Shakespeare certainly places Romeo in Mantua, but he leaves it to your imagination to work out how the location will be shown on stage. For example, in Baz Luhrmann's film, Mantua becomes a run-down trailer park in the desert.

---

presage foretell, promise
bosom's lord heart (or love?)
unaccustomed spirit unusual joy
shadows dreams, illusions
booted in riding boots

immortal part soul
presently took post immediately rode here on horseback
office duty

Act 5 Scene 1
A street in Mantua

Enter ROMEO.

ROMEO If I may trust the flattering truth of sleep,
My dreams presage some joyful news at hand.
My bosom's lord sits lightly in his throne,
And all this day an unaccustomed spirit
Lifts me above the ground with cheerful thoughts.   5
I dreamt my lady came and found me dead
(Strange dream that gives a dead man leave to think!),
And breathed such life with kisses in my lips
That I revived and was an emperor.
Ah me, how sweet is love itself possessed,   10
When but love's shadows are so rich in joy!

Enter Romeo's man [BALTHASAR, *booted*].

News from Verona! How now, Balthasar?
Dost thou not bring me letters from the Friar?
How doth my lady? Is my father well?
How doth my Juliet? That I ask again,   15
For nothing can be ill if she be well.
BALTHASAR Then she is well and nothing can be ill:
Her body sleeps in Capels' monument,
And her immortal part with angels lives.
I saw her laid low in her kindred's vault,   20
And presently took post to tell it you.
O pardon me for bringing these ill news,
Since you did leave it for my office, sir.

There is no word from the Friar. Romeo dismisses Balthasar to hire horses. He resolves to kill himself that night in the tomb with Juliet. But how? The apothecary who sells poisons comes into his mind.

1 'Then I defy you, stars!' (in pairs)

Write the advice you would give to an actor playing Romeo about how to deliver line 24. If the actor asked you what is in Romeo's mind at this moment, what would you say? There is help on page 209.

2 Is Romeo brave or foolish or . . . ? (in small groups)

Well, Juliet, I will lie with thee tonight.

Romeo resolves to kill himself that night in Capulet's monument. Talk together about whether you think this is a brave decision. How else can it be seen? What alternatives might Romeo have?

3 Draw the apothecary and his shop

Lines 37–48 give a detailed description of the apothecary and his shop. Make an imaginative drawing including as much of Shakespeare's description as you can. As you draw, think why such a precise description is given at this point in the play.

4 Show a 'holiday atmosphere'?

The apothecary's shop is shut because it's a holiday in Mantua. One production in the late 1980s made a great show of the holiday festivities going on in Mantua. They were presented as a carnival, with much political protest added (actors wore huge heads of contemporary politicians).

If you were directing the play, would you stage the 'holiday' in some way? Write out the reasons for your decision.

---

import suggest
apothecary druggist, someone who sells ingredients for medicine
weeds clothes
Culling of simples picking herbs to use in medicines

beggarly account poor number
cakes of roses compressed rose petals (for perfume)
penury poverty
present death immediate execution
caitiff miserable, pitiable

ROMEO Is it e'en so? then I defy you, stars!
     Thou knowest my lodging, get me ink and paper,   25
     And hire post-horses; I will hence tonight.
BALTHASAR I do beseech you, sir, have patience:
     Your looks are pale and wild, and do import
     Some misadventure.
ROMEO   Tush, thou art deceived.
     Leave me, and do the thing I bid thee do.   30
     Hast thou no letters to me from the Friar?
BALTHASAR No, my good lord.
ROMEO   No matter, get thee gone,
     And hire those horses; I'll be with thee straight.
                               Exit [Balthasar]
     Well, Juliet, I will lie with thee tonight.
     Let's see for means. O mischief, thou art swift   35
     To enter in the thoughts of desperate men!
     I do remember an apothecary,
     And hereabouts 'a dwells, which late I noted
     In tattered weeds, with overwhelming brows,
     Culling of simples; meagre were his looks,   40
     Sharp misery had worn him to the bones;
     And in his needy shop a tortoise hung,
     An alligator stuffed, and other skins
     Of ill-shaped fishes, and about his shelves
     A beggarly account of empty boxes,   45
     Green earthen pots, bladders, and musty seeds,
     Remnants of packthread, and old cakes of roses
     Were thinly scattered, to make up a show.
     Noting this penury, to myself I said,
     'And if a man did need a poison now,   50
     Whose sale is present death in Mantua,
     Here lives a caitiff wretch would sell it him.'
     O this same thought did but forerun my need,
     And this same needy man must sell it me.
     As I remember, this should be the house.   55
     Being holiday, the beggar's shop is shut.
     What ho, apothecary!

The penniless apothecary sells poison to Romeo even though he knows the penalty for doing so is death. Romeo leaves for Verona and Juliet's tomb, determined to drink the poison there.

---

1 Act out Romeo's meeting with the apothecary (in pairs)

First read through lines 57–86, each partner taking a role. Then talk about how you might stage the action. Think carefully about the state of mind of each character at this moment. Can you show those states of mind in your presentation?

2 The power of gold (in small groups)

Is Romeo's condemnation of gold in lines 80–3 based on bitter personal experience? Make up a mime or short play to show that money (gold) is the cause of the bloody quarrels between the Montagues and Capulets. To see Shakespeare writing at full power in condemnation of gold, see *Timon of Athens* Act 4 Scene 3, lines 26–45.

Choose an extract from the script as a caption for this picture.

---

ducats gold coins
dram dose
soon-speeding gear quick-acting
  poison

trunk body
utters sells
cordial healthy drink

[*Enter* APOTHECARY.]

APOTHECARY   Who calls so loud?
ROMEO Come hither, man. I see that thou art poor.
        Hold, there is forty ducats; let me have
        A dram of poison, such soon-speeding gear   60
        As will disperse itself through all the veins,
        That the life-weary taker may fall dead,
        And that the trunk may be discharged of breath
        As violently as hasty powder fired
        Doth hurry from the fatal cannon's womb.   65
APOTHECARY Such mortal drugs I have, but Mantua's law
        Is death to any he that utters them.
ROMEO Art thou so bare and full of wretchedness,
        And fearest to die? Famine is in thy cheeks,
        Need and oppression starveth in thy eyes,   70
        Contempt and beggary hangs upon thy back;
        The world is not thy friend, nor the world's law,
        The world affords no law to make thee rich;
        Then be not poor, but break it and take this.
APOTHECARY My poverty, but not my will, consents.   75
ROMEO I pay thy poverty and not thy will.
APOTHECARY Put this in any liquid thing you will
        And drink it off, and if you had the strength
        Of twenty men, it would dispatch you straight.
ROMEO There is thy gold, worse poison to men's souls,   80
        Doing more murder in this loathsome world,
        Than these poor compounds that thou mayst not sell.
        I sell thee poison, thou hast sold me none.
        Farewell, buy food, and get thyself in flesh.
                                            [*Exit Apothecary*]
        Come, cordial and not poison, go with me   85
        To Juliet's grave, for there must I use thee.   *Exit*

Friar John tells how an unlucky mischance prevented him delivering Friar Lawrence's letter to Romeo. Friar Lawrence determines to break into Capulet's monument to be with Juliet when she awakes.

1 'Unhappy fortune!' – Friar John's delay

Friar John explains that he was seeking another Franciscan friar to accompany him to Mantua in order to deliver Friar Lawrence's letter to Romeo. He found his brother friar visiting the sick. There disaster struck: the 'searchers' called!

The 'searchers' were health officers of the town appointed to prevent the spread of disease by examining dead bodies to establish the cause of death. They thought that the Franciscans were in a house where plague raged, so refused to allow them to travel ('Sealed up the doors'). This was common practice in London at the time Shakespeare was writing. Work on one or more of the following activities:

a **Echo!** Read lines 5–12 aloud, but add 'unhappy fortune!' after every punctuation mark.

b **Improvise!** (in groups of five or six) Two of the group take the roles of Friar John and his fellow monk. The others are the 'searchers' who refuse them permission to leave the house. Improvise what took place as the searchers refuse to grant the Friars' pleading to be allowed out to travel to Mantua.

c **Act out the scene** (in pairs) Take the roles of Friar Lawrence and Friar John. Act the scene to bring out Friar Lawrence's increasing anguish and his realisation that urgent action is needed.

d **Write the letter** Step into role as Friar Lawrence and write his letter to Romeo. The letter explains the desperate plan he has devised for Juliet's seeming 'death' (see Act 4 Scene 1, lines 89–117).

e **Scene change** The Friar's last line prepares the audience for a scene change to the churchyard. Write or sketch the scene change.

---

barefoot brother Franciscan friar
associate accompany (Franciscans nearly always travelled in pairs)
bare carried
nice trivial

full of charge vastly important
dear import precious meaning
crow crowbar
beshrew blame
corse corpse

Act 5 Scene 2
Friar Lawrence's cell

Enter FRIAR JOHN.

FRIAR JOHN Holy Franciscan Friar, brother, ho!

Enter [FRIAR] LAWRENCE.

FRIAR LAWRENCE This same should be the voice of Friar John.
    Welcome from Mantua. What says Romeo?
    Or if his mind be writ, give me his letter.
FRIAR JOHN Going to find a barefoot brother out,   5
    One of our order, to associate me,
    Here in this city visiting the sick,
    And finding him, the searchers of the town,
    Suspecting that we both were in a house
    Where the infectious pestilence did reign,   10
    Sealed up the doors, and would not let us forth,
    So that my speed to Mantua there was stayed.
FRIAR LAWRENCE Who bare my letter then to Romeo?
FRIAR JOHN I could not send it – here it is again –
    Nor get a messenger to bring it thee,   15
    So fearful were they of infection.
FRIAR LAWRENCE Unhappy fortune! By my brotherhood,
    The letter was not nice but full of charge,
    Of dear import, and the neglecting it
    May do much danger. Friar John, go hence,   20
    Get me an iron crow and bring it straight
    Unto my cell.
FRIAR JOHN Brother, I'll go and bring it thee.   *Exit*
FRIAR LAWRENCE Now must I to the monument alone,
    Within this three hours will fair Juliet wake.   25
    She will beshrew me much that Romeo
    Hath had no notice of these accidents;
    But I will write again to Mantua,
    And keep her at my cell till Romeo come,
    Poor living corse, closed in a dead man's tomb!   *Exit*   30

Paris visits Juliet's tomb to lay flowers and mourn. He is anxious not to be observed, so orders his Page to keep watch. The Page whistles to warn him someone is coming.

---

1 Orders and actions (in pairs)

Face each other, and as one person reads short sections of Paris's lines 1–9, the other mimes each action.

Then repeat, but this time speak only the words of command ('Give', 'Hence', and so on). How many orders does Paris give to his Page? And how do the commands help create a feeling of suspense?

2 Night and churchyards (in small groups)

Shakespeare uses words to create time, place and atmosphere. For example, in line 3 Paris refers to 'yew trees', which are often found in churchyards and are associated with mourning. Sharing the lines between you, speak everything on the opposite page. Emphasise each word and phrase that helps to create the impression of night-time and the graveyard setting (e.g. your first emphasised word would be 'torch').

Follow this by reading aloud each of the words you emphasised. After each word add your own comment as to how it creates an atmosphere of time ('night'), or place ('churchyard').

3 Paris's six lines of mourning – sincere or artificial?

Speak lines 12–17. Do you find them artificial and formal, or do they seem to come from Paris's heart? Does the fact that they rhyme affect your response? It's helpful to compare the lines with Romeo's own mourning later in this scene (lines 85–120).

---

stand aloof go some distance away
yond yonder
lay thee all along lie down
adventure risk it

canopy the stone covering of the tomb (instead of the fabric covering Juliet's bed)
sweet water perfumed water
obsequies funeral rites

Act 5 Scene 3
A churchyard, outside the tomb of the Capulets

Enter PARIS *and his* PAGE [*with flowers and sweet water and a torch*].

PARIS Give me thy torch, boy. Hence, and stand aloof.
        Yet put it out, for I would not be seen.
        Under yond yew trees lay thee all along,
        Holding thy ear close to the hollow ground,
        So shall no foot upon the churchyard tread,   5
        Being loose, unfirm with digging up of graves,
        But thou shalt hear it. Whistle then to me
        As signal that thou hear'st something approach.
        Give me those flowers. Do as I bid thee, go.
PAGE [*Aside*] I am almost afraid to stand alone   10
        Here in the churchyard, yet I will adventure.   [*Retires*]
          [*Paris strews the tomb with flowers.*]
PARIS Sweet flower, with flowers thy bridal bed I strew –
        O woe, thy canopy is dust and stones! –
        Which with sweet water nightly I will dew,
        Or wanting that, with tears distilled by moans.   15
        The obsequies that I for thee will keep
        Nightly shall be to strew thy grave and weep.
               Whistle Boy.
        The boy gives warning, something doth approach.
        What cursèd foot wanders this way tonight,
        To cross my obsequies and true love's rite?   20
        What, with a torch? Muffle me, night, a while.   [*Retires*]

Romeo, determined to force open the tomb, dismisses Balthasar on pain of death. Balthasar resolves to stay and watch. As Romeo begins to force entry, Paris steps forward to challenge him.

1 Masters and servants (in pairs)

Take Romeo's lines 22–42 and carry out an activity similar to Activity 1 on page 178. One person reads, the other mimes every action and echoes each word of command or words that are threatening.

Afterwards divide the lines into four sections: lines 22–7, 28–32, 33–9 and 41–2. Talk together about how each section shows you a different aspect of Romeo's feelings and personality.

2 Why does Romeo lie?

Why does Romeo tell a lie (or two lies) to Balthasar in lines 28–32? Remember, there's no 'right' answer to this, but write a paragraph exploring possible explanations.

3 The language of Revenge Tragedy (in pairs)

In lines 33–9, Romeo uses the hyperbolic (extravagant, 'over the top') language of Revenge Tragedy (see p. 96). His threat ('tear thee joint by joint') and his imagery ('More fierce and more inexorable far / Than empty tigers or the roaring sea') imitates how 'revengers' spoke in such plays. But does he really mean what he says? Talk together about whether you think Romeo is fully serious.

4 A problem of staging

At line 48, Romeo begins to open the tomb. The problem for set designers is that Scene 3 takes place both outside and inside the Capulet monument. When you have read the whole scene, design the stage set. The picture on page 222 shows a Victorian staging, but most of today's designs are far more simple and expressionistic.

---

mattock a kind of pickaxe
wrenching iron crowbar
all aloof far away
dear employment precious business

jealous suspicious
inexorable pitiless
maw stomach
Gorged crammed
apprehend arrest

Enter ROMEO *and* [BALTHASAR *with a torch, a mattock, and a crow of iron*].

ROMEO Give me that mattock and the wrenching iron.
        Hold, take this letter; early in the morning
        See thou deliver it to my lord and father.
        Give me the light. Upon thy life I charge thee,   25
        What e'er thou hear'st or seest, stand all aloof,
        And do not interrupt me in my course.
        Why I descend into this bed of death
        Is partly to behold my lady's face,
        But chiefly to take thence from her dead finger   30
        A precious ring, a ring that I must use
        In dear employment; therefore hence, be gone.
        But if thou, jealous, dost return to pry
        In what I farther shall intend to do,
        By heaven, I will tear thee joint by joint,   35
        And strew this hungry churchyard with thy limbs.
        The time and my intents are savage-wild,
        More fierce and more inexorable far
        Than empty tigers or the roaring sea.
BALTHASAR I will be gone, sir, and not trouble ye.   40
ROMEO So shalt thou show me friendship. Take thou that,
            [*Gives a purse.*]
        Live and be prosperous, and farewell, good fellow.
BALTHASAR [*Aside*] For all this same, I'll hide me hereabout,
        His looks I fear, and his intents I doubt.   [*Retires*]
ROMEO Thou detestable maw, thou womb of death,   45
        Gorged with the dearest morsel of the earth,
        Thus I enforce thy rotten jaws to open,
        And in despite I'll cram thee with more food.
            [*Romeo begins to open the tomb.*]
PARIS This is that banished haughty Montague,
        That murdered my love's cousin, with which grief   50
        It is supposèd the fair creature died,
        And here is come to do some villainous shame
        To the dead bodies. I will apprehend him.
            [*Steps forth.*]

Paris tries to arrest Romeo, but is slain by him. Romeo, dismayed to find whom he has killed, resolves to grant Paris's dying wish, and lays his body beside Juliet's.

---

1 More problems of staging

On the previous page you were invited to design a set for this scene, to show the 'outside' and the 'inside' of the tomb. The lines opposite present two further problems (or opportunities) of staging. First, all the events are being watched by Paris's Page and Balthasar – so where are they? Second, how and where will the fight be staged? Keep these two puzzles in mind when you design the set. Today (as in Shakespeare's time) most designers 'solve' the problems by non-realistic staging. Such stagings ask the audience to use its imagination and to suspend disbelief (that is, to willingly accept non-realistic stagings and events).

2 'Sour misfortune's book!' (line 82)

Who else in the play do you think would join Romeo and Paris in a book of people afflicted by unhappy mischance and accident? Use the character list on page 1 to help you make your choice.

3 Imagery: light in death

Lines 84–6 express elaborate imagery. In architecture a 'lantern' is a glass turret on the roof of a building. Its purpose is to let in light. A 'feasting presence' is a room in a palace where kings received and entertained visitors. In Baz Luhrmann's film, Juliet lay in magnificent state in a cathedral, bathed in the light of thousands of burning candles (see the picture on p. xi in the colour section). That staging shows the difference between film and theatre. Film can present much more realistic settings (see Activity 1 above).

---

unhallowed   unholy
conjuration   appeal, entreaty
Watch   police (but in Shakespeare's time there was no police force like today's. Instead, citizens [the Watch] patrolled the streets at night)

peruse   study
betossèd   disturbed
dead man   (Romeo)
interred   buried

Stop thy unhallowed toil, vile Montague!
Can vengeance be pursued further than death?   55
Condemnèd villain, I do apprehend thee.
Obey and go with me, for thou must die.
ROMEO I must indeed, and therefore came I hither.
Good gentle youth, tempt not a desp'rate man,
Fly hence and leave me. Think upon these gone,   60
Let them affright thee. I beseech thee, youth,
Put not another sin upon my head,
By urging me to fury: O be gone!
By heaven, I love thee better than myself,
For I come hither armed against myself.   65
Stay not, be gone; live, and hereafter say,
A madman's mercy bid thee run away.
PARIS I do defy thy conjuration,
And apprehend thee for a felon here.
ROMEO Wilt thou provoke me? then have at thee, boy!   70
                    [*They fight.*]
PAGE O Lord, they fight! I will go call the Watch.   [*Exit*]
PARIS O, I am slain! [*Falls.*] If thou be merciful,
Open the tomb, lay me with Juliet. [*Dies.*]
ROMEO In faith, I will. Let me peruse this face.
Mercutio's kinsman, noble County Paris!   75
What said my man, when my betossèd soul
Did not attend him as we rode? I think
He told me Paris should have married Juliet.
Said he not so? or did I dream it so?
Or am I mad, hearing him talk of Juliet,   80
To think it was so? O give me thy hand,
One writ with me in sour misfortune's book!
I'll bury thee in a triumphant grave.
A grave? O no, a lantern, slaughtered youth;
For here lies Juliet, and her beauty makes   85
This vault a feasting presence full of light.
Death, lie thou there, by a dead man interred.
                    [*Laying Paris in the tomb.*]

Romeo gazes on Juliet and admires her beauty. He asks Tybalt for forgiveness, and imagines that Death wants Juliet as a lover. To prevent that, and determined to join her in death, he drinks the poison.

1 Romeo's last words (in pairs or individually)

These are the last words Romeo speaks in the play, and he plays with images of death, fateful stars, law and shipwreck. Read the lines through several times, speaking them in different ways. If you choose to work with a partner, share the lines between you. Pick out the lines or phrases that have most appeal for you. Express those lines or phrases in ways that you find imaginatively satisfying.

2 Direct Romeo (in pairs)

Step into role as director and advise the actor playing Romeo how to deliver his final speech. Write the notes you would give him. Identify the different sections of the speech, then suggest actions, expressions, etc. for each. One way of dividing up the speech is: lines 88–91 (end at 'light'ning'); lines 91–6; lines 97–101 (end at 'cousin'); lines 101–5; lines 106–12 (end at 'flesh'); lines 112–18; lines 119–20.

3 Imagery: personifying Death

There are four personifications of Death in Romeo's lines. Identify them and write a sentence on each suggesting what picture or association it conjures up in your mind.

4 What if Juliet wakes?

Romeo's words possess a terrible irony. Unlike the audience, he does not know that Juliet lives. In some productions he sees Juliet showing signs of life just before he dies. This increases the irony of Romeo's last moments as he realises the tragic waste of his life. What do you think of such staging?

---

keepers gaolers, prison warders
light'ning enlivening, relief
ensign flag
paramour lover
set up . . . rest make my full, final commitment (an image from a card game)
yoke restraint

engrossing all-owning ('seal' and 'bargain' echo Romeo's legal imagery of an everlasting contract with Death)
conduct i.e. the poison (but notice that 'conduct', 'guide', 'pilot' and 'bark' [ship] all emphasise Romeo's image of life as a sea journey ending in disaster).

How oft when men are at the point of death
Have they been merry, which their keepers call
A light'ning before death! O how may I   90
Call this a light'ning? O my love, my wife,
Death, that hath sucked the honey of thy breath,
Hath had no power yet upon thy beauty:
Thou art not conquered, beauty's ensign yet
Is crimson in thy lips and in thy cheeks,   95
And Death's pale flag is not advancèd there.
Tybalt, liest thou there in thy bloody sheet?
O, what more favour can I do to thee
Than with that hand that cut thy youth in twain
To sunder his that was thine enemy?   100
Forgive me, cousin. Ah, dear Juliet,
Why art thou yet so fair? Shall I believe
That unsubstantial Death is amorous,
And that the lean abhorrèd monster keeps
Thee here in dark to be his paramour?   105
For fear of that, I still will stay with thee,
And never from this palace of dim night
Depart again. Here, here will I remain
With worms that are thy chambermaids; O here
Will I set up my everlasting rest,   110
And shake the yoke of inauspicious stars
From this world-wearied flesh. Eyes, look your last!
Arms, take your last embrace! and, lips, O you
The doors of breath, seal with a righteous kiss
A dateless bargain to engrossing Death!   115
Come, bitter conduct, come, unsavoury guide!
Thou desperate pilot, now at once run on
The dashing rocks thy seasick weary bark!
Here's to my love! [*Drinks.*] O true apothecary!
Thy drugs are quick. Thus with a kiss I die. [*Dies.*]   120

Balthasar tells Friar Lawrence that Romeo is in the tomb. Entering the vault, the Friar finds the dead Romeo and Paris. Juliet begins to awaken.

1 Speak the lines (in pairs)

Take roles as Friar Lawrence and Balthasar. Read aloud their dialogue in lines 121–39.

How should these lines be spoken? They are shared between Friar Lawrence and Balthasar. There's a theatrical convention that when a line is shared there should be no pauses between the speakers. From your own experience of speaking the words, do you agree?

2 Urgency and fear in the Friar's words (in pairs)

Take each line the Friar says on the opposite page, but say aloud only words and phrases that create an atmosphere of urgency and fear.

You may find it helpful to know that if someone 'stumbled', it would be considered by Elizabethans to be a bad omen (if you 'stumbled', things would begin to go wrong).

3 Balthasar's puzzling words (in pairs)

Balthasar has such a small part that he is often overlooked in theatre productions. Yet he says some curious things to the Friar. Discuss what you think about them:

- 'one that knows you well' – but does he? Friar Lawrence does not seem to know he's Romeo's servant at line 129
- 'half an hour' – does that seem likely?
- why does Balthasar say he dreamed of Romeo and Paris fighting?

Remember: there's no 'right' answer to these puzzles. Talk together about possibilities that you think are dramatically and imaginatively satisfying.

***Enter* Friar** (notice the action shifts to outside the tomb. See p. 180)
grubs worms
intents intended actions
unthrifty unfortunate, unlucky

masterless and gory abandoned and bloodstained
steeped covered
unkind unnatural
lamentable chance sorrowful accident

Enter FRIAR [LAWRENCE] *with lantern, crow, and spade.*

FRIAR LAWRENCE   Saint Francis be my speed! how oft tonight
Have my old feet stumbled at graves! Who's there?
BALTHASAR   Here's one, a friend, and one that knows you well.
FRIAR LAWRENCE   Bliss be upon you! Tell me, good my friend,
What torch is yond that vainly lends his light   125
To grubs and eyeless skulls? As I discern,
It burneth in the Capels' monument.
BALTHASAR   It doth so, holy sir, and there's my master,
One that you love.
FRIAR LAWRENCE   Who is it?
BALTHASAR   Romeo.
FRIAR LAWRENCE   How long hath he been there?
BALTHASAR   Full half an hour.   130
FRIAR LAWRENCE   Go with me to the vault.
BALTHASAR   I dare not, sir.
My master knows not but I am gone hence,
And fearfully did menace me with death
If I did stay to look on his intents.
FRIAR LAWRENCE   Stay then, I'll go alone. Fear comes upon me.   135
O, much I fear some ill unthrifty thing.
BALTHASAR   As I did sleep under this yew tree here,
I dreamt my master and another fought,
And that my master slew him.   [*Retires*]
FRIAR LAWRENCE   Romeo!
[*Friar stoops and looks on the blood and weapons.*]
Alack, alack, what blood is this which stains   140
The stony entrance of this sepulchre?
What mean these masterless and gory swords
To lie discoloured by this place of peace?
[*Enters the tomb.*]
Romeo! O, pale! Who else? What, Paris too?
And steeped in blood? Ah, what an unkind hour   145
Is guilty of this lamentable chance!
[*Juliet rises.*]
The lady stirs.

Romeo and Juliet

Friar Lawrence, fearful of discovery, leaves the tomb, begging Juliet to go with him. She refuses, and stabs herself because she prefers to join Romeo in death. The Watch enter.

1 Friar Lawrence: coward? Or . . . ? (in small groups)

Friar Lawrence tries to take Juliet away, to hide her in a convent. But when she refuses, he simply abandons her. His action increases the sense of Juliet's isolation: she must act her final scene completely alone. Is Friar Lawrence's action callous and self-centred? To help your thinking read lines 151–9 to each other, each person speaking a sentence then handing on. Repeat several times, a different person beginning each reading.

Talk about what these lines tell you about the Friar at this moment: his state of mind, his motives, and his feelings for Juliet.

2 Juliet's final moments

Shakespeare gives Juliet a much shorter 'death speech' than Romeo.

Either show how you would stage her final words to greatest dramatic effect.

Or step into role as Shakespeare and write an additional eight lines for her before she speaks line 169.

You may find it helpful to refer to page 201 and to the picture at the bottom of p. xi in the colour section.

3 'Rust' or 'rest'?

Some critics argue that Shakespeare actually wrote 'rest', not 'rust' at line 170. Which word do you think is more appropriate and why?

4 Should the play end here? (in pairs)

In the nineteenth century, productions often ended with the death of Juliet at line 170. Talk together about what you think a production of the play would gain and lose from ending at this point.

---

comfortable comforting
timeless untimely
churl brute (but how do you think Juliet says the word?)
Haply maybe

restorative medicine (the kiss will 'cure' her of life and restore her to Romeo)
attach arrest

JULIET O comfortable Friar, where is my lord?
　　　I do remember well where I should be;
　　　And there I am. Where is my Romeo?　　　　　　　150
　　　　　　　[*Noise within.*]
FRIAR LAWRENCE I hear some noise, lady. Come from that nest
　　　Of death, contagion, and unnatural sleep.
　　　A greater power than we can contradict
　　　Hath thwarted our intents. Come, come away.
　　　Thy husband in thy bosom there lies dead;　　　　155
　　　And Paris too. Come, I'll dispose of thee
　　　Among a sisterhood of holy nuns.
　　　Stay not to question, for the Watch is coming.
　　　Come go, good Juliet, I dare no longer stay.　　*Exit*
JULIET Go get thee hence, for I will not away.　　　　160
　　　What's here? a cup closed in my true love's hand?
　　　Poison I see hath been his timeless end.
　　　O churl, drunk all, and left no friendly drop
　　　To help me after? I will kiss thy lips,
　　　Haply some poison yet doth hang on them,　　　　165
　　　To make me die with a restorative.
　　　Thy lips are warm.
CAPTAIN OF THE WATCH [*Within*] Lead, boy, which way?
JULIET Yea, noise? Then I'll be brief. O happy dagger,
　　　　　　　[*Taking Romeo's dagger.*]
　　　This is thy sheath;
　　　　　　　[*Stabs herself.*]
　　　　　　　there rust, and let me die.　　　　170
　　　[*Falls on Romeo's body and dies.*]

　　　Enter [*Paris's*] *Boy and* WATCH.

PAGE This is the place, there where the torch doth burn.
CAPTAIN OF THE WATCH
　　　The ground is bloody, search about the churchyard.
　　　Go, some of you, whoe'er you find attach.
　　　　　　　[*Exeunt some of the Watch*]
　　　　　[*The Captain enters the tomb and returns.*]
　　　Pitiful sight! here lies the County slain,
　　　And Juliet bleeding, warm, and newly dead,　　　175
　　　Who here hath lain this two days buried.

Balthasar and the Friar are arrested by the Watch. The Prince and the Capulets enter, disturbed by the commotion and shouting. The Captain tells what he knows.

1 The Captain (in small groups)

For a brief time, the Captain takes command of the stage. Speak all his lines from line 168 to line 201. Then talk together about whether you think an actor should attempt to give the Captain a distinct personality, or whether he should be simply an anonymous officer who makes no personal impact on the audience.

2 The Prince arrives

Look back at the two other occasions when Prince Escales has appeared (Act 1 Scene 1, line 72 and Act 3 Scene 1, line 132). What do those two occasions have in common with this one?

Romeo grieves over Juliet. Now the tragic consequences of the feud between the Montagues and Capulets are about to become clear to everyone in Verona ('all run / With open outcry toward our monument').

---

ground Even the Captain cannot resist a pun. His first 'ground' means 'earth', his second 'ground' means 'reason'

circumstance information
descry perceive, understand

Go tell the Prince, run to the Capulets,
Raise up the Montagues; some others search.

[Exeunt others of the Watch]

We see the ground whereon these woes do lie,
But the true ground of all these piteous woes   180
We cannot without circumstance descry.

Enter [one of the Watch with] Romeo's man [Balthasar].

SECOND WATCHMAN
Here's Romeo's man, we found him in the churchyard.
CAPTAIN OF THE WATCH
Hold him in safety till the Prince come hither.

Enter Friar [Lawrence] and another Watchman.

THIRD WATCHMAN Here is a friar that trembles, sighs, and weeps.
We took this mattock and this spade from him,   185
As he was coming from this churchyard's side.
CAPTAIN OF THE WATCH A great suspicion. Stay the friar too.

Enter the PRINCE [with others].

PRINCE What misadventure is so early up,
That calls our person from our morning rest?

Enter Capels [CAPULET, LADY CAPULET].

CAPULET What should it be that is so shrieked abroad?   190
LADY CAPULET O, the people in the street cry 'Romeo',
Some 'Juliet', and some 'Paris', and all run
With open outcry toward our monument.
PRINCE What fear is this which startles in your ears?
CAPTAIN OF THE WATCH
Sovereign, here lies the County Paris slain,   195
And Romeo dead, and Juliet, dead before,
Warm and new killed.
PRINCE Search, seek, and know how this foul murder comes.
CAPTAIN OF THE WATCH
Here is a friar, and slaughtered Romeo's man,
With instruments upon them, fit to open   200
These dead men's tombs.

The Capulets and Montague enter the tomb to view their dead children. The Prince promises to investigate, and to punish wrongdoers with death. At the Prince's command, Friar Lawrence begins to explain.

1 Another stage set problem

As the Capulets and Montague enter the tomb to see the dead bodies, the practical problem again arises of showing both 'outside' and 'inside' the tomb (see pp. 180 and 182). And once again, modern productions solve the problem by means of a simple, non-realistic setting. But suggest what the other characters might be doing as the Capulets speak their lines 202–7.

2 Lady Montague's death

Montague's announcement that his wife is dead adds an extra layer of poignancy to the play. But Shakespeare may have inserted it in order to free the actor playing Lady Montague to take another part in this scene. Remembering that she would have been played by a boy actor in Shakespeare's time, which character (now on stage) do you think is being 'doubled'?

3 An insensitive Prince? (in pairs)

The Prince's three lines (lines 208–9 and 213) seem very unsympathetic towards Montague's feelings. Explore different ways of saying and staging Prince Escales's lines. Try making him sympathetic to Montague. For example, might he offer a consoling hand? Then make him hard and unfeeling.

4 A tableau of the death scene (in groups of ten or more)

Prepare a tableau to show just how every character is behaving at the Prince's line 216 ('Seal up . . .'). Hold the frozen moment for thirty seconds. Other students identify each character. Which characters are easy to portray and identify and which are more challenging? Why?

---

hath mistane has mistaken (is in the wrong place)
his house its sheath
liege lord
thou untaught (Montague rebukes Romeo)

press . . . grave die before your father
general chief judge
impeach and purge accuse and find innocent

[*Capulet and Lady Capulet enter the tomb.*]
CAPULET O heavens! O wife, look how our daughter bleeds!
This dagger hath mistane, for lo his house
Is empty on the back of Montague,
And it mis-sheathèd in my daughter's bosom!   205
LADY CAPULET O me, this sight of death is as a bell
That warns my old age to a sepulchre.
[*They return from the tomb.*]

Enter MONTAGUE.

PRINCE Come, Montague, for thou art early up
To see thy son and heir now early down.
MONTAGUE Alas, my liege, my wife is dead tonight;   210
Grief of my son's exile hath stopped her breath.
What further woe conspires against mine age?
PRINCE Look and thou shalt see.
[*Montague enters the tomb and returns.*]
MONTAGUE O thou untaught! what manners is in this,
To press before thy father to a grave?   215
PRINCE Seal up the mouth of outrage for a while,
Till we can clear these ambiguities,
And know their spring, their head, their true descent,
And then will I be general of your woes,
And lead you even to death. Mean time forbear,   220
And let mischance be slave to patience.
Bring forth the parties of suspicion.
FRIAR LAWRENCE I am the greatest, able to do least,
Yet most suspected, as the time and place
Doth make against me, of this direful murder;   225
And here I stand both to impeach and purge
Myself condemnèd and myself excused.
PRINCE Then say at once what thou dost know in this.
FRIAR LAWRENCE I will be brief, for my short date of breath
Is not so long as is a tedious tale.   230
Romeo, there dead, was husband to that Juliet,
And she, there dead, that Romeo's faithful wife:

Friar Lawrence tells his story to the Prince: the marriage, the killing of Tybalt, Romeo's banishment, Capulet's attempt to force Juliet to marry Paris, the Friar's desperate plan . . . and much more.

1 Friar Lawrence's explanation of events

Friar Lawrence's story (lines 229–66) provides a valuable summary of events, even though it leaves out his reasons for acting as he did (to unite the families). The language is different from that of much of the rest of the play. It is direct, and easy to follow. There are no puns or wordplay and little imagery. Sometimes this long explanation (which the Friar describes as 'brief'!) is cut in productions of the play. The two following activities will help your understanding of the story (and the action of the play).

a **Point out who is involved** (in groups of eight) Each person takes a part (Friar, Romeo, Juliet, Tybalt, Paris, Friar John, the Nurse, Capulet). Stand in a circle. The Friar slowly reads the lines. Everyone points to whoever is mentioned, for example to the Friar on 'I'; to Romeo and Juliet on 'them' and 'their', and so on. You'll find it fun, and it will vividly remind you of the story. If you want a technical word for this pointing activity, it is *deixis*, pronounced 'deyesis' or 'dakesis'.

b **Act out the story** (in groups of any size) Act out the whole story, showing each action described (for example, marriage, Tybalt's death, Romeo's banishment, and so on). The Friar packs in a tremendous amount of detail: there are at least thirty incidents to 'show'. Try to enact as many as possible.

An alternative is to divide up the different parts of the Friar's explanation. Each group takes a part of the tale to 'show'. For three groups, the sections could be lines 231–42, lines 243–52 and lines 252–64.

---

pined languished, longed for
perforce by force
privy in the secret

ought anything
Miscarried went wrong

I married them, and their stol'n marriage day
Was Tybalt's doomsday, whose untimely death
Banished the new-made bridegroom from this city,   235
For whom, and not for Tybalt, Juliet pined.
You, to remove that siege of grief from her,
Betrothed and would have married her perforce
To County Paris. Then comes she to me,
And with wild looks bid me devise some mean   240
To rid her from this second marriage,
Or in my cell there would she kill herself.
Then gave I her (so tutored by my art)
A sleeping potion, which so took effect
As I intended, for it wrought on her   245
The form of death. Mean time I writ to Romeo
That he should hither come as this dire night
To help to take her from her borrowed grave,
Being the time the potion's force should cease.
But he which bore my letter, Friar John,   250
Was stayed by accident, and yesternight
Returned my letter back. Then all alone,
At the prefixèd hour of her waking,
Came I to take her from her kindred's vault,
Meaning to keep her closely at my cell,   255
Till I conveniently could send to Romeo.
But when I came, some minute ere the time
Of her awakening, here untimely lay
The noble Paris and true Romeo dead.
She wakes, and I entreated her come forth   260
And bear this work of heaven with patience.
But then a noise did scare me from the tomb,
And she too desperate would not go with me,
But as it seems, did violence on herself.
All this I know, and to the marriage   265
Her nurse is privy; and if ought in this
Miscarried by my fault, let my old life
Be sacrificed, some hour before his time,
Unto the rigour of severest law.

Balthasar and Paris's Page tell what they know. The Prince reads Romeo's letter, then calls Capulet and Montague to look on the deadly results of their quarrels.

1 Speak, then act out the three stories (in groups of four to six)

The stories of Balthasar and the Page, and the Prince's report of Romeo's letter are, like the Friar's account, plain narrative, simply expressed.

a In what tone of voice do Balthasar and the Page speak? Fearfully, afraid of punishment? Or . . . ? Experiment with different styles.

b Take the stories of Balthasar (lines 272–7), the Page (lines 281–5) and the Prince (lines 286–90). Act out as much detail as you can of one or more of the stories. You will find each story has at least six or seven 'scenes' that you can re-create.

2 Why include the stories? (in pairs)

Talk together about whether you think these stories add to the play, or could be safely cut from a stage production. If you were directing the play, would you include them? Give reasons for your decision.

3 Write Romeo's letter

What is in Romeo's letter to his father? The Prince reads a brief outline (lines 286–90). Write the full contents of the letter. Try to express Romeo's state of mind at the moment he wrote it, shortly after hearing of Juliet's death.

4 'Heaven finds means to kill your joys with love!'

Do you agree that 'heaven' has killed Romeo and Juliet? Or do you think the tragedy is caused by other reasons?

Pages 212–13 will help you explore why Romeo and Juliet died.

---

still always
in post speedily (post-haste)
make good confirm
tidings news

therewithal with the poison
for winking at your discords for turning a blind eye to your quarrels
kinsmen Mercutio and Paris

PRINCE We still have known thee for a holy man.   270
        Where's Romeo's man? what can he say to this?
BALTHASAR I brought my master news of Juliet's death,
        And then in post he came from Mantua
        To this same place, to this same monument.
        This letter he early bid me give his father,   275
        And threatened me with death, going in the vault,
        If I departed not and left him there.
PRINCE Give me the letter, I will look on it.
        Where is the County's page that raised the Watch?
        Sirrah, what made your master in this place?   280
PAGE He came with flowers to strew his lady's grave,
        And bid me stand aloof, and so I did.
        Anon comes one with light to ope the tomb,
        And by and by my master drew on him,
        And then I ran away to call the Watch.   285
PRINCE This letter doth make good the Friar's words,
        Their course of love, the tidings of her death;
        And here he writes that he did buy a poison
        Of a poor pothecary, and therewithal
        Came to this vault to die, and lie with Juliet.   290
        Where be these enemies? Capulet, Montague?
        See what a scourge is laid upon your hate,
        That heaven finds means to kill your joys with love!
        And I for winking at your discords too
        Have lost a brace of kinsmen. All are punished.   295

Capulet and Montague make up their quarrel. They promise to set up a golden statue of Juliet and Romeo. The Prince closes the play promising pardon for some and punishment for others.

---

1 The golden statue of Romeo and Juliet (in small groups)

You have been commissioned to design the statue. Will it look like the effigies on Elizabethan tombs found in many English churches, or will it be some other design? Talk together about possibilities and then prepare a tableau to show your statue.

After this, each group member sketches the design and adds a suitable inscription at the base of the statue.

2 But is the feud really ended? (in pairs)

Do you think that a promised golden statue really marks the end of the bitter feud? Experiment with Montague's and Capulet's lines 296–304. Can the lines be spoken and acted in ways that show the quarrel will continue? For example, is Montague trying to 'outbid' Capulet, and does Capulet respond by showing he is as wealthy as Montague?

3 Final image (in small groups)

Talk about the last image you wish the audience to see (see the pictures on p. xii in the colour section). Will it be an empty stage? If so, work out how you will get everyone off, including the bodies.

Or you may want the audience to see a final tableau. What is it? Rehearse, and show the class your image of the final moment of the play before the lights fade.

4 Pardoned and punished (a whole-class activity)

Who is responsible for the tragedy? Arrange a trial of some of the major figures who you think might be accused of having a part in the deaths. Appoint a judge, prosecuting and defending counsels. Both sides will be able to call witnesses if they wish. This activity will take time to prepare, so appoint a 'trial day' and do the necessary preparations.

---

jointure marriage settlement (sum of money) made by the bridegroom's father to the bride. (All Capulet now asks from Montague is a handshake and reconciliation)

at such rate be set be held at such high value

Exeunt omnes stage direction meaning everyone leaves the stage

CAPULET O brother Montague, give me thy hand.
        This is my daughter's jointure, for no more
        Can I demand.
MONTAGUE   But I can give thee more,
        For I will raise her statue in pure gold,
        That whiles Verona by that name is known,   300
        There shall no figure at such rate be set
        As that of true and faithful Juliet.
CAPULET As rich shall Romeo's by his lady's lie,
        Poor sacrifices of our enmity!
PRINCE A glooming peace this morning with it brings,   305
        The sun for sorrow will not show his head.
        Go hence to have more talk of these sad things;
        Some shall be pardoned, and some punishèd:
        For never was a story of more woe
        Than this of Juliet and her Romeo.   310
                                  [*Exeunt omnes*]

Looking back at the play
Activities for groups or individuals

1 Show the whole play

Take the Prince's last six lines (lines 305–10) and the Prologue's fourteen lines (on p. 3). Put them together and work out actions that show the development of the whole play. For this activity it is helpful to have a group of ten or more with a narrator.

2 Capulet's dream – the ghosts return

Shakespeare seemed to be fond of ghosts. He wrote some memorable ghost scenes. In *King Richard III*, for instance, all the dead come back in a dream to haunt King Richard.

Work in small groups. Make up a short play entitled 'Capulet's dream' (or 'nightmare'). It brings back all those who have died in the play. You might have each ghost telling why they died, and how they now feel about the feuding families. Don't be afraid to let your imagination run!

3 Obituaries

You have been commissioned to write the obituaries of Romeo Montague and Juliet Capulet for *The Verona Herald*. Talk together about what might be included in an obituary; then settle down to write.

4 Friar Lawrence writes his memoirs

'It's ten years now since the deaths of Romeo and Juliet . . .'. What does the Friar think, looking back over this distance of time? He has had to face up to a cruel irony: he married Romeo and Juliet, hoping that their marriage would end the feud between the Montagues and Capulets. But it was their deaths that caused Montague and Capulet to shake hands. The Friar also has to cope with his abandonment of Juliet in the tomb. What does he now think of that? And what has he been doing in those ten long years? Imagine yourself as Friar Lawrence and write your memoirs.

5 The story of the play – in colour

The pictures in the colour section 'tell the story of the play'. But what is missed out? Suggest three other pictures you would add, giving your reasons.

Juliet's anguish is evident as she cradles the head of the dead Romeo. In the course of the play she has matured from innocent young girl to tragic heroine. She has experienced brief happiness of boundless love, harsh rejection by her parents, betrayal by her Nurse, and the torture of fears aroused by Friar Lawrence's dangerous plan. But she has found the courage to endure the horrors of the Capulet tomb, and now she determines to slay herself, rather than live without Romeo. Use the pictures and script in this edition to help you write an extended essay that traces Juliet's emotional journey through the play.

The story of Romeo and Juliet

There is no limit to the number of ways you can tell the story of Romeo and Juliet. You could write it in a single sentence:

A boy and a girl, from families that hate each other bitterly, fall in love, but everything goes wrong for them and they kill themselves rather than be parted.

Or you might write it in a paragraph, putting in more detail:

The Montagues and Capulets are the two chief families of Verona. For years, they have been enemies in a bitter feud. Their teenage children, Romeo, a Montague, and Juliet, a Capulet, meet by accident at a grand party and fall instantly in love. They marry in secret, but cannot escape the consequences of their families' savage quarrel. Romeo's best friend Mercutio is killed by Tybalt of the Capulets. In revenge, Romeo kills Tybalt and is banished from Verona. Friar Lawrence devises dangerous plans to help Romeo and Juliet live together in happiness, but his schemes go terribly wrong. Romeo, believing Juliet is dead, kills himself to join her in death. Juliet, finding Romeo dead, also kills herself, not wishing to live without him. Their deaths end the quarrels of the Montagues and Capulets.

Or you could tell a much longer story, beginning like this:

Long ago in the Italian city of Verona lived two young people, Romeo and Juliet. They were the children of the city's two leading families, the Montagues and the Capulets . . .

The story you tell depends on many things. Here are just a few:

- how much detail you wish to include (Rosaline? the musicians?)
- the audience for your retelling (young children? examiners?)
- the style in which you tell it (factual? nursery tale? melodrama?)
- the reasons why you tell it (to inform? entertain? teach a moral?)
- how much imagination you use (to add extra scenes, or characters' secret thoughts, to Shakespeare's version).

Remember, there is not one single 'right' story. Every story is a retelling, a different way of recounting what happens. Shakespeare used his imagination to create his own dramatic version of the story he had read. For example, Mercutio is almost entirely Shakespeare's invention, and Paris does not die in other versions.

Is *Romeo and Juliet* true?

There is no simple answer to that question. It all depends on what you mean by 'true'. In thirteenth-century Italy there certainly were two Italian families, the Montecchi and the Capelletti, locked in political struggle. But the Montecchi lived in Verona, and the Capelletti lived in Cremona, sixty miles away! No one knows whether the families had children called Romeo and Juliet.

The story of two young lovers from opposing families was very popular in Italy and France. Myths and folktales about them existed for hundreds of years before Shakespeare. He based his play on a poem published two years before he was born. That poem was an English translation of a French translation of an Italian version!

Although it's probably not true historically, *Romeo and Juliet* is 'true' in other ways. Because it has lasted so long, and because people still find it fascinating, it has a truth in human experience. In every age, young people have fallen in love against their parents' wishes. Where families or societies are in conflict, troubles always lie in store for a boy and a girl from opposing camps who wish to marry. Poets, playwrights and novelists have been irresistibly drawn to write about the plight of such young lovers.

Activities

To help you deepen your understanding of the story of *Romeo and Juliet*, try one or more of the following activities:

1 Write the story as:
   - *either* a mini-saga (in exactly fifty words)
   - *or* a fairytale for young children
   - *or* a short modern novel set in today's times.
2 Collect retellings of the story from theatre programmes or from a book of Shakespeare's stories. Make a list of what's been left out of each. Write an evaluation of one version.
3 Make a list of the ways in which Shakespeare's play is different from any story about Romeo and Juliet.
4 Talk together about the ways in which *Romeo and Juliet* is 'true'.
5 Research other examples of young lovers experiencing huge difficulties because of a clash between their families, cultures or societies.
6 Best of all, act out the play! Form an acting company to rehearse and stage your own version. It can be as long or as short a performance as you wish.

Characters

Juliet, when she first appears, says very little. She is only thirteen, and as the Nurse and her mother talk about her age, she seems innocent and docile. Sometimes she is played as almost tongue-tied, reluctant to take part in adult conversation. She appears to respect her mother's authority. But this thirteen-year-old girl, seemingly so quiet and modest, matures rapidly in her meetings with Romeo. At their very first meeting she allows him to kiss her, and when she appears on the balcony, she is full of longing for him. Throughout the 'balcony' scene she takes the lead, speaking twice as many lines as Romeo. She speaks of her love ('My true-love passion'), and declares it in a memorable image (Act 2 Scene 2, lines 133–5):

> My bounty is as boundless as the sea,
> My love as deep; the more I give to thee
> The more I have, for both are infinite.

Juliet even takes the lead in proposing marriage, and arranges (through the Nurse) to be married the very next day. Her swift 'growing up' into independence is evident in her defiance of her father's demand that she marry Paris. Visiting Friar Lawrence, she displays remarkable courage, first in her determination to kill herself rather than marry Paris, then in willingly accepting the Friar's alarmingly hazardous plan. She returns home and deceives her father, but becomes isolated when the Nurse lets her down, advising her to marry Paris. But even in her isolation she bravely enacts the Friar's plan and drinks the 'poison' that will make her seem as dead. She displays resolute fearlessness when, unwilling to live without Romeo, she kills herself.

Romeo, in his first appearance, declares his love for Rosaline (whom he does not name). This makes him seem a stock character of traditional drama: the melancholy and moody young lover who is rejected by an unattainable woman. But when he meets Juliet there is a progressive deepening of his character (even though evidence of his immaturity and early style of speaking are sometimes found later in the play). The first sign that he will develop into a tragic figure is just before he enters Capulet's mansion for the party at which he will meet Juliet. He fearfully broods on the future (Act 1 Scene 4, lines 106–7):

> my mind misgives
> Some consequence yet hanging in the stars

Although Romeo grows in maturity, he is hasty and impetuous. His moods quickly change. He falls in love at first sight, marries Juliet the next day, and revenges Mercutio's death by immediately slaying Tybalt. His language is sometimes hyperbolic ('that vast shore washed with the farthest sea'), sometimes that of the traditional hero of Revenge Tragedy ('And fire-eyed fury be my conduct now!'). In Friar Lawrence's cell he becomes emotionally childlike and distraught. He seems to lose all self-control in his hysterical outbursts and actions. In Mantua, learning of Juliet's death, his impulsiveness is again evident in his passionate 'then I defy you, stars!' He instantly resolves to kill himself in the tomb with her. But although his state of mind can swing to extremes, his dialogues with Juliet, and his soliloquy before he takes poison, display maturity and his unflinching commitment to Juliet.

Friar Lawrence is like a father figure for Romeo, who confides in him, rather than in his own father, Montague. But the Friar is a puzzling character. His language and actions are open to very different interpretations. Some productions have shown him as shrewd and level-headed, concerned to heal the breach between the Montagues and Capulets. In other productions he has been played as cunning and dishonest, and in others as a bungling, insecure schemer.

On his first appearance he seems a wise moral commentator as he speaks of everything having the capacity for good or evil. He advises caution ('Wisely and slow'), and wishes to use the marriage of Romeo and Juliet to bring peace to Verona. But his deeds do not match his words. He acts hastily, breaking church law by marrying Romeo and Juliet in secret. He devises a plan to deceive Juliet's parents, from whom he conceals her marriage. He risks poisoning Juliet, and abandons her in the tomb at her moment of greatest need. His impulsive actions help cause the death of the lovers.

The Nurse is Shakespeare's development of a character type in classical Greek and Roman drama: the garrulous and bawdy servant. She is a surrogate mother and close confidante of Juliet, for whom she seems to have genuine affection. She acts as a go-between for the lovers, helping Juliet deceive her parents. Her earthy, rambling, repetitive style gives her great stage presence. She brings humour to the play in her frank

enjoyment of sexuality. Her long description of Juliet's childhood is almost always a highlight of any production.

The Nurse sometimes appears to be the most sympathetic character in the play. But for all her likeability, and her close relationship with Juliet, her advice that Juliet should marry Paris seems like a heartless act of betrayal. It leaves Juliet quite isolated.

Mercutio is perhaps the most complex character in the play. Romeo gives a very accurate description of him: 'A gentleman . . . that loves to hear himself talk'. He is an entertainer, clever and witty, but also earthy and coarse. He loves playing with language, particularly when he can give it sexual double meanings. In contrast to Romeo's idealisation of love, Mercutio mocks it, seeing it only as sex. His flights of fancy are full of dazzling invention, but much of his imaginative creativity can also be seen as feverish and neurotic. Examples are his Queen Mab speech, and his dismissal of foreign sword-fencing techniques ('The pox of such antic, lisping, affecting phantasimes').

Mercutio feels intense friendship for Romeo, and possesses a strong sense of male honour. He seems to be always on the edge of looking for a fight. His courage in defending the honour of his friend Romeo results in his death. Some people argue that Mercutio becomes such an engaging character that Shakespeare thought it necessary to kill him off before he completely dominated the play. There is a sense of loss at his death, but perhaps Shakespeare made Mercutio's early death dramatically inevitable as the key to the tragedy, spurring Romeo to revenge.

Tybalt speaks only thirty-six lines in the play, but they create a very consistent character: a man full of anger and aggression. He seems the 'choleric' (angry, fiery) figure of traditional drama, the hot-headed quarreller who feels only rage and a mistaken sense of honour.

Capulet appears at first to be friendly and generous. At the party he reminisces about his youth, and is determined to stop Tybalt making trouble. But he shows a different side to his character when Juliet refuses to marry Paris. He becomes short-tempered and tyrannical, exploding in uncontrollable fury when Juliet refuses to obey him. But when she dies (both in pretence and in reality) he is overcome with grief and remorse.

Lady Capulet seems distant from her daughter. She displays little or no maternal affection. She lacks sympathy for Juliet's feelings ('tell him so yourself'), when Juliet refuses to marry Paris. And she shows little sign of taking Juliet's part or comforting her when she is the target of Capulet's rage. But like Capulet, she too exhibits heartbreak at Juliet's death.

Paris, the Prince and Benvolio have important functions in the design of the play. Paris is the rival suitor to Romeo. Benvolio, the peacemaker, is Romeo's trusted confidant. The Prince is a kind of nemesis for Romeo, sentencing him to banishment. Each character dramatically 'punctuates' the play. Benvolio's narratives recapitulate the action. The Prince's three appearances are always at a moment of crisis, and they structure the play, marking its opening, midpoint and end. Paris's few appearances have consequences for both Romeo and Juliet, hastening their tragedy.

Activities

1 Collect examples of a character's language. Follow a character through the play. Collect lines that you think are typical of him or her. What do those lines tell you about the character? Which six words best describe him or her?

2 Collect examples of a character's actions. Actions, as much as words, are very revealing of character. Make a list of what your character actually does throughout the play.

3 Explore a character's motives in one of the following ways:
   - **'Hot seating'** (in small groups) One person steps into the role of the character. Group members ask questions of the 'why did you do this?' type.
   - **'Psychiatrist's couch'** (in pairs or small groups) One person becomes the character and is psychoanalysed by their partner or other members of the group.
   - **'Autobiography'** Imagine yourself as the character. Write your life story.
   - **'Biography'** Write a biography of a character. Remember, a biographer's own point of view is important. Biographies of Romeo written by Juliet, or Tybalt or Benvolio would be very different.

4 Study the illustrations of Romeo or Juliet in this edition. Which comes closest to your idea of each of them? Write reasons for your selection.

5 Using the information in this section (pp. 204–8), select a character and write an extended essay tracing their progress through the play. Include quotations and examples of their actions.

The oppositions of *Romeo and Juliet*

Oppositions and contrasts abound in *Romeo and Juliet*. You could think of them as themes of the play. The action begins with a violent clash between the feuding families. Throughout the play, divisions and conflicts beset the doomed lovers.

Light versus dark

The play is alive with images of light and darkness. The flash and sparkle of eyes, jewels, stars, fire, lightning, torches, exploding gunpowder, the sun and moon, are set against a darker world of night, clouds, smoke and the blackness of the tomb: 'More light and light, more dark and dark our woes!' Juliet, waiting for Romeo, aches for the sun to set 'And bring in cloudy night immediately'. Romeo sees Juliet's beauty flooding the darkness of the tomb with brilliance: 'her beauty makes / This vault a feasting presence full of light'.

Fate versus free will

Chorus opens the play with a mention of Fate: 'A pair of star-crossed lovers'. The belief that Fate determines our lives echoes through the play. Romeo fears that Fate has unhappy things in store for him if he goes to Capulet's feast: 'my mind misgives / Some consequence yet hanging in the stars'. Juliet fears what inevitably lies ahead as she parts from Romeo: 'Methinks I see thee now, thou art so low, / As one dead in the bottom of a tomb.' Romeo and Juliet struggle to break free of what Fate threatens in dreams and premonitions. 'Then I defy you, stars!' is Romeo's defiant challenge when he hears of Juliet's death.

Love versus hate

Here's much to do with hate, but more with love

Act 1 Scene 1, line 166

The love of Romeo and Juliet is threatened by a society full of hate. Juliet fears for Romeo's safety at the hands of her kinsmen: 'If they do see thee, they will murder thee.' The hateful, hate-full honour code that governs the feuding mafiosi of Verona will destroy Romeo and Juliet, Mercutio, Tybalt and Paris. Love, in Verona's masculine society, is about domination. The macho servants of Capulet joke about sex in violent, aggressive terms. The selflessness of Romeo and Juliet, equal in love, and willing to die for each other, is in strong contrast to the hate that fills Verona.

Death versus life

Death is never far away in the divided world of Verona. The old people brood over it: 'death's the end of all', 'we were born to die'. Young lives are abruptly cut short. Images of death pervade the language: 'death-marked', 'untimely death', 'death-bed', 'canker death', 'Cold death', 'death-darting eye', 'cruel Death', 'detestable Death', 'present death'. Death even becomes a person, shutting up the doors of life, eating the living, fighting on the battlefield. Most memorable of all is the vision that haunts the play, of Death as Juliet's bridegroom: 'Death is my son-in-law, Death is my heir, / My daughter he hath wedded.'

Language versus reality

a rose
By any other word would smell as sweet   *Act 2 Scene 2, lines 43–4*

'What's in a name?' asks Juliet. It's Romeo she loves, and she would love him whatever his name. Shakespeare was intensely interested in the uneasy relationships between words (language) and what they described (experience, things, action, reality). In *Romeo and Juliet*, he shows how language (calling someone a Montague) creates prejudice and hatred. Tybalt is blinded by malice at the very sound of a Montague's voice when he overhears Romeo.

When Lady Capulet compares Paris to a book (Act 1 Scene 3, lines 82–93) or when Romeo early in the play uses the formal language of classical poetry (see p. 16), Shakespeare exposes the differences between words and action, between feelings learned out of a book and emotions learned from genuine experience. *Romeo and Juliet* highlights the tension between words and action, between language and life.

Public versus private

The action of the play shifts from outdoor to indoor, from public to private spaces. In contrast to the violent happenings in Verona's city centre, and the grand occasion of the feast, there are quiet, intimate scenes in the moonlit orchard or in Juliet's bedroom in the Capulet mansion. The shift from public to private, from social spaces to personal meetings, is symbolic of other tensions in the play:

- the loyalties of groups (Montagues and Capulets) versus the loyalties of individuals towards each other (Romeo and Juliet)
- the freedoms of personal love versus the constraints of social life
- male dominance versus the vision of equality of the sexes seen in the love of Romeo and Juliet.

Past versus present

An insistent sense of time echoes through the play. Present time (the fast-moving events the audience sees unfolding on stage) is set against the background of a much longer history. The audience hears of an 'ancient grudge', showing the feud has been going on for years. The Nurse recalls Juliet's childhood: ''Tis since the earthquake now aleven years'. And Romeo imagines his life as a long sea voyage that ends in shipwreck.

Youth versus age

The differences between old and young, between cautious, mature wisdom and youthful impetuous emotion are striking. Romeo's passion is evident: 'I stand on sudden haste'. The contrast with the Friar's advice is vivid as he urges 'love moderately, long love doth so'. But don't think the play is a simple contrast between youth and age. Juliet's father is given to mood swings and sudden outbursts as violent as any in the young people!

Fast versus slow

'Wisely and slow, they stumble that run fast', advises Friar Lawrence. The contrast between passion and caution is evident in the characters (see above), but there are also changes in tempo throughout the play. In Capulet's orchard, time seems to stand still as Romeo and Juliet exchange vows of love. After leisurely beginnings, scenes explode into violent action. Events force the lovers into hasty action. Capulet's decision to bring the wedding forward hurries Juliet into drinking the Friar's potion. News of her 'death' sends Romeo speeding back to Verona – and death.

Dreamtime versus real time

dreamers often lie   *Act 1 Scene 4, line 51*

Dreamtime is quite different from normal time. What happens in dreamtime may or may not be true. Mercutio spins out fantastic stories of the dreams Queen Mab provokes as people lie asleep. Romeo wants to believe what happens in dreamtime: 'my dreams presage some joyful news at hand'. But premonitions are like baleful daydreams, and those of Romeo and Juliet are full of ominous foreboding.

♦ Use the 'oppositions' listed in these three pages as the basis of a long assignment. In it explore how *Romeo and Juliet* dramatises conflicts in society, in personal relationships and in individual emotions. Page 216 has information on antithesis that can help you.

Why did Romeo and Juliet die?

Who's to blame? For hundreds of years people have argued over the reason for the deaths of the young lovers. Why not conduct your own enquiry into the causes of the tragedy? You can investigate in many ways: through mock trials or select committees, or by using the techniques of investigative journalism or television.

Call witnesses (including those who do not speak in the play, for example 'the lively Helena' or Petruchio). Require characters to defend themselves against the charge of being guilty of causing the deaths. Invent other characters who might also have something to contribute: perhaps a householder whose window overlooks Verona's public square; or a boy who had crept into Capulet's orchard to steal fruit.

Don't simply try to pin blame on particular individuals. Seek other reasons for the tragedy. Here are suggestions you can use to investigate what caused the deaths of Romeo and Juliet.

1 Was it fate?

Were the deaths foretold in the stars? There are many suggestions in the play that the deaths were determined by fate. Collect references to the inevitability of the tragedy, for example 'star-crossed' (Prologue, line 6), 'the yoke of inauspicious stars' (Act 5 Scene 3, line 111). You could invent characters' horoscopes – and even call upon an astrologer to give evidence!

2 Was it chance?

Was it just bad luck? Fortune is fickle, so maybe no one is responsible; it was only a series of accidents. Collect examples of chance and accident ('misadventured piteous overthrows'), for example the accidental meeting of Peter, carrying Capulet's invitation list, with Benvolio and Romeo; the non-delivery of Friar Lawrence's letter. Was Mercutio's death just an unhappy chance happening?

3 Was it adolescent passion?

Some critics have laid the blame on the folly of Romeo and Juliet in their youthful haste and passion. But how far do you think it was the lovers' own fault? Is adolescent love at first sight a cause of the tragedy? Collect examples of haste and passion in the play to use as evidence.

4 Was it the feud?

Were the deaths caused by the enmity of the Montagues and Capulets? The two families struggle for power in Verona. Their 'ancient grudge' breaks 'to new mutiny' at the start of the play. A stiff-necked code of honour makes the young men spring to violent, bloody action. Tybalt feels that the 'honour of my kin' has been insulted by Romeo's presence at Capulet's feast. Romeo is provoked into 'fire-eyed fury' by the death of Mercutio. He embraces the revenge code that governs relationships between the two rival factions of the Verona mafiosi.

Collect other examples suggesting the lovers' deaths are caused by the quarrel that fractures the city.

5 Was it fathers?

Verona is a patriarchal city. Fathers hold virtually absolute sway over their daughters. They may give them to whomever they choose, and feel deeply insulted if their daughters dare choose otherwise. Juliet makes that choice and incurs the unmitigated wrath of Capulet:

> go with Paris to Saint Peter's Church,
> Or I will drag thee on a hurdle thither   *Act 3 Scene 5, lines 154–5*

Together with patriarchy goes all the machismo of the young men. They relish crude sexual joking, see love as brutal conquest, and have no understanding of gentler, equal relations between the sexes.

Collect other examples that help you enquire into whether Verona's male-dominated society is responsible for the lovers' deaths.

6 What other causes?

- Is the tragedy caused by love itself? Their love makes Romeo and Juliet feel that meeting in death is the only worthwhile ending. 'Well, Juliet, I will lie with thee tonight' (Act 5 Scene 1, line 34) is Romeo's expression of that love in death.
- Should you question the Friar's motives? He marries the lovers in secret, then devises dangerous plans that will ensure his own part in the affair is concealed. Juliet fears that he might have given her a real poison, 'Lest in this marriage he should be dishonoured' (Act 4 Scene 3, line 26).
- Or might the cause lie in the 'rude will' of human nature? The Friar sees such self-centredness resulting in evil if it gains the upper hand over 'grace' (Act 2 Scene 3, lines 27–30).

Write an extended essay exploring what you think are the reasons for the lovers' deaths. Use these two pages as a resource.

The language of *Romeo and Juliet*

Imagery

Shakespeare seems to have thought in images, and *Romeo and Juliet* abounds in imagery (sometimes called 'figures' or 'figurative language'). Imagery is created by vivid words and phrases that conjure up emotionally charged mental pictures or associations in the imagination. Imagery provides insight into character, and gives pleasure as it stirs the audience's imagination. It deepens the dramatic impact of particular moments or moods.

For example, when Juliet learns that Romeo has killed Tybalt she struggles to express her contradictory feelings. How could such a beloved, beautiful person like Romeo commit so vile a deed? How could such beautiful reality cover such malicious reality? Her outburst (Act 3 Scene 2, lines 73–85) contains at least a dozen images beginning with:

> O serpent heart, hid with a flow'ring face!
> Did ever dragon keep so fair a cave?

Some images recur throughout *Romeo and Juliet*, helping to create a sense of the themes of the play. One example is that of light and dark:

> O she doth teach the torches to burn bright!
> It seems she hangs upon the cheek of night
> As a rich jewel in an Ethiop's ear   *Act 1 Scene 5, lines 43–5*

> The brightness of her cheek would shame those stars,
> As daylight doth a lamp   *Act 2 Scene 2, lines 19–20*

>   her beauty makes
> This vault a feasting presence full of light   *Act 5 Scene 3, lines 85–6*

Some of the play's images are very showy and extravagant, and are often called 'conceits'. One such conceit is in Act 1 Scene 3, lines 82–95, where Lady Capulet gives advice to Juliet to marry Paris. Her conceit is like a sonnet, spun out over fourteen lines (see p. 217). She compares Paris to a book, and begins:

> Read o'er the volume of young Paris' face,
> And find delight writ there with beauty's pen

All Shakespeare's imagery uses metaphor, simile or personification. All are comparisons which substitute one thing (the image) for another (the thing described).

- A **simile** compares one thing to another using 'like' or 'as', for example: 'shrieks like mandrakes' torn out of the earth'; 'And in their triumph die like fire and powder'; 'My bounty is as boundless as the sea, / My love as deep'.

- A **metaphor** is also a comparison, suggesting that two dissimilar things are actually the same. When Romeo says, 'O speak again, bright angel' he implies that Juliet is an angel, some glorious thing to be praised. To put it another way, a metaphor borrows one word or phrase to express another. For example, Benvolio uses all the following as metaphors for swords and sword-fighting: 'piercing steel', 'deadly point to point', 'Cold death', 'fatal points' (Act 3 Scene 1, lines 143–66). And Chorus in the Prologue describes the lovers as 'star-crossed' and their love as 'death-marked'.

- **Personification** turns all kinds of things into persons, giving them human feelings or attributes. Probably the most powerful personification in the play is the image of Death as Juliet's husband-bridegroom. It recurs in different forms:

    And death, not Romeo, take my maidenhead!
    Act 3 Scene 2, line 137

    Death is my son-in-law, Death is my heir,
    My daughter he hath wedded.   *Act 4 Scene 5, lines 38–9*

              Shall I believe
    That unsubstantial Death is amorous,
    And that the lean abhorrèd monster keeps
    Thee here in dark to be his paramour?   *Act 5 Scene 3, lines 102–5*

Check your understanding of metaphors, similes and personification: which is which here?

   'Scaring the ladies like a crow-keeper'
   'When well-apparelled April on the heel / Of limping winter treads'
   'bloody Tybalt, yet but green in earth'
   'Love goes toward love as schoolboys from their books'

- ◆ Find several examples of metaphors, similes and personification in the play. Write them out, and say why they appeal to you. Suggest the atmosphere they create, or how they help to build up a sense of what a character is like.

- ◆ Also, listen carefully to other people's language. You'll hear hundreds of metaphors and similes!

Antithesis and oxymoron

Antithesis is the opposition of words or phrases against each other, as in 'More light and light, more dark and dark our woes!' (Act 3 Scene 5, line 36). This setting of word against word (e.g. 'light' versus 'dark') is one of Shakespeare's favourite language devices. He uses it in all his plays. Why? Because antithesis powerfully expresses conflict through its use of opposites, and conflict is the essence of all drama.

In *Romeo and Juliet*, conflict occurs in many forms: Montague versus Capulet, love versus hate, the bridal bed versus the grave, and all the other oppositions listed on pages 209–11. Antithesis intensifies that sense of conflict. For example, Friar Lawrence's first speech (Act 2 Scene 3, lines 1–30) contains at least fifteen antitheses as he gathers plants and ponders on the potential for good and evil in every living thing ('baleful weeds' versus 'precious-juicèd flowers', 'tomb' against 'womb', 'Virtue' against 'vice', and so on).

In another speech full of sharply contrasting antitheses, Capulet grieves for Juliet (Act 4 Scene 5, lines 84–90). He contrasts the happy preparations for the intended wedding with the mourning rites that now must mark her death. The first two lines set 'festival' versus 'funeral':

All things that we ordainèd festival,
Turn from their office to black funeral

A special kind of antithesis is **oxymoron**. Here, two incongruous or contradictory words are placed next to each other, as in 'cold fire' or 'bright smoke'. Oxymoron comes from two Greek words: *oxys* meaning 'sharp' and *moros* meaning 'dull'.

At the end of the 'balcony' scene Juliet uses a memorable oxymoron to describe her feelings: 'Parting is such sweet sorrow' ('sweet' versus 'sorrow'). Romeo, on his first appearance, seeing the signs of the brawl, speaks a dozen oxymorons as he reflects on love and hate (Act 1 Scene 1, lines 167–72). His reflection begins with two oxymorons, setting 'brawling' versus 'love', and 'loving' versus 'hate':

Why then, O brawling love, O loving hate

◆ Work through the play collecting as many examples of antitheses and oxymorons as you can. Write an extended essay showing how these two language devices help create the sense of conflict in *Romeo and Juliet*. There are shorter activities on antitheses on pages 2 and 164, and on oxymorons on page 14.

Sonnets

At about the same time as Shakespeare wrote *Romeo and Juliet*, he was probably writing his *Sonnets*. There are several sonnets in the play:

- Chorus at the start and end of Act 1
- Lady Capulet's praise of Paris (Act 1 Scene 3, lines 82–95)
- Romeo and Juliet's first meeting (Act 1 Scene 5, lines 92–105)
- their next four lines are the start of another sonnet.

A Shakespearian sonnet is a fourteen-line poem. Each line usually contains ten syllables. The sonnet has three quatrains (each of four lines) and a couplet:

- the first four lines (rhyming ABAB)
- the next four lines (rhyming CDCD)
- the next four lines (rhyming EFEF)
- a couplet (two lines) to finish (rhyming GG).

◆ Turn to the Prologue. Identify the rhymes ('dignity'/'mutiny', 'scene'/'unclean', and so on) and match them with the rhyme scheme above.

Write your own sonnet

The quickest way to learn to write a sonnet is to have one in front of you and to write a parody of it. Turn to the Prologue and complete the following sonnet by carefully fitting the last twelve lines to the rhythm and rhyme scheme of Shakespeare's language:

Two classrooms, quite unlike in atmosphere,
Inside this building, (where I write this rhyme),

The sonnet tradition

The language of *Romeo and Juliet* shows the strong influence of the Italian poet Petrarch (1304–74). He became very popular with English poets in the time of Queen Elizabeth I. They drew on Petrarch's themes and style to write about courtly love.

Romeo's love for Rosaline echoes the major theme of Petrarch's poetry: a young man's unrequited love of an unattainable and disdainful woman. Romeo was infatuated with Rosaline, but she rejected all his advances. In Act 1 Scene 1, lines 199–207, and lines 219–29, you can see other influences of the sonnet tradition: neat rhyming; elaborate conceits (for example, metaphors of war); and the wordplay of wit, puns and repetition.

You can find more help with sonnets in the Cambridge School Shakespeare edition of *The Sonnets*.

Verse and prose

Although it has a good deal of rhyme, most of *Romeo and Juliet* is written in blank verse: unrhymed verse with a 'five-beat' rhythm (iambic pentameter). Each line has five iambs (feet), each with one stressed (/) and one unstressed (×) syllable:

$$× \quad / \quad × \quad / \quad × \quad / \quad × \quad / \quad × \quad /$$

But soft, what light through yonder window breaks?

The 'five-beat' rhythm (or metre) is often obvious, but at other times, notably in the 'balcony' scene, it is less prominent.

Prose was traditionally used by comic and low-status characters. High-status characters spoke verse. But the Nurse (low-status) speaks a good deal of verse when she is with high-status Lady Capulet and Juliet. Also, Romeo, Mercutio and Benvolio (all high-status) use prose in Act 2 Scene 4 (probably because their talk is 'comic'). And although the conventional rule is that tragic death scenes should be in verse, Mercutio, at the point of death, speaks in prose.

◆ Choose a verse speech and speak it to emphasise the metre (five beats). Then speak it as you feel it should be delivered on stage. Finally, write four to eight lines of your own in the same style.

Listen! It's all around you!

Shakespeare created some very familiar expressions in *Romeo and Juliet*:

star-crossed lovers	if love be blind
parting is such sweet sorrow	as true as steel
above compare	cock-a-hoop
light of heart	as gentle as a lamb
in a fool's paradise	past help
what's in a name?	on a wild goose chase
what must be shall be	we were born to die
I will not budge	stiff and stark
where have you been gadding?	on pain of death
let me alone	the weakest go to the wall
fortune's fool	go like lightning
a rose by any other word (often	a plague on both your houses
misquoted as 'name')	where the devil?
would smell as sweet	

◆ Use these familiar expressions to make up a short story. Include other familiar sayings you find in *Romeo and Juliet*.

Repetition

Repeating words or phrases was a favourite device of Shakespeare's. Repetition can heighter tension and add depth to both drama and character. For example, when Juliet opposes her mother in Act 3 Scene 5, lines 114–17:

LADY CAPULET The County Paris, at Saint Peter's Church,
    Shall happily make thee there a joyful bride.
JULIET Now by Saint Peter's Church and Peter too,
    He shall not make me there a joyful bride.

- ◆ Collect more examples of repetition in the play. Dramatise a few to show their effect.

Puns – something to find out

A pun is a play on words which sound similar but have different meanings. Shakespeare was fascinated by puns – especially in *Romeo and Juliet*. Mercutio revels in punning, often of a sexual nature. Even at the point of death he can't resist punning: 'Ask for me tomorrow, and you shall find me a grave man' (Act 3 Scene 1, lines 89–90).

- ◆ Does every character in the play use puns? Discover the first pun each character uses. For example, Gregory and Sampson pun on 'colliers'/'choler'/'collar' at the very start of Act 1 Scene 1.

Shakespeare – and other writers' stories and language

Shakespeare almost always took the ideas for his plays from someone else's writing. He brilliantly transformed whatever he worked on. He found the idea for *Romeo and Juliet* in Arthur Brooke's poem *The Tragicall Historye of Romeus and Juliet*, written in 1562. But Brooke's long poem was pretty dull! Here are Brooke's lines about Juliet just before she drinks the potion:

The force of her imagining, anon did wax so strong,
That she surmised she saw out of the hollow vault,
(A grisly thing to look upon) the carcase of Tybalt,
Right in the self same sort, that she few days before
Had seen him in his blood embroiled, to death eke wounded sore.

Shakespeare vividly rewrote Brooke's image of the dead Tybalt:

Where bloody Tybalt, yet but green in earth,
Lies fest'ring in his shroud   *Act 4 Scene 3, lines 42–3*

Romeo and Juliet in performance

Romeo and Juliet at the Globe

In Shakespeare's day, Juliet, the Nurse and other female parts were played by boys. There were no elaborate sets on the bare stage of the Globe Theatre. Only a few props were used (swords, chairs, etc.), but the actors wore attractive and expensive costumes, usually the

'Hold thy desperate hand!' In the Globe's production the Nurse was played by a male actor.

fashionable dress of the times. The Globe Theatre has now been rebuilt on London's Bankside, close to the site on which it first stood. Many of the productions there are staged as Shakespeare's Elizabethan audiences probably saw them. In 2004, *Romeo and Juliet* was performed in Elizabethan costume. The picture opposite shows Romeo kneeling over the 'dead' Juliet, and about to drink the poison. In the picture above, the Nurse and Friar Lawrence struggle to seize the dagger from Romeo. The Globe also welcomes international companies, and the picture below shows a moment from a Brazilian adaptation, *Romeu & Julieta*, which featured jugglers, stilt-walkers, musicians, and William Shakespeare himself! Can you find him in the picture?

Eighteenth-century stagings of *Romeo and Juliet*

In the eighteenth century, David Garrick's rewritten version of *Romeo and Juliet* was very popular. He cut much of the dialogue, but added a funeral procession (see p. 169) and a final conversation between Romeo and Juliet in the tomb. The play was acted in the fashionable costumes of the day, as you can see in the picture.

Spranger Barry as Romeo and Miss Nossiter as Juliet, Covent Garden, London, 1753.

Nineteenth-century stagings of *Romeo and Juliet*

In the nineteenth century, productions of *Romeo and Juliet* became obsessed with historical accuracy. Period costumes and settings were designed with meticulous attention to detail. Pick out features in the picture below which show attempts to re-create twelfth-century Verona on stage.

Henry Irving's 1882 production at the London Lyceum. Identify lines in Act 5 Scene 3 which match this picture.

Modern productions

Modern productions have displayed a huge variety of ways of staging *Romeo and Juliet*. But nearly all use a single basic set that can be quickly adapted to enable the play to flow swiftly from scene to scene. Such sets avoid lengthy breaks for scene-shifting. Even though locations shift from place to place, the flow of action is continuous.

All kinds of transformations of Shakespeare's play have been made. There is a ballet by the Russian composer Serge Prokofiev (see p. 224), an opera by Gounod (see the picture on p. xi in the colour section), and an American stage musical and film, *West Side Story*, with music by Leonard Bernstein (see p. 6). The Italian film director Franco Zeffirelli used images of youth and beauty in Renaissance paintings as an inspiration for his 1968 film (see the picture on p. xii in the colour section). The film director Baz Luhrmann (see the pictures on pp. vi, xi and 225) sharply distinguished the feuding families by their clothes. The Montagues wore casual beachwear (e.g. colourful Hawaiian shirts). The Capulets wore expensive designer clothes, ornamental jewellery and bullet-proof vests.

Prince Escales rebukes the Capulets (left) and Montagues (right) in the play's first scene. Study the costumes and set of this 1995 Royal Shakespeare Company production and suggest what impression of Verona and its feuding families the designer wishes to create.

Romeo and Juliet dance together in the Bolshoi Ballet's 1993 production of Prokofiev's ballet.

In 2003–4, the Icelandic theatre company Vesturport staged their production at London's Young Vic and Playhouse theatres. It featured trapeze artists and fire-eaters. Here, in the party scene, Juliet stands triumphantly on Capulet's shoulders, with Tybalt on her right.

In Baz Luhrmann's film *William Shakespeare's Romeo + Juliet*, 1996, Juliet leans on the balcony and longs for Romeo. Claire Danes was sixteen years old when she played Juliet in the film. Find a line in Act 2 Scene 2 as a caption for this picture.

Stage your own production of *Romeo and Juliet*

Talk together about the period and place in which you will set your play: medieval Italy? a present-day place where conflict exists between two social groups? a 'timeless' setting? Then choose one or more of the following activities. Your finished assignment can be a file of drawings, notes and suggestions, or an active presentation.

- Design the set – how can it be used for particular scenes?
- Design the costumes – look at past examples, but invent your own.
- Design the props – furnishings and hand props (e.g. swords).
- Design a lighting and sound programme – for one or two scenes.
- Design the publicity poster – make people want to see your play!
- Design a 'flyer' – a small handbill to advertise the production.
- Design the programme – layout? content? number of pages?
- Write character notes for actors' guidance.
- Work out a five-minute presentation to show to potential sponsors.

Visit a production of *Romeo and Juliet*

Shakespeare wrote *Romeo and Juliet* to be acted, watched and enjoyed – not to be studied for examinations! So visit a live performance. Prepare for a school or college visit using the following:

- Everyone chooses a character (or an incident or scene) to watch especially closely. Write down your expectations before you go. Report back to the class on how your expectations for 'your' character or scene were fulfilled or challenged.
- Choose your favourite line in the play. Listen carefully to how it is spoken. Does it add to your understanding?
- Your teacher will probably be able to provide one or two published reviews of the production. Talk together about whether you should read the reviews before or after you see the play for yourself. After the visit, discuss how far you agree or disagree with the reviews.
- Write your own review. Record your own perceptions of what you actually saw and heard – and your feelings about the production.

Two points to remember:

- Preparation is always valuable, but too much can dull the enjoyment of a theatre visit.
- Every production is different. There's no such thing as a single 'right' way to 'do' Shakespeare – but you might think that there are 'wrong' ways!

What the dickens!

The Royal Shakespeare Company mounted a memorable production of Charles Dickens' *Nicholas Nickleby*. In it there was a performance of the last scene of *Romeo and Juliet*. But the RSC turned it into a very happy ending! Romeo and Juliet awoke to life. They hadn't really poisoned or stabbed themselves. Paris was similarly unharmed. Benvolio appeared, and revealed he was really a girl, Benvolia! Paris instantly fell in love with her and proposed marriage! Only Tybalt wasn't granted a reprieve into life.

Use this version as your inspiration to create your own happy ending to the play. Work together in pairs or small groups. Write the script based on Act 5, choose your parts, rehearse your lines – and put on a performance!

How to play the Prince

In the RSC *Nicholas Nickleby* version of *Romeo and Juliet*, the Prince was very drunk – and very funny! In Baz Luhrmann's film, Escales becomes Captain Prince of the Verona Beach police force, and he arrives by helicopter at the death scene. Take the Prince's three appearances (Act 1 Scene 1, Act 3 Scene 1 and Act 5 Scene 3), decide the setting of your play, and work out how you would play the Prince. Deliver your lines!

Romeo and Juliet: a website

Work in a group. Design a website for the play. Pool ideas to decide what to include: for example, illustrations, graphics, quotations, character studies.

Illustrations – your preferences

Look through all the photographs in this edition. Select the five you like best. Write a paragraph on each saying why you enjoy it.

Show the relationships

Look at the list of characters on page 1, and use it to help you design the cast list for your performance. Be sure to make the relationships of the characters as clear as possible.

Make your own video of a scene from *Romeo and Juliet*

Choose a scene or incident. Find a space in the school or college grounds, learn your lines, rehearse your scene – and shoot it!

William Shakespeare
1564–1616

1564 Born Stratford-upon-Avon, eldest son of John and Mary Shakespeare.

1582 Marries Anne Hathaway of Shottery, near Stratford.

1583 Daughter, Susanna, born.

1585 Twins, son and daughter, Hamnet and Judith, born.

1592 First mention of Shakespeare in London. Robert Greene, another playwright, described Shakespeare as 'an upstart crow beautified with our feathers . . .'. Greene seems to have been jealous of Shakespeare. He mocked Shakespeare's name, calling him 'the only Shake-scene in a country' (presumably because Shakespeare was writing successful plays).

1595 A shareholder in The Lord Chamberlain's Men, an acting company that became extremely popular.

1596 Son Hamnet dies, aged eleven.

Father, John, granted arms (acknowledged as a gentleman).

1597 Buys New Place, the grandest house in Stratford.

1598 Acts in Ben Jonson's *Every Man in His Humour*.

1599 Globe Theatre opens on Bankside. Performances in the open air.

1601 Father, John, dies.

1603 James I grants Shakespeare's company a royal patent: The Lord Chamberlain's Men become The King's Men and play about twelve performances each year at court.

1607 Daughter, Susanna, marries Dr John Hall.

1608 Mother, Mary, dies.

1609 The King's Men begin performing indoors at Blackfriars Theatre.

1610 Probably returns from London to live in Stratford.

1616 Daughter, Judith, marries Thomas Quiney.

Dies. Buried in Holy Trinity Church, Stratford-upon-Avon.

The plays and poems

(no one knows exactly when he wrote each play)

1589–95 *The Two Gentlemen of Verona, The Taming of the Shrew, First, Second and Third Parts of King Henry VI, Titus Andronicus, King Richard III, The Comedy of Errors, Love's Labour's Lost, A Midsummer Night's Dream, Romeo and Juliet, King Richard II* (and the long poems *Venus and Adonis* and *The Rape of Lucrece*).

1596–9 *King John, The Merchant of Venice, First and Second Parts of King Henry IV, The Merry Wives of Windsor, Much Ado About Nothing, King Henry V, Julius Caesar* (and probably the *Sonnets*).

1600–5 *As You Like It, Hamlet, Twelfth Night, Troilus and Cressida, Measure for Measure, Othello, All's Well That Ends Well, Timon of Athens, King Lear.*

1606–11 *Macbeth, Antony and Cleopatra, Pericles, Coriolanus, The Winter's Tale, Cymbeline, The Tempest.*

1613 *King Henry VIII, The Two Noble Kinsmen* (both probably with John Fletcher).

1623 Shakespeare's plays published as a collection (now called the First Folio).